Studies in Eighteenth-Century Culture

Volume 41

Studies in Eighteenth-Century Culture

Volume 41

Studies in

Eighteenth-Century Culture

Volume 41

Published by The Johns Hopkins University Press for the
American Society for Eighteenth-Century Studies

The Johns Hopkins University Press
Baltimore and London
2012

Printed in the United States of America on acid-free paper.
9 8 7 6 5 4 3 2 1

The Johns Hopkins University Press
2715 North Charles Street
Baltimore, Maryland 21218-4363
www.press.jhu.edu

ISBN 978-1-4214-0562-9
ISSN 0360-2370

Articles appearing in this annual series are abstracted and indexed in *Historical Abstracts* and *America: History and Life*.

Contents

Editor's Note

Absence and Presence and Categories Between

What is in or not in a text or a visual experience? And what is the relationship between what is present and what is absent? These questions may seem more productive for the self-reflexive and theoretical projects of the twentieth- and twenty-first centuries than the eighteenth. Yet, in fact, a range of questions about what is present, what is absent, what exists between the text and its context, what appears and disappears through movement, what is inside the frame and outside it, and what audiences make of the apparent, the absent, and the implied are among the themes that serendipitously and subtly link the eleven essays in this forty-first volume of *Studies in Eighteenth-Century Culture*. While some of the authors in this collection explicitly employ theoretical models that address presence/absence, all of the contributors rely on and strongly enrich the historical, the material, the contextual, and the concrete. This is a collection that engages significant and sophisticated interpretive questions, but each essay does so, first and foremost, by examining texts, objects, other material phenomena, and historical conditions on their own terms.

This volume's subjects are far-ranging, stretching from the Habsburg and Celtic fringes to London, Paris, and the early American Republic, representing work in art and architectural history, intellectual and cultural history, literature, media studies, gender studies, and more. Each essay of course offers fresh insights into its particular topic, whether Jonathan Swift or the German rococo, and each will naturally appeal to its respective specialist audience. But, perhaps by chance or by the power of the zeitgeist, these eleven essays, selected from a competitive pool of contenders, have become a coherent whole that is ultimately interconnected by shared methodological and thematic concerns that speak to a broad audience of eighteenth-century scholars.

Volume 41 is particularly fortunate to include three essays in visual studies. In her examination of the under-studied French female painter Marie-Éléonore Godefroid, whose group portrait of the Ney brothers illustrates this volume's frontispiece, Jennifer Germann argues that visual cues and biographical clues can provide information that has the power to complicate or even subvert the overt subject matter of an image. Godefroid's depiction of the Ney boys—presumably an obvious example of nascent male bonding through strictly masculine pursuits of militarism and political life—is, according to Germann, not simply or only a record of male homosocial relations. It is, surprisingly and paradoxically, evidence of *female homosocial* relations. By tracing familial, social, and institutional relationships in Revolutionary and Napoleonic France, Germann uncovers the pivotal role that women played together when they forged alliances as artists and patrons, assistants and hostesses. Though visually absent from this portrait of men, women are pivotal in the construction of this painting and many others through their own homosocial ties, according to Germann.

Michael Yonan's analysis of the Wieskirche, a pilgrimage church in southern Bavaria (constructed, 1745-1754), examines absence and presence as essential experiences in an intertwined architectural and theological strategy. Typically written off as gaudy and derivative of finer French examples, central European rococo churches, argues Yonan, were innovative and creative. The Wieskirche, for one, used the ornate, elaborate rococo as an essential, dynamic component in worship, spiritual renewal, and theological argument. While the Wieskirche's seemingly derivative rococo may initially appear an overwhelming and meaningless display of everything all at once, Yonan reveals how everything is not entirely visible. Rather, components appear and recede in relation to one another as humans move through architectural spaces and view paintings, friezes, sculptures, and decorations framed, revealed, and occluded by one another. As one example, when worshipers walk through the ambulatories of the Wieskirche, paintings of miracles appear and disappear in relation to the rococo framing devices and architectural structures. The process of "walking and looking" that allows imagery to present itself and then disappear, Yonan argues, visually and experientially complements and embodies the Christian message and Catholic liturgical practices.

Sandro Jung's work on the English illustrator, Thomas Stothard, explores a greatly over-looked textual form—the pricey illustrated pocket-diary of the late eighteenth- and nineteenth-centuries—that offered large empty spaces of blank paper to its well-heeled owner to be filled with memoranda, schedules, or sketches. Framing the pages are series of elaborate, original pictorial vignettes. As Jung demonstrates, the imagery, though pleasing and beautiful in its own right, made word-less reference to great English literature and contemporary poems and novels. Knowing what the image might point to, whether Chaucer or William Cowper, heightened the enjoyment for the sophisticated owner. But these depictions sometimes distorted or reinvented the original work by removing or softening its original critical intent. Though, for example, George Crabbe's poems critiqued socio-economic conditions, Thomas Stothard transformed scenes from *The Seasons* into bucolic and sentimental representations of romanticized laboring classes. The educated consumer of the expensive, illustrated diaries could take pleasure in recognizing the reference to an important poetic critique of contemporary society, but Stothard's depictions effaced the original criticism and ultimately facilitated a less jarring relationship between image and the memoranda to eventually be written on the blank spaces.

Sandro Jung illuminates how the pleasure in Thomas Stothard's exquisite work relied on its affluent consumers' sophisticated knowledge about reading and their ability to understand based on their ability to invoke unnamed literary references. Catherine Keohane takes up this issue of "reading" and reading between the lines as signs of class and status in her exploration of the laboring-class poet Anne Yearsley and her one-time patron Hannah More. In her own close reading of Yearsley's "Clifton Hill" and More's "Prefatory Letter" that served to introduce and frame Yearsley's volume, Keohane argues that the poet was better read and critically far more sophisticated than More portrayed her in the letter. Rather than simply expand the list of literary texts that Yearsley was actually familiar with compared to More's list, Keohane shows that the poet's subtle references to and transformations of contemporary authors' works provided a powerful critique of the limited understanding possessed by didactic, condescending elites. More's portrayal of Yearsley's reading, riddled with absences, helped to simplify the poet; Yearsley's subtle references to additional, but unnamed works, helped to reveal how poorly her former patron (and elites in general) could see, read, and understand others.

As Keohane provides fresh insights into the relationship between texts and social relations, so too does David Brewer in his analysis of George Colman the elder's 1760 play, *Polly Honeycombe*. Reading the farce as a source to challenge a series of widely presumed binary relations and theoretical frameworks in modern scholarship, Brewer proposes that print and/or theater versus personhood are not oppositional categories, but in an endless play of reciprocal creation. He also challenges the position that before the rise of the novel "people were supposedly externally oriented and 'theatrical' up to 1740, and then they turned inward, and the modern subject was born." Brewer uses *Polly Honeycombe* itself—a farce about reading, romance, acting, and identity—to argue for the continuing presence and vitality of the theater in the age of the novel, the dynamic relationship between stage and print, the paradoxical relationship between the quixotic and self understanding, and the unexpected theoretical utility of farce.

Dorothee Birke challenges another literary opposition articulated by Gérard Genette between the text and the "paratext." Birke explores whether the paratextual—titles, chapter headings, illustrations, notes, preface, the material features of books, etc.—is actually separated from and primarily supplementary to the text itself in her examination of the chapter titles in three mid-century novels. Genette argued that the paratextual element of chapter-titles fell increasingly out of fashion in nineteenth-century novels because they drew attention away from the text and reminded readers they were reading books. Birke argues that "in the eighteenth century they had an important function: namely, they contributed to the reflection of the function and purpose of an emerging form of writing," and she shows three different evolving paratextual strategies of Henry Fielding, Sarah Fielding, and Charlotte Lennox. Chapter titles provided numerous functions central to the reader's understanding of and enjoyment of the novel, including their ability to impart different layers of meaning to readers of varying levels of sophistication and wit. She proposes that a more naïve reader can read Charlotte Lennox's *The Female Quixote* earnestly as "a didactic novel," but the sophisticated reader grasps the ironic and critical narrative stance of the work through the alternating "modes" of the novel's chapter titles—some descriptive, some silly, and some self-reflexive—which create "frictions" between text, paratext, and meaning.

As Dorothee Birke views the relationship between text and paratext as "playfully set up," so too does Zeina Hakim emphasize the playful game between author and reader in such texts as *Mémoires et aventures d'un homme de qualité qui s'est retiré du monde* (1728-1731) by Antoine François and *La Vie de Marianne* (1731-1742) by Pierre de Marivaux. Hakim meticulously examines how these two fictional works played with claims to "true" stories. Many eighteenth-century fictional works proclaimed themselves to be "real" by presenting themselves as a collection of authentic letters recovered and presented by an editor; in some works, as in the case of Rousseau's *La Nouvelle Héloïse*, readers were encouraged to believe the fiction was really true. Hakim argues that Prévost and Marivaux had different intentions with their invocations of authenticity. She proposes that in their works the claim to truthfulness was not actually designed to convince readers that the texts were verifiably true. Instead, Marivaux and Prévost structured their works' claims to authenticity in ways that deliberately played with their readers' expectations and reading practices. The more they asserted their status as authentic renderings of real life, the more these texts reminded their readers that they were in fact reading fiction.

Marc Lerner's study of the William Tell legend, its many eighteenth-century rewritings, and its invocation in moments of political action also challenges the status of fiction and reality in an eighteenth-century world that embraced historical change. Tracing the tale from its earliest Swiss incarnation in fifteenth-century sources through its multiple eighteenth-century appearances to its many and varied early nineteenth-century staging throughout Europe and the Americas, Lerner illuminates this to have been an unusually potent transnational, political symbol. The William Tell story's survival and utility, Lerner shows, reflected its flexibility as it could serve political ideologies across the spectrum, from radical democracy to conservative patriotism, from individual liberty to the general will, and so forth. As Lerner shows, versions changed in meaning largely because certain features and details were variously highlighted or made absent. Most strikingly, "William Tell" served as political shorthand for numerous causes, so much so that rebels and revolutionaries would occasionally dress as or name themselves after the Swiss hero, blending legend and life. When staged in its multiple versions, the story rarely served as a purely historical tale, but rather reflected its audiences' contemporary political desires, thus perpetually renewing itself for living needs.

Katrina Berndt reads Sir Walter Scott's historically fictional *Redgauntlet* in light of Adam Ferguson's theories of civilization and progress to examine the reinvention of the past for the needs of the present. Contrary to the received view of Scott, Berndt argues that he did not embrace a wholly nostalgic view of Scotland's history, including its Jacobite past, nor did he fully accept David Hume's and Adam Smith's models of commerce and progress that would carry Scotland, as part of Great Britain, to ever civilized heights. Rather, Berndt argues that Scott was influenced by Ferguson's more tumultuous model of historical change in which conflict rather than harmony served as the necessary motor to invigorate society and social relations. The absence of conflict, whether militaristic or political, softened the polity and prevented its citizens from realizing their potential. For Scott, then, the Jacobite rebellion of 1745 was neither a romantic tragedy nor evidence of Scottish backwardness. Instead, it was, as realized through *Redgauntlet*'s characters—including a fictionalized Bonnie Prince Charlie who ultimately renounces Jacobitism—a dynamic opportunity that invigorated both Scotland and England as parts of a larger British polity.

Danielle Spratt similarly employs political economic theory in her reading of Jonathan Swift's *The Travels*, *A Modest Proposal*, and other writings. Here, she examines Gulliver as an over-zealous economic projector whose "narration depicts the creation, control, and circulation of commodities between both colonized and colonizing peoples and nations." As he energetically foists his "political anatomy" on the bodies of the people and creatures he meets as he travels, his body—monstrously large or small or strange—becomes in turn an object of curiosity and commerce and soon an uncategorized "freak of nature." Objectified and put in the service of various Brobdignagian and other schemes, Gulliver's body can be read as the dehumanized status of the Irish people as so many bodies to be bred, transported, and indentured in contemporary political economy and English colonial policy.

Julie Henigan explores the relationship between the English and the Irish, elites and plebeians, and print and oral culture in her detailed study of the Irish ballad. Challenging assumptions that the Irish ruling class and the poor "inhabited two wholly discrete cultural worlds, one literate and the other oral," Henigan illuminates a dynamic relationship between printed ballads—largely English in origin—and oral culture in eighteenth-century Ireland. Newspaper advertisements, ballad collection prefaces, the songs themselves, as well as social relations between elites and the peasantry at festivals, sporting events, and in the household as masters and servants all collectively revealed a fluid impact of oral and popular culture on print and the ultimate dominance of the Irish on the ballad form throughout the British Isles and North America by the late eighteenth century.

Clearly many themes, methodological concerns, and research problems link these eleven essays beyond what can be highlighted here, but it is worth noting that they each offer insights to readers beyond their particular fields and disciplines. The interdisciplinary and transnational power of this volume's essays reflects the spirit of the American Society for Eighteenth Century Studies and the incisive reports offered by dozens of outside scholars and an energetic and engaged editorial board. I am grateful to the members of the *SECC* board and dozens of outside readers who provided extensive, precise, sometimes creative, and often very challenging reports to the large pool of authors who submitted work for consideration. I thank both the authors and members of the board for their dedication to this project, most especially David Macey for his exceptional work with individual authors. I am also grateful to all the editors of *SECC* reaching back to the 1990s, especially Jeff Ravel and Tim Erwin, for their advice and suggestions in strengthening this collection. Ultimately, thanks to the very hard work of all involved in volume 41 of *SECC*, this has become a work that responds to and greatly animates vital problems in the long eighteenth century.

The Wieskirche: Movement, Perception, and Salvation in the Bavarian Rococo

MICHAEL YONAN

Despite the recent widespread scholarly reassessment of eighteenth-century rococo art, Bavarian rococo churches remain architectural ugly stepsisters. Widely known and unfailingly referenced in every art-historical survey text, rococo religious architecture nonetheless remains virtually unstudied within current Anglo-American scholarship, a situation that persists despite significant advancements in methodological and interpretive schemas helpful for confronting secular rococo design. Perhaps modern viewers continue to perceive these churches' abundantly ornamented interiors as little more than hysterical adaptations of an originally refined, visually seductive decorative mode characterized by the French elite *hôtel*. Raising its head as well is the possibility, implicit in some statements about the Bavarian rococo I have encountered, that to many observers these buildings confirm German bad taste, that they reveal a Teutonic obsessiveness with detail and a tiresome fascination with irrelevant complexity, qualities that obliterate the restrained gracefulness of their Gallic counterparts.

It was not always this way. The 1960s in particular saw a sustained scholarly interest in eighteenth-century German religious architecture among Anglo-American scholars, and during that time a number of prominent architectural historians directed serious scholarly attention to these buildings. The most surprising among them is Henry-Russell Hitchcock, well known as the documenter of the International Style and a high priest of architectural modernism. Mostly forgotten today is that Hitchcock published two substantial books on eighteenth-century Bavarian churches, one a collection of miscellaneous essays and the other a monographic treatment of the Zimmermann brothers.[1] Hitchcock's legacy in this area has not been great, however, and few modern studies of the rococo even mention his work, let alone build on it. Casting a long shadow over English-language understanding about the religious rococo is Karsten Harries's 1983 study, *The Bavarian Rococo Church: Between Faith and Aestheticism*.[2] Written by a prominent philosopher of art and architecture, Harries's book is a multivalent thematic analysis, with chapters devoted to individual spiritual and aesthetic qualities typical of the German rococo as a whole. Harries concerns himself less with the outfitting of any single church than with establishing the Bavarian rococo church typologically. It is an important and rich contribution to the scholarly literature, one filled with insights into the interrelationship between meaning, ornament, and space. That said, Harries's book shows its age as well as its philosophical genealogy. It relies on stylistic categories that today feel dated and its integration of aesthetic and historical observations seems insufficient in light of current knowledge about eighteenth-century culture. Nonetheless, Harries's book remains the best-developed investigation of this material in English and my debt to it in this essay shall soon become clear. In German-language scholarship, one finds a multitude of local and regional studies and several classic surveys, but few serious attempts to rethink or recategorize these buildings in new ways, and to my knowledge no scholarship that tries to revisit these churches in light of the many scholarly insights on French rococo art and architecture that have appeared recently.[3]

Whatever the underlying reasons for this neglect, its consequences are clear: there is no other corner of eighteenth-century European art in which so much important material remains unknown or understudied. I offer this essay as a preliminary contribution to a reengagement with rococo religious architecture, one that seeks to demonstrate its potential for enriching our broadening picture of eighteenth-century art. I shall do so by directing my analysis through perhaps the best known of these buildings, the Wieskirche or "Church in the Meadow." (fig.1) Located in a rural area of southern Bavaria, the Wieskirche was erected as a pilgrimage church between 1745 and 1754; it owes its strikingly beautiful design to the combined efforts of the architect Dominikus Zimmermann (1685–1766) and his elder brother, the painter and stucco carver Johann Baptist Zimmermann

Figure 1. Dominikus Zimmermann, Wieskirche, 1745–1754. Exterior view. (Photo: Marburg/Art Resource, NY)

(1680–1758).[4] Scholarly writing about the Wieskirche has emphasized its sophisticated treatment of interior space, in particular the way its masses and voids create a sense of aerated permeability that critics of architecture term "lightness."[5] (fig. 2) Indeed, the church's manipulation of light effects to produce gradations of brightness and shadow, its suffusion of light with spiritual values, and the apparent dematerialization of substance that results, are certainly among the building's most sophisticated design characteristics. Rather than understand this phenomenon as a purely formalist achievement, as the scholarship has often done, I shall argue that spatial permeability advances an eschatological theology related both to the church's function as a pilgrimage destination and as a modification of Enlightenment conceptions of sensation and knowledge. For rather than present Catholic doctrine as universal dogma, which one would expect an

Figure 2. Dominikus and Johann Baptist Zimmermann, Wieskirche. Interior. (Photo: Erich Lessing/Art Resource, NY)

early modern church to do, the Wieskirche instead presents salvation as a process, one that unfolds metaphorically through the experience of moving through its interior. Movement is more than just a stylistic quality enacted in the church's rocaille ornamentation; the rococo ornament's incitement of movement stages a particular human relationship to the divine.[6] In showing this, I shall suggest something more fundamental about Germanic applications of rococo ornament, namely that the Germans understood the rococo as an essentially spatial decorative mode and that their rococo forms engage issues of place and space differently and to a greater degree than their French counterparts. Indeed, they rely on such qualities intrinsically, and the Wieskirche illustrates how and why that is the case.

To begin, we might acknowledge that it has become cliché in discussions of early modern religious architecture to claim that a striving toward movement is one of its defining characteristics. From this perspective, the Bavarian rococo church appears the inheritor of Counter-Reformational urges in which architects incorporated curving architectural forms, semantic complexities, and spatial illusionism into their buildings to stimulate piety among believers and convince the potentially wayward of the church's sustained vitality. This lineage leads back at least as far as Francesco Borromini's seventeenth-century Roman churches, buildings whose spatial dynamism metaphorically visualizes spiritual passion. Yet the Bavarian rococo derives much from a French-inspired conception of the elite interior, rococo spaces that likewise insist upon movement to register their full visual and semantic content. That most emblematic of Parisian rococo rooms, the Salon de la Princesse in the Hôtel de Soubise, demonstrates how rococo forms permit a fluid relationship between movement and meaning. The shifting planes of the room's material surfaces, which vary from glass to mirrors to painted and gilded woodwork to oil paintings, invite the eye to bounce from surface to surface in unsettled, disruptive, yet potentially highly pleasing sensational permutations. These qualities of spatial malleability, fragmentation, and transformability relate in this context to the intrigues, embarrassments, and pleasures of elite sociability. Following Marian Hobson, art historians have designated this quality *papillotage*, a flickering effect reminiscent of a butterfly's flitting wings that arises from constantly shifting perceptions of light, surface, and space.[7] Motion is central to how a rococo room such as the Salon de la Princesse achieves *papillotage*, and indeed we can position motion dialectically in relation to such a room's inhabitants and their senses. The room's surfaces invite motion in order for their visual complexity to be perceived, even as motion reveals new combinations of sensations, always unstable, that animate the space. Therefore one might say that the rococo aesthetic principles employed in the Salon de la Princesse both invite movement and rely upon it to achieve their fullest effects.

It may seem a lengthy trip from an urban French elite interior to a rural German pilgrimage church, and indeed formulating the differences and connections between rococo ornamental applications in these two geographical arenas has been a major knot in the scholarly literature.

But the distance may not be as great as it first seems. Many francophone architects and designers relocated to Central Europe's major cultural centers; Parisian and Lorrainian artists and architects were active at all of the major German courts, from Berlin to Vienna, where they found ample patronage due to the Germanic nobility's fondness for French-inspired decorative designs. In Bavaria especially, the ties to French artistic culture were strong and strengthened further after Elector Max Emanuel's decade-long exile in Paris during the Wars of Spanish Succession.[8] Max Emanuel brought the Belgian-born architect François de Cuvilliés the Elder (1695–1768) back with him to Munich in 1715. After 1725, Cuvilliés held the position of *Hofbaumeister* at the electoral court there and published an extensive series of ornamental print books detailing rococo designs for wall decorations, furniture, and various luxury objects.[9] Johann Baptist Zimmermann worked alongside Cuvilliés on various projects in Munich, including the justly renowned interior of the Amalienburg, and therefore there is at least one direct link between the Wieskirche and the elite secular rococo.[10] French ornamental prints were likewise avidly collected among the artistically savvy in German-speaking Europe, which indicates that the likely routes of transmission were multiple and diverse.[11] For my purposes, it is enough to note that the Wieskirche employs similar shifting spatial complexities in its interior as does the Salon de la Princesse, but its function as a place of worship, combined with the specific metaphors and symbolism of its decoration, lends its ornament an entirely distinct purpose and a different effect.

Before we pursue this idea, however, it might help to know a little about how the Wieskirche came to be built. Its construction falls within a larger trend to outfit Catholic southern Germany with parish, abbey, and pilgrimage churches during the eighteenth century. This process resulted in hundreds of newly built or renovated religious spaces, many of them employing a rococo decorative format, that in toto amount to a major campaign to reassert the region's Catholic identity and rearticulate its ecclesiastically based social structure. This occurred both through new church and abbey construction instigated by the region's ecclesiastical class and through the development of new religious edifices to respond to burgeoning displays of popular piety.[12] The Wieskirche represents a mix of both processes in a single site. It was built to commemorate a wooden statue of the flagellated Christ first used in local religious processions. (fig. 3) This marionette-like effigy was cared for by a pious woman named Maria Lory, a widowed innkeeper resident near the Bavarian town of Steingaden, who claimed one day to experience a miracle: while praying before the statue, she looked up to see it crying real tears. We know of this from a chronology prepared by

Figure 3. Balthasar Augustin Albrecht and Egid Verhelst the Elder, High Altar of the Wieskirche. (Photo: Marburg /Art Resource, NY)

a later abbot at Steingaden, Marianus Mayr, written around 1759, in which he asserts that this apparently miraculous event took place on 14 June 1738[13]. As word traveled of Maria Lory's experience, pilgrims flocked to the area to venerate the holy image; many of these were sick or crippled individuals who came to pray for divine intercession against their ills.[14] The site's renown spread quickly, so fast in fact that the local ecclesiastical authorities struggled to monitor and appropriately direct the burgeoning crowds' enthusiasm. A small, simply decorated chapel was erected near Steingaden in the early 1740s; it was consecrated and mass first held there on 17 March 1744. The growing throngs of pilgrims quickly exceeded its capacity, for which reason the local ecclesiastics commenced with plans to erect a more commodious new church. They did so with the blessing of the presiding abbot, one Hyazinth Gassner, but his death in March 1745 rendered the project an orphan and the religious practices transpiring at Steingaden unsupervised. Mayr succeeded Gassner, assuming control over the new church after obtaining permission from the electoral court in Munich in June 1745.[15] Somewhat later the Steingaden religious authorities realized that the church required diocesan approval as well, and therefore work on it halted until an official commission could visit the site and report on its holiness. That visit took place from 14 to 16 September 1745.

It is worth pausing for a moment to reflect on what this series of events portended. The situation at Steingaden—swelling crowds of worshippers and pilgrims gathering at an only intermittently supervised site, displaying passionate religious fervor toward an unsubstantiated miracle, with chapels being built without proper church authorization—represented a highly problematic constellation of activities for the regional ecclesiastical authorities. Understanding why involves recognizing the complicated intellectual culture that existed within eighteenth-century Bavarian religious communities. The critical literature on Bavarian rococo architecture has tended to caricature the region as a lingering enclave of simplistic medieval piety, its people obstinately devout and dominated by a "peasant mentality" lacking in sophisticated conceptions of human affairs. This view has transmuted into an assessment of Bavaria as somehow anti-Enlightenment in mindset. Harries in particular has described Bavaria in these terms, noting that it lacked a strong middle class of the kind that fueled public discourse elsewhere in Europe, that the Catholic church remained powerful in the region, and that the former continental cultural significance of its major cities like Nuremberg and Augsburg had dwindled. The implication of such a characterization is that social conditions hindered the development of an Enlightenment-friendly culture, and the exuberant spiritualized decoration of Bavarian churches seems to substantiate this further.[16] Yet Bavaria's ecclesiastical class was involved profoundly in an intellectual reconsideration of religious expression, one parallel to societal reflections promulgated elsewhere and that has been characterized recently as the "Catholic Enlightenment."[17] The abbeys of the Pfaffenwinkel region, where the Wieskirche ultimately would be erected, were sites of significant inquiry into the interrelationship between theology and Enlightenment natural philosophy, often considered as overlapping intellectual domains whose correspondences enabled modification of divine understanding in light of new, proto-scientific thinking. These perhaps were not the bold speculations of Genevan, Parisian, or London-based philosophers, but neither were they a passive acceptance of outdated beliefs.[18] A major figure in this movement, one who strove to promote an ecclesiastical Enlightenment in Bavaria, was the Augustinian theologian and priest Eusebius Amort (1692–1775). He was resident at Polling Abbey, located a few miles to the northeast of Steingaden, and was a member of the committee that examined Maria Lory's "miracle" in September 1745. His intellectual pedigree inflected his interpretation of what he encountered there. Amort had befriended Pope Benedict XIV Lambertini while in Rome between 1733 and 1735 and he shared with the pontiff a desire to see devotional excesses curbed in the visualization of Catholic faith, a position he expounded in multiple writings on spirituality and the miraculous. It turns out that Amort's and Benedict's shared view of religious passion as an essentially earthly phenomenon had great implications for the Wieskirche's design.[19]

Amort postulated that most of what seemed to be paranormal, extraordinary phenomena like visions or revelations could be explained through recourse to two possible causes: trickery or natural effects. Only a very small number of apparent miracles were actually divine in origin. He developed this idea by extrapolating ideas out of Pope Benedict's lengthy and influential disquisition on the subject, a tract entitled *De Servorum Dei beatificatione et beatorum canonizatione,* in which Benedict provided rules for determining the authenticity of apparently miraculous occurrences and subsequently the beatification of those experiencing them, rules it should be noted that the Catholic Church still employs today.[20] Amort had absorbed and applied Benedict's thinking about these issues in his investigations of the German Catholic mystic Crescentia of Kaufbeuren; in a treatise entitled *De revelationibus, visionibus, et apparitionibus privatis,* published just a year before he became involved at Steingaden, Amort explored how personal revelations of God could be explained as the result of logical, earthly sources.[21] The gist of this process is that no phenomenon can be credited as miraculous until all possible natural or diabolical explanations have been investigated carefully and eliminated. Only then, after all other possibilities have been denied, can an event be deemed a divine intervention.[22]

Amort's assessment of divine revelation in his *De revelationibus* served him well when he traveled to Steingaden.[23] Amort regarded the miraculousness of Maria Lory's weeping statue with skepticism, but he simultaneously appreciated it as an incitement to good works. He did not believe that the miracle was real—the statue's teardrops were fake, he surmised, and their traces on the sculpted Christ's face made by a painter.[24] He even went so far as to express a wish that the statue remain in storage, brought out for view only on special occasions and at the local abbot's discretion. But Amort acknowledged that in this instance popular devotion had instigated an efflorescence of piety and public good, and for those reasons he ultimately condoned and authorized worship at the Wieskirche site.[25] Further supporting his approval was the pilgrims' focus on a representation of the suffering Christ and not on a relic of dubious origin or on Maria Lory herself. This directed the masses' devotional energies into a proper outlet, one very close to the traditional function of art in Catholic worship. Even Amort himself was moved by the statue's primitive beauty, so much so that he composed a spontaneous Latin couplet on its sentimental impact.[26]

But Amort's efforts in defining Maria Lory's "miracle" as an actually non-miraculous instigator of good works did not end there. In 1746, after the Zimmermann brothers had begun construction on the new church, it was Amort who supported the publication of the official ecclesiastical record of the "miracle," called in various editions the *Gnadenblum* or *Gnadenbüchlein*.[27] In it, the book's anonymous author argues against understanding Maria Lory's vision as miraculous and instead characterizes it and the subsequent outpouring of devotional piety as *Guttaten*, or good works. He further paraphrases Benedict's *De Servorum* directly in despiritualizing miracles generally and subjecting the seemingly miraculous to careful scrutiny.[28] As the *Gnadenblum* phrases it:

> Es ist derohalben wohl zu mercken, daß ein Miracul oder Wunderwerck eygentlich seye ein ungewöhnlich wunderliche Begebenheit wider, oder über die Kräfte der Natur, oder wenigstens die Arth und Weiß, wie sonsten die Natur zu würcken pfleget, so beschreibet, und theilet die Miracul ab der Heil. Thomas von Aquin; zu deme wird eine dergleichen ungewöhnliche Begebenheit vor ein Miracul offentlich nit erkennet, es sey dann ein Sach, daß selbe durch offentlichen Process von Bischoffen, oder seinem Vicario bewähret; dann es kan offtermahlen geschehen, daß ein Sach für ein Miracul gehalten weilen einem oder auch anderen Menschen die natürliche Ursach nit bekannt, welches nach des gelehrten Pignatelli nit erklecklich; massen die natürliche Ursach nit nur einen, oder auch mehrerem, sondern nach möglicher menschlicher Wissenschaft allen unbekannt seyn muß.[29]

The *Gnadenblum*'s text therefore justifies the role of an educated clergy versed to determine the truly miraculous, and in fact it was exactly this kind of culture that existed in Bavaria's cloisters and that Amort sought to promote in his administrative and educational activities. It also applies natural philosophy to human activity in its call for the ostensibly divine to undergo tests of human reason and its recommendation that nature explain most occurrences deemed miraculous.

It was this project of de-mystifying the Steingaden miracle that inflected the Wieskirche's design in the year before the laying of its foundation stone on 10 July 1746. The intermittent months between that date and the previous autumn's diocesan assessment are difficult to fill in. At some point the Zimmermann brothers were brought into the project, possibly even before Mayr became abbot, and the exact manner of their involvement there is today only imperfectly understood. Amort's involvement is likewise difficult to confirm, even though several surviving letters attest to his interest in activities at Steingaden and his careful conceptualization of the site's religious character.[30] Whether Amort could have influenced the church's design, or whether the design supervision fell to Mayr, or came from the architects themselves, remains unclear. Regardless of how its design came into existence, the church that the Zimmermann brothers built harmonizes remarkably well with Amort's thinking as expressed in his letters, his theological tracts, and the *Gnadenblum* whose publication he supported, and for these reasons his possible direct influence on the church is worth considering. That the architects themselves were likewise drawn to the site's allure has long been known, and Dominikus Zimmermann particularly displayed a strong personal attachment to this architectural project.[31] He relocated permanently to the area in 1752, built himself a small house there where he lived out his days, and worshipped regularly in the church he built. His son Franz even married the widowed Maria Lory. Yet for all the commitment of the architect to his project and to the devotional significance of the site, the character of the Wieskirche's interior harkens to Amort, since as I shall now demonstrate, something other than a pure expression of miraculous wonder is operational in its design.

It has often been noted that Zimmermann constructed the Wieskirche's interior to present a dramatic effect upon first entering its nave.[32] (fig. 2) If the church exemplifies divine wonder, it does so principally from this vantage point. Its decoration and interior organization appear unified there and some commentators have suggested that a perception of spatial coherency occurs at that spot as well. But the church's full complexity cannot be understood from that position, since it is ultimately a deceptive one; too much remains invisible initially and only becomes viewable as one moves into and through the church's interior. The introductory perception of decorative coherency therefore turns out to be false, and the miraculous event it seems to celebrate likewise soon emerges as complicated by the church's spatial arrangement. In the Wieskirche interior, surfaces shift, perceptions of solid and void vary, and new combinations of decorative data and imagery emerge and partially cohere, a point noted by Harries in his analysis of the church.[33] One might in this respect recall the Salon de la Princesse, whose interior surfaces demand movement as much as do the Wieskirche's, but here movement spiritualizes the interior since spatial progression repeatedly places religiously themed ornamental and pictorial iconography into view. This process achieves its most meaningful coordination in the building's apse, specifically in the relationship of the high altar to the ambulatory that encircles it. Ambulatories are of course a commonplace design element of pilgrimage churches, since they allow visitors to navigate around the altar without disturbing the ceremony of the mass. Zimmermann's design for the ambulatory and apse at the Wieskirche involved constructing a pseudo-arcade; two stories of joined columns and pilasters create a balcony-like effect that surrounds the altar area on either side, while also allowing considerable visual penetration between the apse and its surrounding spaces.[34] (fig. 4) This architectural configuration animates the process of walking in front of and around the altar, something pilgrims would typically do, and makes those moments of walking and looking into a false culmination of the entire pilgrimage experience, a point I shall explain further momentarily. In short, what Zimmermann accomplished here is to transform walking and looking into a metaphor for Christian faith and its relationship to a partially discernable yet unquestionably confirmed divine.

To see this, one can begin by noting that the apse arcade separates the altar from the ambulatory, but typically for rococo architecture it does not so much divide these spaces as emphasize their permeability, suggesting transitions and inviting views from one area to the next. This is especially true when one walks through one arm of the ambulatory and looks into the apse proper; when doing this, a surprising thing happens. Here I beg the reader's patience, since still images of a building's interior can never convey the full experience of actually moving through it. Atop the colonnaded balcony that demarcates the apse on either side are three rococo cartouches that frame openings in the apse wall. These voids hang in midair and punctuate the wall's vertical orientation. Looking upward from the ambulatory on the same side they appear simply as abstracted decorative forms; but looking across the apse from one arm of the ambulatory to the other, one sees *through* these freestanding rococo frames onto the church's exterior wall behind them. (fig. 5) Their undulating scrolls, rocaille forms, and waves allow light to pass through, which contributes to the church's complex interior lighting, and again typically of the rococo this involves much indirect and diffused light to create a sense of divinity. This is possible because there are irregularly shaped windows in the ambulatory

Figure 4. Wieskirche, upper choir, looking north. (Photo: Marburg/ Art Resource, NY)

Figure 5. Wieskirche, upper choir, looking north. (Photo: Marburg/ Art Resource, NY)

that correspond exactly to these rocaille-framed openings; as one moves through the space, light from these windows is partially directed through these frames to illuminate areas of the apse's center.[35]

But these hanging cartouches also act as moving frames for art. Painted on the walls several feet behind them are a series of paintings.[36] Three of these scenes appear in each leg of the ambulatory and correspond exactly to the three cartouches on each side. (fig. 6) They depict individual moments from the life of Jesus and illustrate his mercy and charity toward the suffering. These include representations of him healing the sick, the deaf, the paralyzed, the blind, the leprous, and even the dead as exemplified by the raising of Lazarus. They are simply painted and, despite being representations of miracles, are remarkably devoid of supernatural

Figure 6. Wieskirche, choir looking north with view toward windows (Photo: Marburg/Art Resource, NY

iconography. As one moves through the ambulatory, these scenes come in and out of view; they are not uniformly visible from any single spot, but must be observed while moving in order for their pictorial content to become evident. One first sees the open rococo frame with an empty wall behind it, then as one walks a picture emerges within and behind that freestanding frame, only to subsequently disappear again as one moves further to reveal once again an unadorned white wall. (fig. 5 and 6) The effect is not unlike that of watching a solar eclipse—the optical experience begins at one side and comes into view gradually before disappearing again at the opposite edge. The architecture here frames its pictorial subjects and does so in an exuberantly three-dimensional manner, thereby vitalizing the meanings conveyed in the art by demanding motion as part of the religious experience. Furthermore the architecture thematizes partiality, fragmentation, and ephemerality as central components of its spiritual experience. In that respect the Wieskirche insists upon a fourth dimension, time, for its message to unfold.

That these scenes frame the apse is significant in that they set up a relationship to the statue of the flagellated Christ, the object of the pilgrim's worship, which is located in a shrine at the high altar and is the *pièce de resistance* of the pilgrim's experience. In arranging scenes of charity around the apse, the church's space three-dimensionalizes the common representation of the object in popular devotional prints. The *Gnadenblum* begins with a picture of the Christ statue surrounded by images of his good deeds, and in that regard the Wieskirche's architecture resembles a devotional print transformed into a three-dimensional space.[37] Commentators have repeatedly remarked on how distinctive is this combination of architectural, ornamental, and painted components within the history of architecture, although Zimmermann's design is neither new nor unique. It resembles Piedmontese experiments with permeable space typified by Vittone or Juvarra, and the inclusion of wittily cartouched paintings and spatial play likewise again recalls the Salon de la Princesse.[38] In explaining them, Harries simply notes their oddness and the element of the unexpected they bring to the experience of the church: "Die Wies is full of surprises—here I only want to call attention to the curious openings in the upper ambulatory, which reappear, fantastically transformed, below the choir vault, providing shifting frames for the ambulatory's small frescoes."[39] Carl Lamb describes them as the fitting culmination of the pilgrim's journey, as the realization of all that the pilgrim longed for in their slow perambulation to the holy image.[40] Yet my observation suggests that this is not the case; the holiest area of the Wieskirche does not provide a resolution to anything, but in a typically rococo way culminates in spatial and semantic complexity. The only possible resolution of this experience will occur in the mind of the pilgrim, and likely after exiting the church. Perception and imagination fleetingly resolve what sensory experience of the church's interior presents as partial and unconfirmed.

Christ's charity is of course an entirely appropriate theme for the decoration of a pilgrimage church, one that attracted sick or ailing worshippers alongside those who sought penance for their sins. But divine mercy is presented to those visitors not as fact, but rather as activity; not as a tangible thing that art illustrates, but as something temporally bound, partially detectable, and ongoing, in other words as an undertaking. In this regard, a strict division between the miracles of Christ's life and our ability to perceive them is put into play. We see these stories illustrated for us in the church's decoration, but the architectural mode of their conveyance places us at a remove from comprehending them perfectly. The viewer's understanding of the miraculous is therefore moderated or qualified through the Wieskirche's architecture. We can never perceive of these miracles as straightforward representational wholes; they only take on that status when we move, and ultimately in our imagination.

More than one observer has used the metaphor of theater to explain exactly how this process of understanding through art works. Harries has described Bavarian rococo churches in their entirety as reminiscent of the theater in that the pilgrim/worshipper acts as an actor who gives life to the concepts represented in the church's decoration through his presence.[41] That is certainly true, as my discussion above demonstrates, but more to the point is that the divine is presented in them not as comprehensible totally through human sensation, but always remaining to some degree beyond full apprehension, a status that the worshipper's motion activates and seems to resolve, but actually only reinforces as partially perceptible and distant. Salvation is known through representation, here as in any Catholic church, but one can comprehend it only fragmentarily, that is unless one moves. It is knowable, but must be energized by the worshipper's physical transportation through the space.

Harries sees theatrical affects like this as both enforcing and destructive of devotional aesthetics, arguing that "...the rococo, at least in Bavaria, can be understood as a playful potentiation of the baroque that at the same time implies its negation. *In the rococo the baroque destroys itself*."[42] Here Harries is arguing against the sometime assertion that the Bavarian rococo represents the waning of religious piety in an Enlightened world, a point with which my earlier discussion concurs entirely. He continues: "Its play with perspective is more than an aesthetic game; it is part of a last successful attempt to create a genuinely religious art that knows about the insufficiency not only of art, but of the visible. The Bavarian rococo's unwillingness to simply adopt illusionism [...] does not stem from an inability to take the theatre seriously. Quite the contrary. Because the Bavarian rococo continues to take the theatre so seriously, because it is unwilling to subject it to the rule of perspective, it cannot accept that pictorialization of the theatre."[43] Harries notes here that by shifting away from a perspectival system in which art is viewed from fixed positions to the operational spatiality of the Bavarian church, such churches reveal profound devotion in what appears to be aesthetic play. Harries's argument, couched in abstract philosophical and stylistic terms, enables a valuable conclusion: that a new understanding of the human interaction with and comprehension of the divine is represented through the Wieskirche's theatricalization of space. That newness is a belief in the human mind's ability to understand the natural world and comprehend it rationally, a procedure that does not invalidate the divine, but redefines its relationship to human sensation. The divine is there, and the Wieskirche makes it apparent, but not through straightforward picturing. Spatial play through rococo ornament and art transforms the divine to a new sensational logic, one in which the actual miraculousness of Jesus' acts are confirmed as inscrutable.

Harries is at pains to show how this change related to a rationalist mindset that nonetheless rests on Catholic conceptions of belief. The seventeenth century, he argues, went too far in its glorification of theatrical effects in religious architecture, to the point of using visual and spatial complexity to recreate the divine in sensual, phenomenal terms.[44] The Bavarian rococo, in contrast, is aware that the divine can only be known insufficiently and imperfectly, that there are limits to our senses' ability to comprehend it. Harries seems therefore to argue against the predominant deist strain of eighteenth-century religious thought that tried to argue for a knowable, rationally provable God. The Wieskirche's motion-activated interior complicates Harries's view more than he recognizes, since the ambulatory frames promote a sense of a mystical divine yet simultaneously draw attention to our sensory capability for understanding it transitorily. It is not quite right to say that the divine exists either in our world phenomenally or is beyond our understanding; the Wieskirche puts the divine somewhere in between these antipodes in a typically eighteenth-century way, and in fact leaves its exact nature at once sensorily detectable and difficult to locate. It is there, we can sense it partially, but never completely and never as a totally convincing illusion of the real. It is miraculous, yet knowable, and perceptible yet ephemeral all at once.

Seventeenth-century churches, edifices constructed a century closer to Counter-Reformational ardor, reinforce faith through the process of seeing and perceiving. In the Wieskirche, however, vision is divided and partial. The pilgrim must believe that the rest is there, since he knows it and has just seen it, and his perceptions enable him to remember that which he once saw but is now out of view. He acts on faith, and in that respect the Wieskirche's architectural complexity encourages and stimulates belief not through representing before the worshipper, but in the mind of the worshipper after they have moved through the church. The church is not wonder revealed, at least not after the initial moment of entry, but rather wonder ongoing in the sensations of the believer. The pilgrim's movement through the church stimulates that action, but also metaphorizes it. There is therefore a shift here from the Catholic doctrine of art as illustration of Christian truths, as a text for the illiterate believer, to art as a prompt for belief. Art incites faith as action through motion.

Piety is very much the point of this building's decorative program, but that piety is not presented as something finite, coherent, and ultimately clear in its implications. Rather, the actions of the worshipper are required to effectuate it, and I think that message makes particular sense in the context of a pilgrimage church whose congregation may only have worshipped here for a limited period within a much longer spiritual life. The deeper purpose of a religious pilgrimage is not to worship at a holy site, but rather to return home spiritually transformed, altered in one's faith and righted on the path toward salvation.[45] That transformation requires work through good deeds; it cannot simply occur in the act of being a pilgrim, but must be reenacted continually in a gradual movement toward eternity. The Wieskirche prepares the believer for further activity later in life through emphasizing his role as an active agent in a spiritual journey. The church's ceiling fresco, which represents Judgment Day about to take place and which vertically associates the door to eternal life with the entry vestibule of the church, only makes the connection between future salvation and the worshipper's actions more explicit. For just as life, viewed through a Catholic lens, is a series of choices that bring the believer closer to or farther from salvation, so does the Wieskirche present salvation as a series of changing visions that are not stationary, but become whole or dissolve through passage within its interior. Harries calls this an outgrowth of a rural peasant mentality, one in which the worshipper is "in the grip of higher powers that he could not control and not fully understand."[46] But to my eyes it simply a reassertion of certain fundamental Catholic beliefs, grounded firmly in a rational sense of self positioned in dialogue with an inexplicable yet only incompletely perceptible divine. Human sensation is rational enough to identify that the divine exists beyond it, and in that sense perhaps there is a trace strain of inadvertent deism in the church's ornamental theology.[47]

I would suggest further that this interpretation of the Wieskirche's effects is fundamentally an Amortian one. The Wieskirche renders the divine inscrutable except for its actuation in human activity. Good works, rather than a straightforward celebration of the miraculous, ultimately is the order of the day. The apparent miraculous unity of the church's interior turns out to be a false perception, one that further exploration and understanding of the church's interior reveals as a misapprehension. Knowledge prevails over uninformed wonder. Likewise, the apparent culmination of the pilgrim's experience at the altar and ambulatory results in ambiguity, inciting further investigation and contemplation in the pilgrim's post-pilgrimage life. The apparently miraculous—be it Jesus' good deeds or Maria Lory's vision—are compromised through the church's rococo indeterminacies, which draw attention to the pilgrim's ability to perceive of the divine, as well as the limits of doing so. And the miraculous as such becomes an illusion in the mind of the pilgrim, one insistently irresolute in the church's decorative program but attaining fleeting coherency in the pilgrim's imagination. The importance of good deeds through future human activity, and not unchanneled divine intervention, become what this church ultimately celebrates in its rococo semantic and spatial complexity. Furthermore, the existence of the divine is promoted, even glorified, but in terms that recast the passionate baroque miracle into a controlled phenomenon while still acknowledging its unfathomable genesis. Christopher Johns has noticed a similar tension in eighteenth-century Italian painting, which was influenced by teaching missions and religious sermons that desired to "rationalize faith while retaining its revelatory mystique."[48] The Wieskirche achieves exactly this by locating the miraculous within the worshipper's evanescent imagination. The building represents a hedge between pure belief and pure knowing, and only in the pilgrim's actions can that conundrum, at least temporarily, be resolved.

In conclusion, I'd like to parse out some of the preceding argument's implications. It should be clear that rococo arabesques and cartouches were not incorporated into the Wieskirche solely to be decorative, although they are decoration and function on the level of adorning the interior and pleasing viewers with their beauty. They also act as intermediaries between the worshipping inhabitant and the concepts at work in the church's spiritual content.[49] That intermediary role exceeds simply framing or accompanying; it dislocates the viewer's previous psycho-spatial sense of his relationship to the sensate world and whatever lay beyond. It is in this respect that the rococo church can be understood as intervening into the believer's place within a larger spiritualized cosmos. Many churches do this with their interior decoration, but the Wieskirche emboldens the worshipper's process of psychic regeneration more than most; it requires and celebrates the worshipper's inner perceptions of the divine, and the result is greater devotional agency that relates, I have tried to demonstrate, to Enlightenment Catholicism. Speaking more broadly, rococo spatial and semantic ambiguity is used here for a specific set of concerns emergent from the spiritual, social, political, and doctrinal concerns of this site. Other eighteenth-century rococo churches may display similar characteristics, but the flexibility of rococo aesthetics permitted a wide range of applications and implications that operated on the level of the individual building. Positing a general set of tenets for all rococo religious architecture, or worse, lumping these buildings together into an undifferentiated mass, glosses over the precise concerns that rococo forms illuminated for a society that saw in them an opportunity to express profound spiritual and social matters. It is my hope that future scholarship will view Bavarian and Central European rococo churches not simply as reckless derivatives, but as buildings where rococo ornamentation's full potential was understood and put to work.

NOTES

1. Sincere thanks to Jeffrey Collins, Christopher Johns, and Alistaire Tallent for their contributions to my thinking about this subject. Henry-Russell Hitchcock, *Rococo Architecture in Southern Germany* (London: Phaidon, 1968); and *German Rococo: The Zimmermann Brothers* (Baltimore: Penguin Books, 1968). These volumes collect diverse essays that Hitchcock published in 1950s and 1960s. A current summary of the field is Ulrich Leben, "German Rococo: From Cuvilliés in Munich to Nahl in Potsdam," in *Rococo: The Continuing Curve*, ed. Sarah D. Coffin, et al. (New York: Cooper-Hewitt National Design Museum, 2008), 136–49.

2. Karsten Harries, *The Bavarian Rococo Church: Between Faith and Aestheticism* (New Haven: Yale University Press, 1983).

3. The classic survey being Norbert Lieb, *Barockkirchen zwischen Donau und Alpen* (Munich: Hirmer, 1953). Noteworthy as well are the studies of Hermann Bauer, including *Rocaille: Zur Herkunft und zum Wesen eines Ornament-Motivs* (Berlin: Walter de Gruyter, 1962); *Der Himmel im Rokoko: Das Fresko im deutschen Kirchenraum im 18. Jahrhundert* (Regensburg: Pustet, 1965); *Rokokomalerei* (Mittenwald: Mäander, 1980); and *Johann Baptist und Dominikus Zimmermann: Entstehung und Vollendung des bayerischen Rokoko* (Regensburg: Pustet, 1985). A most welcome recent exception to this situation, focusing on sculpture, is Christiane Hertel, *Pygmalion in Bavaria: The Sculptor Ignaz Günther and Eighteenth-Century Aesthetic Art Theory* (University Park, PA: Pennsylvania State University Press, 2011).

4. Carl Lamb, *Die Wies* (Munich: Süddeutscher Verlag, 1964), remains the reference monograph on the building. See also Bauer, *Zimmermann*, 58–63.

5. See, for example, the lengthy disquisitions on light provided by Lamb, *Die Wies*, 84–85 and 101–106, and the intepretative analysis of space and light offered by Hermann Bauer, "Zur Bedeutung der Wieskirche," in *Die Wies: Geschichte und Restaurierung*, ed. Michael Petzet (Munich: Bayerisches Landesamt für Denkmalpflege, 1992), 73–80.

6. This sense of eighteenth-century interior space as a promulgator of movement is explored in a recent collection of essays: *Architectural Space in Eighteenth-Century Europe: Constructing Identities and Interiors*, ed. Denise Amy Baxter and Meredith Martin (Farnham: Ashgate, 2010), especially 1–4, albeit with a focus on secular architecture.

7. Marian Hobson, *The Object of Art: The Theory of Illusion in Eighteenth-*

Century France (Cambridge: Cambridge University Press, 1982), 47–61; and for *papillotage* as metamorphosis, see Mary D. Sheriff, "Seeing Metamorphosis in Sculpture and the Decorative Arts," in *Taking Shape: Finding Sculpture in the Decorative Arts*, ed. Martina Droth (Los Angeles: Getty Publications, 2009), 158–65.

8. During which Max Emanuel participated in the building boom that took place in and around Paris in the 1710s and 1720s. For his palace at Saint-Cloud, see Max Tillmann, "*Très belle, agréable et bien meublée*: The Electoral Palace at Saint-Cloud in the Early Eighteenth Century," in Baxter and Martin, *Architectural Space*, 35–55; and Tillmann, *Ein Frankreichbündnis der Kunst: Kurfürst Max Emanuel von Bayern als Auftraggeber und Sammler* (Munich: Deutscher Kunstverlag, 2009).

9. Wolfgang Braunfels, *François Cuvilliés: Der Baumeister der galanten Architektur des Rokoko* (Munich: Süddeutscher Verlag, 1986), 111–15.

10. Braunfels, *François Cuvilliés*, 210–11. See also Horst Mellenthin, *François Cuvilliés' Amalienburg: Ihr Bezug zur französischen Architekturtheorie* (Munich: Tuduv, 1989).

11. Alastair Laing, "French Ornamental Engravings and the Diffusion of the Rococo," in *Le stampe e la diffusione delle immagini e degli stile*, ed. Henri Zerner (Bologna: Editrice Clueb, 1979), 109–27. Laing argues that craftsmen transmitted rococo forms to Germany in advance of prints. For recent assessments of this subject, see Sarah D. Coffin, "Radiating Rococo: The Dissemination of Style through Migrating Designers, Craftsmen, and Objects in the Eighteenth Century," in *The Continuing Curve*, 102–35; and Philippe Poindront, "Augsbourg, centre de reproduction de gravures d'ornement parisiennes au XVIIIe siècle," *Histoire de l'art* 61 (October 2007): 27–37.

12. Mary Lee Nolan and Sidney Nolan, *Christian Pilgrimage in Modern Western Europe* (Chapel Hill: University of North Carolina Press, 1989), 106–7. The authors note that the largest number of new pilgrimage sites created in post-reformation Europe was not in Italy or Spain, but rather Catholic Central Europe. Forty-nine new religious sites appeared there between the middle-sixteenth and late-eighteenth centuries, which exceeds thirty for the same period in Italy, twenty-six in Iberia, and twenty-one in France. They likewise note that the Germanic lands developed a particular inclination toward shrines devoted to images of Jesus, a point made in connection to the Wieskirche by Thomas and Helene Finkenstaedt in two related publications: *Der Wies-Heiland. Seine Devotional-Kopien und verwandte Andachtsbilder des Christus an der Geisselsäule* (Würzburg: Bayerische Blätter für Volkskunde, 1981); and *Materialien zur Wies-Wallfahrt* (Würzburg: Bayerische Blätter für Volkskunde, 1981), both published in association with the Bayerisches Nationalmuseum.

13. Thomas Finkenstaedt, "Das Gnadenbild des Gegeißelten Heiland auf der Wies und sein Rahmen: Wallfahrt und Baugeschichte," in Petzet, *Die Wies*, 45–46. See also Finkenstaedt, "Zur Baugeschichte der Wieskirche." *Jahrbuch des Vereins für christliche Kunst in München* 11 (1980): 109–15.

14. Thomas and Helene Finkenstaedt, *Die Wieswallfahrt. Ursprung und Ausstrahlung der Wallfahrt zum Gegeißelten Heiland* (Regensburg: Verlag F. Pustet, 1981), 86–89. The pilgrimage began as a mostly local and regional phenomenon, but

after the first prints of the Wies statue were produced in the middle 1740s, pilgrims began flocking to the site from across continental Europe. One source, dating from 1779, describes them as hailing from Germany (including Austria and Switzerland), Bohemia, Hungary, and the adjacent provinces of eastern France and northern Italy. Surviving documentation also permits an understanding of their number. The Wies parish kept records on communicants, whose yearly total peaked at 39,000 in 1762. This indicates that by the 1760s, Wies had developed into a pilgrimage destination of international stature and significance.

15. Lamb, *Die Wies*, 29. Mayr obtained consent in June, and there survives a letter dated 7 December 1745 that mentions Dominikus Zimmermann's plan for the church choir, indicating that the architect was involved in the project by that date and building underway. A nearly contemporary letter from Amort likewise mentions the choir area under construction in fall 1745.

16. Harries, *Bavarian Rococo Church*, 197.

17. Christopher M. S. Johns, "Gender and Genre in the Religious Art of the Catholic Enlightenment," in *Italy's Eighteenth Century: Gender and Culture in the Age of the Grand Tour*, ed. Paula Findlen, Wendy Wassyng Roworth, and Catherine M. Sama (Stanford, CA: Stanford University Press, 2009), 331–33, with additional bibliography.

18. Finkenstaedt, *Die Wieswallfahrt*, 49.

19. On Amort, see Georg Rückert, *Eusebius Amort und das bayerische Geistesleben im 18. Jahrhundert* (Munich: Verlag Franz X. Seitz, 1956); and Karin Precht-Nussbaum, *Zwischen Augsburg und Rom. Der Pollinger Augustiner-Chorherr Eusebius Amort (1692–1775). Ein bedeutender Repräsentant katholischer Aufklärung in Bayern* (Paring: Augustiner-Chorherr Verlag, 2007).

20. Benedict, *De Servorum Dei beatificatione et beatorum canonizatione* 4 vols (Bologna, 1734–38).

21. Eusebius Amort, *De revelationibus, visionibus, et apparitionibus privatis* (Augsburg, 1744). The book subsequently appeared in Italian editions, including a Venetian one in 1750. See Finkenstaedt, *Wieswallfahrt*, 51, and for Amort's interest in mysticism generally see Rückert, *Eusebius Amort*, 21–31.

22. Such caution may have been necessitated by the German predilection for religious shrines associated with seemingly spontaneous miracles. See Nolan and Nolan, *Christian Pilgrimage*, 241–49. Almost half of the 459 miracle shrines documented in Europe are located in predominantly German-speaking regions. A detailed historical study of later German holy apparitions, demonstrating their remarkable tenacity across the centuries, is David Blackbourn, *Marpingen: Apparitions of the Virgin Mary in Nineteenth-Century Germany* (New York: Alfred A. Knopf, 1994).

23. Finkenstaedt, *Wieswallfahrt*, 62.

24. To some degree, Amort's statements evoke the tradition of having an ecclesiastical official play devil's advocate during the authentication of spiritual occurrences; such a figure was deemed essential in processes of canonization. It should be noted, however, that Amort's thoughts about the apparent worldliness of the Wies "miracle" are not isolated comments, but emerge from a sustained critique

of the miraculous that began with Benedict and that Amort developed in his writings over decades.

25. Finkenstaedt, *Wieswallfahrt*, 52.

26. Finkenstaedt, *Wieswallfahrt*, 62–64. Amort's couplet reads: *Tam grato Capiti, nur membra informia sponsas?/Nam Caput es nobis, nos tibi membra sumus.*

27. The anonymous publication's proper title is *Neu-entsproßene Gnadenblumen auf der Wis* (Augsburg: Anton Maximilian Heiss, 1746). A modern reprint appeared in 1999 from Verlag Anton H. Konrad, Weissenhorn.

28. *Gnadenblum*, 16–17. The book's anonymous author then directly references Benedict XIV on the subject of converting sinners. *Gnadenblum*, 17 forward.

29. "It is therefore good to recognize that a miracle or wondrous event could simply be an unusual, rare occurrence, or be driven by the powers of nature, or at the least through the art and manner that nature tends to work; so are miracles related to us and described by St Thomas Aquinas. Furthermore we cannot easily distinguish an unusual occurrence of this kind from a true miracle, and therefore it is a matter that can be determined only through the public inquiry of bishops or their deputies. Then again it sometimes occurs that something is taken for a miracle when people don't know its natural causes, which after the understanding of the educated Pignatelli [Pope Innocent XII], we know happens considerably often. One must assess natural causes not only by one or by several possibilities, but instead by all possible human knowledge, before something is declared to have a miraculous origin." *Gnadenblum*, 14–15. The translation is mine.

30. Transcribed in Finkenstaedt, "Das Gnadenbild," 49; and Finkenstaedt, *Wieswallfahrt*, 62–65.

31. Lamb, *Die Wies*, 17.

32. Lamb, *Die Wies*, 49.

33. Harries, *The Bavarian Rococo Church*, 155.

34. Lamb, *Die Wies*, 91–95 and 102–05.

35. Perfecting the mechanics of this spatial arrangement appears to have preoccupied the Zimmermanns to a special degree. Few architectural drawings survive from their studio, but one that can be traced to them with reasonable certainty is a drawing of the interior apse wall looking into the ambulatory, in other words precisely the view analyzed here, now housed at the Städtisches Museum Weilheim, Germany. The drawing illustrates how the three open rococo cartouches relate to the windows and paintings in the ambulatory behind them, as well as to the apse interior below. For an illustration, see Petzet, *Die Wies*, 190; and for a discussion, Alois Epple, ed., *Dominikus Zimmermann: Zur 300. Wiederkehr seines Geburtsjahres* (Munich and Zurich: Schnell & Steiner, 1985), 38–39.

36. On the Wieskirche's interior imagery, see Anna Bauer-Wild, "Das Bildprogramm der Wieskirche," in Petzet, *Die Wies*, 53–58. The inventor of the church's program, which Bauer-Wild notes was conceived with unusual semantic coherency, remains unknown, but likely was a representative from the nearby Steingaden abbey. Likewise is the precise authorship of these six paintings unclear, but that they were made under Johann Baptist Zimmermann's direct supervision is beyond doubt.

37. Lamb, *Die Wies*, 69–70.

38. Richard Pommer, *Eighteenth-Century Architecture in Piedmont: The Open Structures of Juvarra, Alfieri, and Vittone* (New York: New York University Press, 1967). Pommer, 68, notes that this conception of "open architecture" had parallels and legacies in central European architecture, particularly in Kassel and Vienna.

39. Harries, *The Bavarian Rococo Church,* 139.

40. Lamb, *Die Wies*, 70.

41. His argument is actually considerably more complex than this, since he finds in Bavarian churches multiple overlapping layers of stages. Harries, *The Bavarian Rococo Church*, 120–21.

42. Harries, *The Bavarian Rococo Church*, 121, emphasis in the original.

43. Harries, *The Bavarian Rococo Church*, 149–50.

44. Harries, *The Bavarian Rococo Church*, 154.

45. The literature on pilgrimage has characterized spiritual transformation in varied ways. One influential perspective comes from Victor and Edith Turner, *Image and Pilgrimage in Christian Culture* (New York: Columbia University Press, 1978), who stress the concept of *communitas* as the mental and social state that provides the desired spiritual self-understanding. A contrasting view appears in John Eade and Michael J. Sallnow, eds, *Contesting the Sacred: The Anthropology of Christian Pilgrimage* (London: Routledge, 1991), where the authors argue that pilgrimage is a more individually motivated experience and that the holy shrine is a site of contestation and conflict.

46. Harries, *The Bavarian Rococo Church*, 201.

47. Which is not to say that the church or its builders espoused such deistic possibilities knowingly. German theology flirted with deism for much of the eighteenth century, and some German thinkers sought to meld the results of modern natural philosophy with theology into what Thomas P. Saine has termed an "astonishing syncretism" of divergent intellectual strains. This "physicotheology" thrived despite persistent public resistance against anything openly termed deism. See Saine, *The Problem of Being Modern, or The German Pursuit of Enlightenment from Leibniz to the French Revolution* (Detroit: Wayne State University Press, 1997), 187–89 and 193–98.

48. Johns, "Gender and Genre," 339.

49. On rococo ornament as pictorial intermediary, see Bauer, *Rocaille*, 61–63.

Print Culture, Marketing, and Thomas Stothard's Illustrations for The Royal Engagement Pocket Atlas, 1779–1826

SANDRO JUNG

This article will offer an account of a now very rare late eighteenth- and early nineteenth-century pocket diary-cum-almanac, which was targeted at a multifarious audience largely from the middling ranks of British society: *The Royal Engagement Pocket Atlas*. As a contribution to the history of the ephemeral book, it briefly sketches the variety of illustrated pocket books in the 1790s and then examines both the marketing strategies employed by its publisher and the importance of book illustration—particularly the vignettes of Thomas Stothard—in the formation of a canon of literary texts at the end of the eighteenth century. My central concern is to investigate the ideologically representative meanings of Stothard's illustrative paratexts and relate them to proliferating cultures of consumerism. Focusing on the genesis, fashioning, and long "life" of the *Royal Engagement Pocket Atlas*, the article will explore both the interpretive narratives of the printed designs and the cultural phenomenon of the almanac among the middle and upper classes as an ephemeral, but desirable product belonging to the expanding world of eighteenth-century print culture.

A practically unexplored market for pocket diaries for the middle and upper classes emerged in the last three decades of the eighteenth century, which offered a new product, the so-called "pocket-book." Containing not only calendar and diary pages but material for instruction, ruled memorandum pages, and "cash accounts" as well, these books (of up to 150 pages in length) were fashionable late eighteenth-century middle-class accessories. The pocket book is a hybrid genre that incorporates features from such earlier genres as the almanac offering information on important dates of the year but also including information that is more directly aimed at the middle classes. The replacement of the astrological pages, weather forecasts, and agricultural advice with ruled pages to be used as diaries positioned the pocket book as a publication for the professional and middle classes, as well as the aristocracy. In the course of the genre's history in the late eighteenth and nineteenth centuries, special class-specific sections reflecting the different needs, interests, and concerns of the users of these pocket books were introduced. The books' diary sections—now ornately embellished with engraved illustrations—derived primarily from more functional pocket and memorandum books such as *The Universal Cash Book and Newcastle Pocket Diary* which was declared to be "Suited to Every Gentleman's and Tradesman's Business" and sold at one shilling sixpence in the 1770s. Although the titles of these publications frequently designate themselves as "almanacs," only the cheapest among them still carried the extensive material relating to prophecies, astrology, and the seasonal cycle that characterised earlier almanacs, which were first advertised and issued by the Stationers' Company in the seventeenth century and would remain popular into the nineteenth.[1] The pocket book, exemplified by the carefully illustrated *Royal Engagement Pocket Atlas*, by way of contrast, was not aimed to be an instrument of business or astrology, but an object of consumer pleasure and device for social engagement.

The pocket diary as an ephemeral print cultural genre has not yet received much systematic scholarly attention, although Jenny Batchelor has insightfully examined a related genre, the pocket book for women.[2] The neglect of the pocket diary in general by scholars can be explained by the scarcity of surviving copies with only a few scattered across collections in Britain and North America. No major research collection holds a complete or even near complete run of any of these ephemeral publications nor is there even a catalog or source that has compiled all the individual copies held in the world's archives and libraries. The English Short Title Catalog (ESTC), for example, is missing some of the copies I have traced. WorldCat has records of eleven different copies of the *Pocket Atlas*,[3] while Copac references a further seven.[4] I have two different volumes in my possession—the atlases for 1810 and 1825—and have traced two more in archives in the United Kingdom.[5] Owing to the scarcity of copies of the *Pocket Atlas* any critical investigation must necessarily be tentative. An added problem in the study of such ephemeral publications is the need to examine the actual material objects, their binding, paper, and general layout, as well as any traceable palimpsests that cannot be approached through databases such as ECCO whose digital imaging is unsatisfactory for the study of illustrations and other materiality-specific elements of books. Despite the limitations here, studying the known individual copies, their annotations, and the newspaper advertisements that describe each new annual number's special features illuminates the nature of these ephemera, not to mention the interplay between readers and texts.

The most prominent of these pocket diaries featured engraved illustrations, while other, more cheaply produced diaries such as *Crosby's Royal Fortune-Telling Almanack; or, Ladies Universal Pocket Book*, selling at one shilling ("bound in red") or one shilling sixpence ("Gilt extra with Pockets"),[6] included a single full-page engraving designed by Isaac Cruikshank, the father of the better known George Cruikshank. Pocket almanacs such as *The Royal Repository, or Polite Pocket Diary* (produced between the early 1790s and 1838)[7] and *The Polite Repository or Pocket Companion* (produced between 1781 and the 1870s) featured engraved plates of landscapes, architectural structures, and stately homes, the latter based on original work by the eminent garden designer Humphry Repton.[8] Illustration was marketed as a material asset, and in the advertisement for his pocket diary, the proprietor of the *Royal Repository* emphasized that it was "embellished with an emblematical Frontispiece and Twelve other capital Engravings."[9] During the early 1790s a number of new pocket books such as *Le Souvenir, or, Pocket Remembrancer* (1792–1803, after which time it was published under the revised title of *Le Souvenir, or, Pocket Tablet*) were conceived and built upon the format that the earlier illustrated pocket diaries had defined. J. Godwin, the bookseller publishing *Le Souvenir*, advertised the first volume in November 1791 as

> A New, Elegant, and Superb POCKET BOOK, entitled LE SOUVENIR, or POCKET REMEMBRANCER, embellished with Twelve elegant Engravings by Heath, after Drawings by Burney and Dodd, selected from English History, and Twelve Miscellaneous Engravings by Milton and Landseor; consisting of Gentlemen's Seats, Views in the Isle of Wight, &c. &c. From Drawings by Nattes, Barrow, and J. Nixon, Esq. to which is subjoined Monthly Memorandum Pages, and a complete cash account for each month.[10]

The pocket diary was initially priced at three shillings sixpence in "Paper Boxes" but from November 1793 was available at the cost of "3s. 6d. in a neat Case, and may be had in a Variety of Bindings, to any Price."[11] In 1797 the bookseller increased the price to four shillings to accommodate "the great Advance on Stamps."[12]

Out of the various pocket diaries on the late eighteenth-century market, *The Royal Engagement Pocket Atlas* distinguished itself in several respects: it was the first among the illustrated pocket diaries and it uniquely took the illustration of literary texts, such as, among others, Thomas Parnell's *The Hermit*, James Thomson's *The Seasons*, and Sir Walter Scott's novels and poetry, as its annual subject; it established a pattern of paratextual composition that would be found in the later pocket books of the period and it used marketing strategies—explicitly stated in the bookseller's advertisements—which were largely imitated by the producers of similar publications. The explicit targeting of an audience is clear from its beginning. In October 1778, the Southampton-based stationer and bookseller, Thomas Baker, advertised the first 1779 number of this up-market diary in duodecimo format, specifically flagging that it was "Calculated for the politer circles":

> It is presumed the utility of this little performance, in having 365 commodious divisions for the engagements of the year, the uncommon elegance of its execution, on near 40 copper-plates, by that celebrated artist Mr. [John] Hall, with an equal number of pages, replete with useful information for the pocket, in the neatest type the metropolis could furnish, and the whole comprized in a case not exceeding the size of a moderate letter, will merit the patronage and encouragement of a polite and judicious Public.[13]

In January 1779, Baker advertised the publication again, and, at the same time, noted its immediate commercial success, describing that the "uncommon demand for the Atlas bespeaks real merit, and [...] the noble and refined arts of printing and engraving are truly and masterly exemplified."[14]

Thomas Baker was an astute bookseller who specialised in issuing works of local interest including *The Southampton Guide* (1772), the Rev. Richard Warner's *The History of the Isle of Wight* (1775), devotional poetry and sermons, one novel, *Moreton Abbey, or the Fatal Mystery* (1786) by Harriet Chilcot Meziere, and John Bullar's popular *A Companion in a Visit to Netley Abbey* (1800). He has also been associated with the printing of the *Hampshire Chronicle* and was the proprietor from 1767 of a circulating library in Southampton.[15] His *Pocket Atlas* was to have a long life, running from 1779 to 1826. Initially printed by S. Couchman in Southampton, by 1800 the *Pocket Atlas* was printed in London. Baker's first London agent was

Thomas Beecroft who was "appointed as the Wholesale Vender for Great Britain,"[16] but in 1782, his place was taken by William Marsh, Stationer; not only did Marsh act as Baker's agent, he also simultaneously became the co-publisher of the atlas. Baker must have relied on Marsh's distribution of the publication in the metropolis, and their publishing partnership was to last until the final number of the atlas in 1826.

In terms of its formal structure, *The Royal Engagement Pocket Atlas* changed little over the course of the publication's existence. It always included twenty-four diary pages (consisting of two pages for each month), information on important societal events throughout the year, lists of the members of the Royal family, the "Crowned Heads of Europe," archbishops, bishops, and deans, as well as maps of the world and Great Britain. The earliest volumes carried elaborate printers' ornaments such as floral borders, garlands, and other decorative headpieces designed by Edward Edwards who, in the 1780s and 1790s, also produced extensive visual material for John Bell's and Charles Cooke's series of editions of "The British Poets." All the volumes also carried a full-page engraved frontispiece featuring the mythological figure of Atlas, but this figure evolved over time with every number of the publication printing a new version of the design.[17] (fig. 1a) (fig. 1b) (fig. 1c) In the case of the pocket atlas for 1788, the wrapper consisted of thicker paper (two conjoined sheets into which the binding cords were integrated) on which the engraved full-page plate of Atlas was printed; the back cover page featured a female writing, a cherub, and a male figure in the background, as well as a caption giving the publisher's information. The title page was unique in that it featured another full-page engraved heraldic image incorporating the royal lion, unicorn, and crest, amplifying the more modest original title-page design of the atlas for the year 1779. (fig. 2) The whole was placed into a natural setting with a sophisticatedly executed tree on the left (especially in the top half) and more foliage in the foreground. Other early mythologizing plates featured cornucopias as media to emphasize the range of information that Baker's publication provided. (fig. 3a) and (fig. 3b) In the first three years of its publication, Baker's *Pocket Atlas* developed into a desirable ephemeral item featuring high-quality illustrated vignettes that clearly distinguished itself from other, cheaper diary almanacs. As we will see below, it would be the vignettes from 1783 forward—based on the drawings of Thomas Stothard—that would make *The Royal Engagement Pocket Atlas* an especially appealing print object.

The initial three numbers of the *Pocket Atlas* still retained the (traditional almanac-specific) pictorial references to the zodiac in the vignettes at the heads of the memorandum pages. In the first number, the general font was significantly smaller than in later volumes of the atlas, and, altogether, there

Figure 1a. Full-page plate depicting Atlas carrying the globe, *The Royal Engagement Pocket Atlas* for 1790. Reproduced by permission of the Lilly Library, Bloomington.

Figure 1b. Full-page plate depicting Atlas carrying the globe, *The Royal Engagement Pocket Atlas* for 1788. Reproduced by permission of the British Museum.

were twelve vignette designs only, which were divided into three areas, the center giving a zodiacal image for the month concerned with the left and right areas focusing on, among other subjects, seasonal, agricultural and hunting activities. In Baker's earliest volumes, the vignettes were much smaller at 6.4 cm by one (fig. 4) than those printed in the volumes from the mid-1780s at 5 cm by 2.5. The 1782 atlas reproduced a series of vignettes featuring "capital portraits, designed by [Thomas] Stothard [...], of the whole Royal Family, which alone far exceed the price of the book."[18] (fig. 5) By November 1782, Baker had further enlarged his description of the volume by advertising it as "the most elegant, useful, and portable Pocket Atlas, for Ladies and Gentlemen, that ever appeared in Europe; and the polite circles have ever distinguished the Atlas by their kindest approbation."[19]

Baker described *The Royal Engagement Pocket Atlas* for 1781 in a newspaper advertisement as "the most elegant and useful Almanack ever

Figure 1c. Full-page plate depicting Atlas carrying the globe, *The Royal Engagement Pocket Atlas* for 1820. Reproduced by permission of the British Museum.

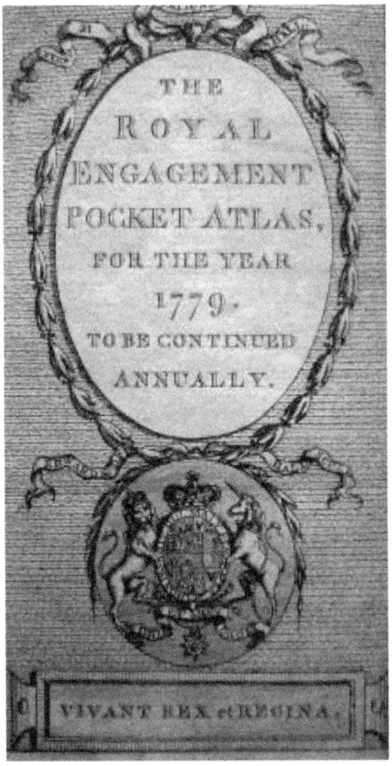

Figure 2. Title page of *The Royal Engagement Pocket Atlas* for 1779. Reproduced by permission of Wigan and Leigh Archives.

yet offered to the Public. The engravings are entirely new, and exceedingly masterly, and allude chiefly to the most remarkable and spirited Actions of the present War." Baker noted that the price ranged from three shillings sixpence to five guineas, "according to the mounting."[20] Later in the year, Baker's advertisements laid out a range of prices starting again at three shillings sixpence with increasingly fine morocco bindings for five shillings sixpence, seven shilling sixpence, and ten shillings sixpence, "or in a much higher stile at the pleasure of the purchaser."[21] The recurrent theme emphasized in advertisements for the *Pocket Atlas* was its elegance, but in November 1792, Baker altered his standard advertisement to add, "Proprietors [...] are gratefully sensible of the distinguished partiality bestowed on that favoured publication, to endeavour that each succeeding work, as far as lies in their power, exceed the former one in neatness, utility, and elegance."[22]

Indeed, "utility" appealed to consumers of the atlas, who recorded appointments, engagements, invitations, and visits to balls, the theatre, or the

Figure 3a. Allegorical frontispiece. *The Royal Engagement Pocket Atlas* for 1795. Reproduced by permission of The British Museum.

Figure 3b. Allegorical frontispiece. *The Royal Engagement Pocket Atlas* for 1798. Reproduced by permission of The British Museum.

opera. Occasionally they drew little cartoons or tried to copy the characters from the designed vignettes. (fig. 6) The everyday use of this beautifully illustrated pocket diary as an object of social intercourse and sociability and its being carried about by men and women as a both useful and fashionable accessory defined its consumable nature. Once its use as a temporary diary had been exhausted, it was easily discarded and replaced with the new edition of, according to Baker, the even more "elegant" *Pocket Atlas* of the following year. In one respect, the atlas was reduced to its functionality and exemplified, through its illustrations and generally decorative makeup, the financial status of its owner who could purchase a disposable print object far more expensive than many editions of the texts the atlases invoked with their illustrative vignettes.

Despite their disposable nature, not all pocket books were discarded after the year was over when they no longer served to record engagements.

Figure 4. Head vignette. *The Royal Engagement Pocket Atlas* for 1799. Reproduced by permission of Wigan and Leigh Archives.

Figure 5. Head vignette. *The Royal Engagement Pocket Atlas* for 1781. Reproduced from a copy in the author's possession.

Surviving copies show that owners routinely recorded the preoccupations of their leisure hours rather than the commitments of their professional lives in the diary pages, which may have given the books a sentimental value. Elizabeth Inchbald's 1792 copy of the atlas (now at the Folger Shakespeare Library) records with whom she dined and what public events she attended, rather than a schedule.[23] Perhaps she kept it as a memento. Other owners reused parts of their atlases, for instance, when they cut out the vignettes and inserted them in Grangerized, extra-illustrated copies of the literary work that they had originally interpreted visually while yet others built up extensive albums featuring these excerpted illustrations from a range of popular diaries-cum-almanac. Individual copies of pocket books could be embellished with costly materials such as silk, precious stones, or metals, transforming *The Royal Engagement Pocket Atlas* into a desirable commodity for elite consumption, as well as a lasting record of a pleasurable year.

Indeed, Baker's advertised descriptions of the atlas indicated that he marketed each volume as a collectable with potential value beyond its ephemeral purpose of scheduling activities. Embellishing copies cost as much as five guineas, according to Baker's advertisements, and the process transformed the function of these volumes from ephemeral social tools to lasting keepsakes. Enhancing their pocket atlases with expensive and ornate bindings, sometimes using mother-of-pearl, owners turned these mechanically reproduced objects into unique, hand-crafted treasures of high-cultural consumption. (fig. 7) Once transformed from mass-produced print commodities to distinct treasures reflecting an owner's individuality, they became *objets d'art* possessing what Walter Benjamin theorized in terms of "aura," the cultic value that distinguishes the unique and original artwork from the mass-produced copy.[24] I have come across only two copies of these well preserved and luxuriously decorated atlases, which were clearly marked as personalised items for gift exchange.[25] But even those consumers who did not transform their copies into unique and costly luxury objects could choose different bindings and slipcases to suit their taste and budget. Each copy of the atlas came with a slipcase—"a very commodious Case for the pocket"—according to Baker's 1778 advertisement.[26] The earliest slipcase traced for the pocket atlas is made from card and covered with blue paper; it featured a glued-on label with the word "Atlas" but this early format of the slipcase would change for the standard format of a cream-coloured slipcase bearing the printed title of the publication in either green, brown, or black. (fig. 8) The case of the 1788 *Pocket Atlas* in the British Library is ornately decorated with morocco leather applications in ebony, red, green, and blue, extensive gilt tooling and scrollwork, as well as emblematic miniature devices in the shape of birds, lions, and flowers. A case for an 1809 atlas, also in the British Library, is bound in a (cheaper, more common) leather wallet with pencil holder and an integrated wallet that could accommodate such folded materials as letters.[27]

What truly set Baker's pocket diary apart from others on the market and inspired owners to invest in costly bindings, slipcases, decorations and to save portions of it was each annual volume's beautifully executed copper-engraved vignettes by William Angus based on designs by Thomas Stothard (1755–1834) that were added beginning in 1783.[28] Twenty-four illustrative copper-engraved vignettes in the shape of ovals or rectangular boxes were placed at the head of the twenty-four diary pages.[29] Each of Stothard's images captured a scene from English literature including the classics and popular contemporary works. When Baker incorporated the vignettes to *The Royal Engagement Pocket Atlas* in 1783, he raised this ephemeral publication far above the competition.

When Baker commenced the publication of the *Pocket Atlas*, the field of book illustration was expanding rapidly with new engraving and etching technologies becoming available to produce higher-standard work that could be marketed at a lower cost than traditional high-quality engraved matter.

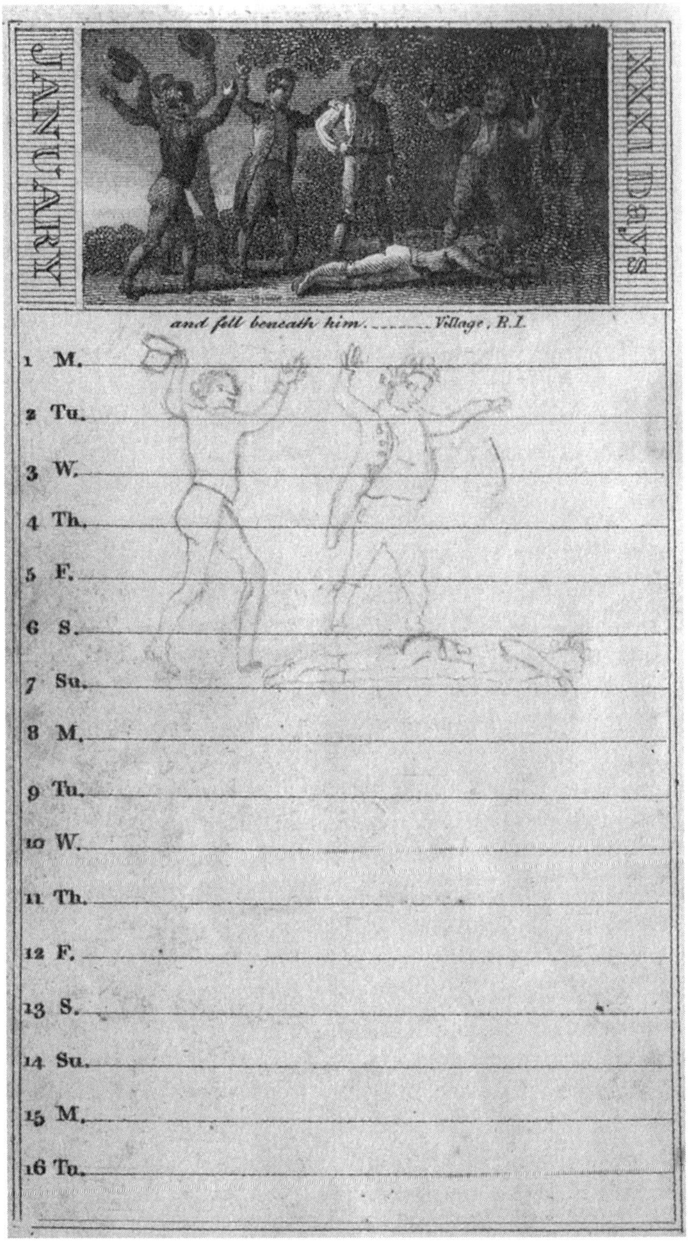

Figure 6. Memorandum page. *The Royal Engagement Pocket Atlas* for 1811. Reproduced from a copy in the author's possession.

Thomas Stothard was well suited for the demanding project of providing Baker with more than two dozen illustrations each year, as he had rapidly established himself as one of the foremost designers for illustrated books. From the mid-1780s, he produced illustrations for most literary classics, alongside the successful, commercial work that he exhibited annually at the Royal Academy, of which he was elected a Fellow in 1794 and Librarian in 1814. Not infrequently Stothard drew several series of designs for different editions of one and the same text. Given that Baker did not specialise in publishing *belles lettres* and that Stothard, since 1780, had already been successfully employed as an illustrator by James Harrison (and produced 148 designs for Harrison's *Novelist's Magazine*),[30] it is possible that Stothard was responsible for the choice of literary subjects and therefore not only acted as illustrator but also as advisor to the bookseller.

Although a complete list of the subjects of Stothard's designs for *The Royal Engagement Pocket Atlas* is not yet known, I have reconstructed an almost complete list which corrects previous conjectural work by A. C. Coxhead, the author of an early twentieth-century, foundational account, *Thomas Stothard, R.A.: An Illustrated Monograph* (1906).[31] The only other scholar that has worked on the illustrations of the atlas, Nancy Finlay, has concentrated particularly on Stothard's wash drawings of designs for the volumes that portrayed scenes from James Thomson's *The Seasons* and Thomas Parnell's "The Hermit" in the Graphic Art Collection at Princeton University Library.[32] Because she did not have access to the published copies of the atlas, Finlay's dating of the drawings has necessarily had to be tentative. Having not physically examined the British Library copy for the year 1806 also led her to erroneously identify one set of drawings as illustrating Oliver Goldsmith's *Vicar of Wakefield*.[33] In fact, the 1806 copy at the British Library allows us to identify those vignettes as illustrating *Edward* (1796) by John Moore, the author of *Zeluco* (1789).[34] Coxhead's examination of Stothard's work for the *Pocket Atlas* relied on the studying the proof sheets of the publication in the Balmanno Collection in the British Museum, but these proofs do not include all the illustrations printed in the various numbers of the atlas. Frequently, these proofs lack the Atlas figure, the allegorical plates, or the later full-page plates illustrative of literary subjects that Stothard provided for the volumes. According to Coxhead, the full-page plate illustrating the volume's chosen literary text occurred for the first time in 1804, with the illustration of William Somervile's didactic poem, *The Chace* (1735). Considering the incompleteness of the proofs in the Balmanno Collection and the possibility of some sheets depicting Atlas figures having been added to the wrong sets of proofs of the vignettes, Coxhead's findings should be treated with caution: I have found nine full-

Figure 7. Ornate cover of an almanac. Reproduced from a copy in the author's possession.

Figure 8. Label of the slipcase for *The Royal Engagement Pocket Atlas* for 1780. Reproduced from a copy in the author's possession.

page plates in different published numbers of the atlas that his list did not include. While the materials at Princeton and the British Library have their limitations, another source, previously unexamined by scholars, provides significant new material for our understanding of Stothard's illustrative work for *The Royal Engagement Pocket Atlas*: the Houghton Library at Harvard holds an album of 113 drawings by Stothard that depict images for untraced volumes of Baker's pocket diary.[35] These images represent an essential source for a large-canvas study of Stothard as a literary illustrator and his conception of these designs' complex narratives of fashion and taste.

It is of course impossible to examine Stothard's more than 1100 engraved vignette designs (excluding those designs that appear on the memorandum pages and the full-page plates) in the space of an article. Nonetheless, we can use some examples from his oeuvre to examine the ways in which they contribute to our understanding of the ideological and paratextual meanings of book illustration, particularly because Stothard often illustrated the same literary text several times for different annual numbers of *The Royal Engagement Pocket Atlas* and for other publishers' volumes of poetry and fiction. In at least two instances before 1800, Stothard illustrated the same text twice for the *Pocket Atlas*: in 1786, he produced "Vignettes [...] descriptive of some of the most striking Picturesque Scenes in Milton's celebrated Poem, L'Allegro,"[36] a text he illustrated again for the atlas of 1788. Similarly, in

1793 and 1796, he designed different visual narratives of James Thomson's *The Seasons,* which, in the course of the decade, would be illustrated in nine different editions of the poem.

Altogether, Stothard's extended and complex visual narratives are among the most significant paratextual interpretations of some authors' works; as a body of visual interpretations, the designs for the volumes of the *Pocket Atlas* frequently contributed to re-introducing a rarely illustrated early eighteenth-century poem such as Thomas Parnell's "The Hermit" or to fostering the reputation of a popular production such as *The Pleasures of Memory* (1792) by Samuel Rogers, Stothard's long-time patron, whose poem he illustrated, with two plates, for its edition publication in 1794 and the *Pocket Atlas* in 1808. Stothard illustrated Rogers's long poem *Italy* for Baker's 1825 volume and, in 1830, was joined by J. M. W. Turner to illustrate *Italy* on a grander and more ambitious scale than ever before in an edition published by Thomas Cadell.[37] In his illustrations of "The Hermit" for the 1791 volume of the *Pocket Atlas* Stothard demonstrated his ability to capture vividly the spiritual message of Parnell's poem, beginning with two oval vignettes of the hermit and concluding with one in which he confronts the transfigured angel. (fig. 9a) (fig. 9b)

Baker repeatedly described his targeted audience as belonging to the "politer circles," which signified more than their financial ability to afford the *Pocket Atlas*, that is their cultural ability to make sense of the illustrated matter. Initially, Baker used generalized (almanac-specific) printing ornaments in the first three numbers of the atlas, but then moved on to commission ambitious and sophisticatedly executed designs. In their depiction of events from the history of England and scenes from British literature the illustrative paratexts of the numbers of the pocket atlas relied on, and appealed to, readers' familiarity with the texts illustrated. Baker's title therefore represented a unique kind of publication that was distinctly different from an illustrated anthology such as *Roach's Beauties*, published in numbers in 1794–95, which reprinted excerpts and episodes from well-known literary texts and offered the reader an illustrative full-page plate per number. Like an anthology, the *Pocket Atlas* was an index to taste, but its function went beyond its printing of illustrations of very recent literary texts not yet incorporated into the canon. As Finlay describes, "the subjects selected for illustration reflect the changing literary taste of the period, ranging as they do from Thomson and Cowper in the early 1790's, through Byron and Scott in the 1820's."[38] Stothard would have been acutely aware of, and sensitive to, the currency of some texts and would most likely have tried to capture an interpretation in his designs that had already been confirmed by the polite taste of the future purchasers of the *Pocket Atlas*.

While up to the mid-1790s, the atlas featured established classics such as Geoffrey Chaucer in the 1784 volume,[39] John Milton, James Thomson, and Samuel Richardson (whose *Sir Charles Grandison* was illustrated),[40] Baker in the following years also printed designs for works of such popular poets as Anna Seward and William Cowper whose *Louisa* (1784; by 1792, the volume had reached its fifth edition) and *The Task* (1785) were illustrated in the 1792 and 1801 annual numbers of the atlas respectively. While after 1800 the advertisements for the *Pocket Atlas* were shorter than previously, the publication appeared to be able to draw on an established clientele that would continue to purchase the volumes until the mid-1820s.[41]

Baker's adeptness at responding speedily to the publication of a "bestseller" was reflected in his 1802 decision to commission from Stothard designs to illustrate Robert Bloomfield's *The Farmer's Boy* (1800). For Baker's 1810 volume Stothard provided eleven designs for George Crabbe's long poem, *The Village* (1783), which had not yet and would not otherwise be illustrated in any edition before the mid-1830s. The remaining rectangular designs illustrated moments and scenes from Crabbe's recent *Parish Register* (1807). Given the complex social subject matter of *The Village*, its departure from the depiction of idyllic pastoral, its exhortative tone, and the realism of the acuteness of contemporaneous poverty, the poem may seem an odd choice for illustration in that a literal transposition into visual poetics could have run the risk of jarring consumers' ideological sense of their class position. Without translating the text literally, Stothard mediated their possible readings of Crabbe's poignant, poetic critique of elite classes, their luxury, and their treatment of the poor inside and outside the workhouse, and softened Crabbe's critiques into a series of sentimental images. The poet had emphasized that in the anti-pastoral realm of *The Village* "Rapine and Wrong and Fear usurp'd her [Nature's] place, / And a bold, artful, surly, savage race."[42] By visually collapsing Crabbe's lengthy and precise descriptions of poverty and its baneful effects into more generalized, less class-specific images, and by adding only half- or one-line captions to his vignettes, Stothard reinvented Crabbe's meanings. Frequently, he reduced the textual imagery and transformed a tale such as that of the poor old man into a contemplative vignette, rather than an accurate and sorrowful rendering of the suffering of impoverished old age: (fig. 10a)

> For yonder see that hoary swain, whose age
> Can with no cares except his own engage;
> Who, propt on that rude staff, looks up to see
> The bare arms broken from the withering tree;
> On which, a boy, he climbed the loftiest bough,
> Then his first joy, but his sad emblem now.[43]

Figure 9a. Head vignette. *The Royal Engagement Pocket Atlas* for 1799. Reproduced from a copy in the author's possession.

Figure 9b. Head vignette. *The Royal Engagement Pocket Atlas* for 1799. Reproduced from a copy in the author's possession.

The vignette portrays this relationship between the "hoary swain" and the tree he can no longer climb. Stothard places the bent man leaning on his staff and the tree in the compositional center. The tonal sophistication of the design turns the lighter right hand side of the tree trunk into a mirror of the declining life of not just this old man, but rather every man. Stothard does not depict the brokenness of the tree that Crabbe had highlighted as a parallel to the old man's decline and losses. Rather, the dark outline on the left of the man's figure echoes the dark outline of the huge and solid oak on the left; the dark, heavy lines help to foreground him as physically solid and thoughtful as he looks into the mirror of a tree, but in his design, Stothard

Figure 10a. Head vignette. *The Royal Engagement Pocket Atlas* for 1811. Reproduced from a copy in the author's possession.

Figure 10b. Head vignette. *The Royal Engagement Pocket Atlas* for 1799. Reproduced from a copy in the author's possession.

downplays Crabbe's original metaphorical parallelism between an aging, lonely, and infirm man and the "withering tree."

In these designs Stothard eliminated any controversial messages from the poem to create instead a visual narrative that featured pastoral and Georgic elements. In the case of Stothard's second vignette for February 1810, Crabbe's three field laborers with scythes resemble William Hamilton's illustrations of Georgic scenes in *The Seasons* issued by J. M. S. Tomkins in a 1797 edition rather than the poet's original broken-down peasants. Likewise, Stothard's first vignette for February 1810 portrays Crabbe's text as a tale of men eager to save a foundering vessel, rather than a narrative depicting the plunder of a wrecked ship, as the poet intended. (fig. 10b) He transforms the scene into one of maritime tragedy mended by humanitarian succour from one portraying a local population whose poverty compels them to prey on those at the mercy of the natural forces. In all, Stothard reformulated the original poem's realism and appeal to action through visual interpretations that compositionally altered the relation between impoverished subjects and privileged readers. By portraying the poor in sentimental, but effectively conservative vignettes, Stothard removed what Baker's audience might consider the offensive exhortative tone that characterized Crabbe's tale. To users of the *Pocket Atlas* unfamiliar with the poem, Stothard's revisions in sentimental, Georgic, or tragic terms of scenes from *The Village* effected an ideological reorientation that offered an unproblematic rendering of the tale and could therefore be more pleasingly marketed to affluent consumers choosing ephemeral pocket books and diaries.

Baker's successful marketing of his pocket diary depended to a large degree not only on the particular qualities of the material pocket book but the possibilities that consumer culture allowed his customers to fashion the pocket book into an artwork that, once opened, revealed the explicit skill of Stothard's designs. He effectively negotiated the hazards of the market for the illustrated book by offering the best product for a niche market and recruiting Stothard to produce ever new and original designs for his *Pocket Atlas*. Stothard provided high-cultural, even conservative interpretations when he illustrated texts for Baker, but these were in striking contrast to those he designed for illustrated volumes that were targeted at a broader audience at relatively low prices. The designs he furnished for John Stockdale's 1793 edition of *The Seasons*, featuring fourteen full-page plates, for example reveal a different ideological reading strategy for a different target audience of consumers and readers. Stockdale's edition was, by no means, a cheap edition, but it occupied the middle range of editions between P. W. Tomkins's ornate folio edition with large-format furniture plates after work by William Hamilton and engraved by Francesco Bartolozzi on the one hand and the cheap pocket editions by Cooke, Bell, and Wenman at the lower end.[44] Stockdale's edition sold for nine shillings in boards, ten shillings sixpence in calf gilt, and fifteen shillings in morocco with gilt back and edges. Compared to the vignettes of the *Pocket Atlas*, however, Stothard's plates for John Stockdale's 1793 edition were markedly less sophisticated in their handling of line and cross patterning to achieve depth and tonality. Importantly, Stothard's designs for Stockdale predated his vignettes for Baker and, for the first time, significantly varied the poem's painterly matrix by identifying iconographic moments from areas such as the realms of domesticity, the family, and lower-class working life that had not previously featured in illustrated editions of Thomson's work.

By the time that Stockdale issued his edition of Thomson's poem, other illustrators had established a visual matrix of repeatedly illustrated iconographic moments in *The Seasons*. But Stothard did not include a depiction of one of the most easily recognised interpolated episodes, the signature story of the lovers Celadon and Amelia, as the depiction of Amelia's death through lightning would have disrupted the harmony and life-affirming designs of happy country and family life advocated by his series of fourteen plates for Stockdale's volume. The story of the death of Amelia had been popularized by Richard Wilson's painterly rendering of Thomson's tale, *A Summer's Storm* (1760), and its 1766 version as a furniture print superbly engraved by William Woollett. The story also served as the subject for William Williams's *Thunderstorm with the Death of Amelia* (1784) and other paintings well before William Hamilton adopted the tale for his flamboyant painting of the two lovers, which was reproduced in engraved form in Tomkins's folio edition. [45]

Apart from full-scale paintings, Thomson's tale had also been realized in edition-format and served as a frontispiece to Robert Morison's 1790 edition of *The Seasons*. Stothard illustrated the tragic tale in miniature for the 1793 number of the *Pocket Atlas*. The juxtaposition between Stothard's original wash-drawing for the engraved vignette and the final printed image reveals the skill of both designer and engraver dynamically working together. (fig.11a) (fig. 11b) Stothard's two separate series of designs for Baker's pocket diary captured the kaleidoscopic nature of *The Seasons*, a characteristic that was translated impressively when, in 1842, Longman issued an illustrated edition with seventy-seven wood-engraved designs by a range of different illustrators.

Stothard illustrated *The Seasons* for several formats and publishers. For instance, Finlay has identified two vignettes by Stothard, related to his illustrations for Baker's *Pocket Atlas* that were integrated in the frontispiece of the 1793 Perth edition issued by Robert Morison.[46] She also has described different organising principles in Stothard's 1793 vignettes compared to those he designed for the 1797 *Pocket Atlas*. His 1793 "selection of scenes strictly followed the verse order of *The Seasons*" but "the subjects for the British Museum proofs [i.e. the designs for the 1797 number] were chosen to correspond logically with the appropriate months."[47] While Stothard on the whole harmonized contradictions, as in his illustrations of Crabbe's *The Village*, he interpreted Thomson's long poem in terms of its tonal and modal hybridity, emphasizing its thematic, ideational, and ideological range. His designs for Stockdale's 1793 edition did not deploy the specific captions that other publishers used. His Musidora, a bathing figure featured in the interpolated episode of Damon and Musidora in "Summer," remained unnamed, but the plate carried the simple caption: "Bathing." Thomson's tale of "The Perishing Man" from "Winter" was retitled "The Perishing Traveller," and did not depict, as most illustrators (particularly Henry Fuseli) did, the dying man but rather a man walking through snow at night in search of shelter. Stothard made his design of the tale of the man perishing in the snow more specific for the 1793 number of the *Royal Engagement Pocket Atlas* by adding a caption which no longer stressed the wanderer's identity but his progress through the snow, describing him as "flouncing through the drifted heaps." By the time both numbers of Baker's pocket atlas were issued, Thomson's tales were widely known—especially to the upper classes who had at their disposal costly visualizations such as Woollett's furniture print of Wilson's painting and other renderings of the tale of the perishing man such as the plate for "Winter" in John Murray's 1778 edition of *The Seasons* or Nathan Drake's 1788 painting of the subject.

Thomas Stothard was the most important illustrator at the end of the eighteenth century who issued multiple literary designs for a range of editions and periodical or annual publications, including the *Lady's Magazine* and *Le Souvenir* along with his work for Baker's *Pocket Atlas*, and numerous publishers' volumes of poetry and fiction. His work contributed to forming a uniform canon that could be linked modally and generically by means of the illustrations that publishers added to their editions. In an attempt to reconcile earlier models of primitive literature and the formally more polished productions of the eighteenth century, the book trade employed paratextual strategies to render a polite canon of literature.[48] Stothard's own contribution to this process of canon formation is significant, if under recognized. He illustrated Chaucer for Baker's *Pocket Atlas,* reinterpreting *The Canterbury Tales* in refined and genteel terms that he had first established in his fourteen designs for Bell's edition of Chaucer (1782–83).[49] Alice Miskimin states that "Stothard's Gothic images are gratifying, easy-to-read illustrations that belong to a new level of discourse: particular best-selling fiction and its narrative tradition." He "expurgated Chaucer, finding the recognizable commonplace and the familiar sense—safe for the general audience."[50] In appropriating Chaucer's work as contemporary, he furnished designs that differed little from illustrations of such eighteenth-century texts as Richardson's and Thomson's. In so doing, Stothard's visual paratexts become essential signifiers of cultural coherence and literary continuity.

In the *Pocket Atlas* for 1799 Stothard's illustrative paratexts of *The Deserted Village* were strikingly different from earlier illustrations. Earlier, the headings of the memorandum pages had used a range of scrollwork ornaments, but by 1799 Stothard offered highly finished vignettes that featured, among other subjects, owls on a background of rich foliage and

Figure 11a. Wash drawing for vignette depicting Celadon and Amelia. Reproduced by permission of the Princeton University Library.

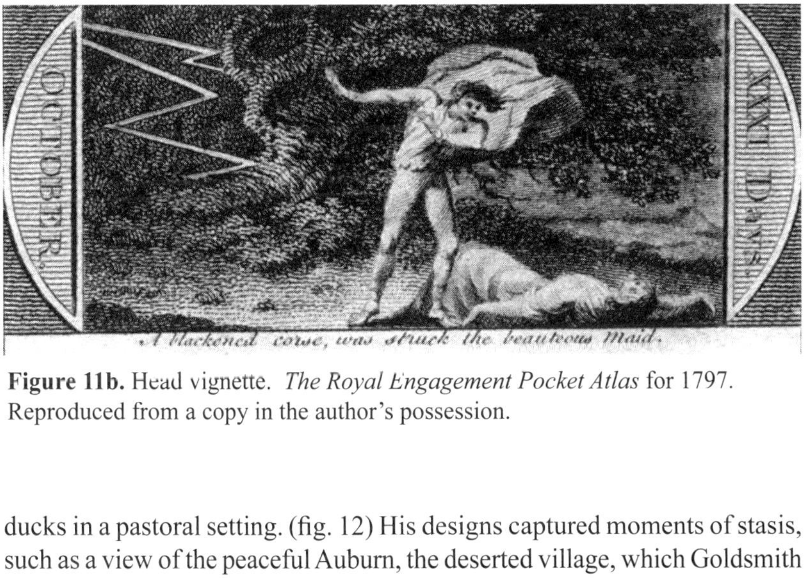

Figure 11b. Head vignette. *The Royal Engagement Pocket Atlas* for 1797. Reproduced from a copy in the author's possession.

ducks in a pastoral setting. (fig. 12) His designs captured moments of stasis, such as a view of the peaceful Auburn, the deserted village, which Goldsmith modelled on his native Lissoy. From the idyllic view of the hamlet, Stothard turned his attention to the representation of the different generations, the children playing under the kind gaze of their elders. He contrasted scenes of domestic activity and peace with scenes of strife and poverty. Equally, he represented individualized characters and, through his designs, constructed a community of villagers. Of particular interest is the second plate for October in which Stothard depicted a moment of drama and fear, reminiscent of his design of the Celadon and Amelia tale in the 1793 number of the pocket atlas. Similarly, one of his June designs introduced the angel figures that

Figure 12. Head vignette. *The Royal Engagement Pocket Atlas* for 1796. Reproduced by permission of the Glasgow University Library.

he had deployed in his illustration for Thomas Heptinstall's 1798 edition of Edward Young's *Night Thoughts*. In other words, Stothard transformed Goldsmith's contemporary village deserted because of lamentable socio-economic forces into a sentimental, vaguely historical space of plump animals, beautiful foliage, playful children, hard-working farmers, and watchful grandparents and angels.

As Baker's agent, Marsh would have made sure that the *Pocket Atlas* was available as widely as possible and that customers could draw on a wide range of binding and casing designs to enhance the appearance and desirability of their pocket diaries.[51] When they used their pocket diaries, perhaps many times a day, middling and elite consumers encountered Stothard's illustrated imagery over and over, which functioned to create a visual imaginary of an emergent "canon." *Pocket Atlas* owners may have spent time familiarizing themselves with the literary passages that Stothard's illustrations depicted, but they also indirectly absorbed these images repeatedly as they used their diaries to record and remind themselves of their personal engagements and notes. Baker was both culturally sensitive and commercially savvy as he capitalized on the work of popular and beloved authors, for instance selecting Sir Walter Scott's novels for no less than nine different numbers of the *Pocket Atlas*, and advertising these volumes not only in England but in Scotland as well.[52] Ultimately, these pocket books would have represented status symbols indicating that their owners were fashionably up-to-date while also constituting what Maxine Berg has termed "semi-luxuries."[53] When individualized, they could serve as personal indices of taste, leisure, and wealth, but above all, they demonstrated that this ephemeral genre could be both useful and elegant and play a part in the construction of polite identity at the end of the eighteenth and the beginning of the nineteenth centuries.

Stothard's skill as a designer of book illustrations is best appreciated when examining the vignettes for the *Royal Engagement Pocket Atlas*. As Coxhead noted long ago: "They certainly bear eloquent witness to his supreme ability of grouping his figures, and of telling his story by attitude, where facial expression is almost impossible, as well as his almost unvarying fidelity to the text."[54] The range of visual responses Stothard produced both for Baker and for editions of literary texts on which he worked from the early 1780s to the mid-1820s reveal him as a sensitive reader and visual translator of the literature of his time, but, like Baker his publisher, also a very astute businessman who could effectively market his skill in the ever proliferating world of print culture.

NOTES

Acknowledgements: The research for this article was made possible by the award of a Princeton University Library Fellowship that enabled me to work in the Graphic Arts Collection. I am also grateful for an overseas-conference grant and a research grant to work in the Houghton Library, Harvard University. I am indebted to the staff of the libraries and archives I have used for my research, specifically the staff at the Beinecke Rare Books and Manuscripts Library, the British Library, the British Museum, the Houghton Library, the Lilly Library, the Princeton University Library, the University of Liverpool Library, and the Wigan and Leigh Archives.

1. See Brian Maidment, "Re-Arranging the Year: The almanac, the day book and the Year Book as Popular Literary Forms, 1789–1860," *Rethinking Victorian Culture*, ed. Juliet John and Alice Jenkins (Basingstoke: Macmillan, 2000), 91–113. See also, Jill Alloway, "Paper Ghosts: the almanack and year book, 1790–1860" (Ph.D. thesis, University of Huddersfield, 2004).

2. See Jenny Batchelor, "Fashion and Frugality: Eighteenth-Century Pocket Books for Women," *Studies in Eighteenth-Century Culture*, 32.1 (2003): 1–18. Batchelor examines the ideological inscription of these pocket books, specifically the ways in which woman are instructed to record (and, by doing so) regulate their expenditure. She notes: "Pocket books fashioned themselves as indispensable shields against the economic and moral trials [...] by directing women to be perpetually accountable for their own limited finances" (2) but also by "instruct[ing] their readers in the etiquette of polite and fashionable life" (5).

3. Copies are given by year of publication, with the holding library in brackets: 1780 (Lilly Library, Indiana University), 1782 (National Library of Wales), 1788 (British Library), 1790 (Beinecke Library, Yale), 1793 (Folger Shakespeare Library), 1794 (Harry Ransom Center, University of Texas at Austin), 1796 (British Library),

1799 (Glasgow University Library), 1800 (Victoria and Albert Museum, London), 1805 (British Library), and 1816 (British Art Center, Yale),

4. 1779 (Society of Antiquaries of London), 1781 (National Library of Wales), 1793 (Liverpool University Library), 1795 (Bodleian Library, Oxford), 1796 (Bodleian Library, Oxford), 1800 (Lambeth Palace, London), and 1808 (Bodleian Library, Oxford).

5. 1779 (Wigan and Leigh Archives, Lancashire), 1824 (Norfolk Record Office, Norwich).

6. (London: printed for B. Crosby, No. 4, Stationers'-Court, Ludgate-Sreet, 1795), title-page.

7. *The London Literary Gazette, or, Journal of Belles Lettres, Arts, and Sciences* (1833) carried an advertisement for *The Royal Repository*, stating that copies of the publication "may be had in a variety of bindings suitable for Christmas or New Years' presents" (797).

8. The first advertisement for the *Polite Repository* that I have been able to trace was published on 13 November 1780 in *London Courant and Westminster Chronicle*. This early advertisement does not mention illustrative plates but states that the almanac is embellished "with ornamental ruled pages for memorandums." In the following year, on 15 November 1781, the *London Chronicle* carries an advert stating that the *Polite Repository* is "Embellished with elegant Engravings for each Month." While the general text of the advertisement listing the features of the almanac remains practically the same, in 1782 the advertisement (*Morning Herald and Daily Advertiser*, 18 November) offers more explicit information on the subject that is illustrated: "Ornamented with elegant Historical Engravings to each month, and a View of Gibraltar, with the burning the Spanish floating batteries, at their grand attack, September 13, 1782." The designs of country seats that are associated with Repton from the early 1790s are already mentioned in a 1783 advertisement (*St. James's Chronicle or the British Evening Post*, 11 December) in which the pocket book is described as containing "twelve elegant Views, of different Noblemen's and Gentlemen's Seats, engraved by Mr. Taylor, from Original Drawings by Messrs. Hearne, Tomkins, Robertson, and Steuart." On Repton's designs for the publication, see Nigel Temple, "Humphry Repton, Illustrator, and William Peacock's *Polite Repository*, 1790–1811," *Garden History*, 16.2 (1988): 161–73.

9. *The Star*, 27 December 1791.

10. *World*, 12 November 1791. The same advertisement also mentions another pocket diary, the *Pocket Museum*, "containing twelve Views of Gentlemen's Seats."

11. *St. James's Chronicle or the British Evening Post*, 21 November 1793.

12. *St. James's Chronicle or the British Evening Post*, 16 December 1797.

13. *London Chronicle*, 20 October 1778.

14. *Morning Post and Daily Advertiser*, 1 January 1779.

15. Christine Y. Ferdinand, *Benjamin Collins and the Provincial Newspaper Trade in the Eighteenth Century* (Oxford: Oxford University Press, 1997), 70 and n26.

16. *St. James' Chronicle, or the British Evening Post*, 6 January 1780.

17. From 1809, the Atlas figure is no longer centralised but occupies merely the upper half of the title-page; with one knee on the ground, he balances the globe on his shoulders. He appears to be the center piece of a greater architectural structure, with two classical pillars flanking him, and a large pedestal not only carrying him but also featuring a tapestry on which the title of the publication is engraved. This design was also produced by Stothard.

18. *Gazetteer and New Daily Advertiser*, 16 November 1781.

19. *Morning Post and Daily Advertiser*, 19 November 1782.

20. *Lloyd's Evening Post*, 15 November 1780; this is the first advertisement for the atlas I have located.

21. *Morning Chronicle and London Advertiser*, 16 November 1781.

22. *St. James' Chronicle or the British Evening Post*, 20 November 1792.

23. Folger Shakespeare Library; call number W.a.239–240.

24. See Walter Benjamin, *Das Kunstwerk im Zeitalter seiner technischen Reproduzierbarkeit*, ed. Burkhardt Lindner (Stuttgart: Reclam, 1989), 19–20.

25. Both sold at Christie's in 2009 and 2010.

26. *The Royal Engagement Pocket Atlas for the Year MDCCLXXX* (Southampton: published by Thomas Baker, 1780), 2.

27. The copies in my possession are bound into a similar wallet but lack the additional wallet.

28. Michael Bryan, *Dictionary of Painters and Engravers, biographical and critical*, enlarged by George Stanley (London: H. G. Bohn, 1849), 27.

29. The oval format was used until 1791, and from the following year Baker adopted the rectangular vignette to frame Stothard's designs. One of the characteristics of the vignettes in the 1780s is that that they were substantially smaller than those issued from the 1790s.

30. For a very brief bibliographical account of Stothard's early career as a book illustrator, see Hanns Hammelmann and T. S. R. Boase, *Book Illustrators in Eighteenth-Century England* (New Haven: Yale University Press, 1975), 68–71. Their dating of Stothard's work for *The Royal Engagement Pocket Atlas* is incorrect.

31. A. C. Coxhead, *Thomas Stothard, R.A., an Illustrated Monograph* (London: A. H. Bullen, 1906); Shelley M. Bennett, *Thomas Stothard: The Mechanisms of Art Patronage in England circa 1800* (Columbia: University of Missouri Press,1984), does not mention the *Pocket Atlas*.

32. See Nancy Finlay, "Thomas Stothard's Illustrations of Thomson's *Seasons* for the *Royal Engagement Pocket Atlas*," *Princeton University Library Chronicle*, 42.3 (1981): 165–77; "Thomas Stothard's Illustrations for Parnell's 'Hermit,'"

Princeton University Library Chronicle, 45 (1984): 174–77, and "Parnell's 'Hermit': Illustrations by Stothard," *The Scriblerian*, 18.1 (1985): 1–5.

33. Finlay, "Stothard's Illustrations of Thomson's *Seasons*," 166.

34. British Library; shelfmark P.P.2470.p.

35. Houghton Library; shelfmark: f MS Typ 791.

36. *General Evening Post*, 19 November 1785.

37. Adele M. Holcomb, "A Neglected Phase in Turner's Art: His Vignettes to Rogers's *Italy*," *Journal of the Warburg and Courtauld Institutes*, 32 (1969): 405–10.

38. Finlay, "Parnell's 'Hermit,'" 4.

39. Stothard had already designed fourteen plates to illustrate the Chaucer volume of Bell's Poets of Great Britain. On Stothard's work on Chaucer, see Mark Greenberg, "The Canterbury Pilgrims by Stothard and Blake: An Account with Reproductions in *The Architect*," *Notes & Queries*, 23 (1978): 401–02, and Betsy Bowden, "Transportation to Canterbury: The Rival Envisionings of Stothard and Blake," *Studies in Medievalism*, 11 (2001): 73–111.

40. Stothard had already illustrated *Sir Charles Grandison* for volumes 10 and 11 of Harrison's *Novelist's Magazine*.

41. "This neat little WORK, the first of the Kind ever introduced to the Public, needs no encomium; the great and increasing demand the Proprietors have hitherto met with, sufficiently evinces its general utility; no pains or expence [sic] have been spared to render it more complete every session." See *World*, 22 December 1791.

42. George Crabbe, *The Village* (London: printed for J. Dodsley, 1783), 8, lines 109–10.

43. Crabbe, *The Village*, 13, lines 181–86.

44. See Sandro Jung, "Visual Interpretations, Print, and Illustrations of Thomson's *The Seasons*, 1730–1797," *Eighteenth-Century Life*, 34.2 (2010): 23–64 and Sandro Jung, "Print Culture, High-Cultural Consumption, and Thomson's *The Seasons*, 1780–1797," *Eighteenth-Century Studies*, 44.4 (2011): 495–514; see also, Ralph Cohen, *The Art of Discrimination: Thomson's 'The Seasons' and the Language of Criticism* (London: Routledge & Kegan Paul, 1964).

45. See Sandro Jung, "Painterly 'Readings' of *The Seasons*, 1766–1829," *Word & Image*, 26.1 (2010): 68–82.

46. See Finlay, "Stothard's Illustrations of Thomson's *Seasons*," 167.

47. Finlay, "Stothard's Illustrations of Thomson's *Seasons*," 168.

48. The strategies of canon formation have been traced by Jonathan Brody Kramnick, *The Making of the English Canon: Print-Capitalism and the Cultural Past, 1700–1770* (Cambridge: Cambridge University Press, 1998), and Thomas F. Bonnell, *The Most Disreputable Trade: Publishing the Classics of English Poetry, 1765–1810* (Oxford: Oxford University Press, 2008).

49. See Alice Miskimin, "The Illustrated Eighteenth-Century Chaucer," *Modern Philology*, 77.1 (1979): 26–55, esp. 40–49.

50. Miskimin, "The Illustrated Eighteenth-Century Chaucer," 40–41, 43.

51. While Baker registered the *Pocket Atlas* with the Stationers' Company in 1779 and submitted nine copies, there are no records of the overall print run of the publication. I am grateful to Sue Hurley for examining the *Stationers' Register* for me.

52. The *Pocket Atlas* prints Stothard's illustrations of Scott's works within one to three years of their original publication, thereby indicating Scott's canonic status as a modern professional author. A list of the illustrated texts follows. The first date is that of original publication, the second that of illustration in the pocket atlas: *The Lay of the Last Minstrel* (1805/1807), *Marmion* (1808/1809), *Lady of the Lake* (1810/1812), *Bridal of Triermain* (1813/1815), *Guy Mannering* (1815/1817), *Ivanhoe* (1819/1821), *Kenilworth* (1821/1822), *The Pirate* (1822/1823), and *Peveril of the Peak* (1822/1824). Unlike earlier numbers, these volumes were advertised in Scotland also. See, for instance, the advertisement for the 1807 volume of the *Pocket Atlas*, illustrating Scott's *Lay of the Last Minstrel*, which was published in the *Caledonian Mercury*, 18 December 1806.

53. Maxine Berg, "New Commodities, luxuries and their consumers in eighteenth-century England," *Consumers and Luxury: Consumer Culture in Europe, 1650–1850*, ed. Maxine Berg and Helen Clifford (Manchester: Manchester University Press, 1999), 69.

54. Coxhead, 52.

Tracing Marie-Éléonore Godefroid: Women's Artistic Networks in Early Nineteenth-Century Paris

JENNIFER GERMANN

Marie-Éléonore Godefroid's life and work is caught in the paradox that faces historians of women's lives. Well known and respected in artistic and elite circles during her lifetime, she was quickly forgotten after her death. While there is plentiful evidence of an active career in the records of the Salons, few of her works have survived or, at least, remain attributed to her. Her biography exists in a few scattered secondary sources written long after her death, based on a now-lost autobiographical text. If anonymous was a woman, her sister has a name but no oeuvre to give her life a context. How do we begin to trace the life and career of a woman artist whose work is largely lost and whose career path was forged outside the traditional focus of the discipline of art history? These are two different, but not unrelated problems, as I will demonstrate. In this essay, I propose to give texture to Godefroid's life and surviving work by pursuing her interpersonal relations, particularly with women. I argue that Godefroid's connections to elite women in Napoleonic France can enrich our understanding of the ways that women in general and this woman in particular utilized homosocial relationships to survive and, at least in some sense, prosper. These networks also provide an avenue of historical access to the life and work of women in the art world, albeit in a fragmentary and provisional state.

Perhaps ironically, given my argument, the visual focus of my essay will be an image of young boys, not women, and thus one that has been read by others as a statement about relations between men. Godefroid's *The Sons of Marshal Ney* (Berlin, Gemaeldegalerie, Staatliche Museen, 1810) (fig. 1) has become a minor icon of art produced by a woman. Godefroid's painting, shown in the Paris Salon of 1810 and called the "Portrait en pied des enfans de M.gr le maréchal duc d'Elchingen" in the *livret*, presents Joseph Napoléon, Michel Louis, and Eugène Ney in fancy dress as if arrayed on stage.[1] Joseph, the eldest child, aged eight, is in the center framed by the curtain, his feet inscribed within a circular red paving stone. His hat is festooned with white feathers, wearing a white silk-fringed tunic with a blue sash over white silk stockings tucked into black boots, an outfit echoed by Michel, the second son. Joseph displays the sword hung from a belt slung across his chest. Eugène, aged two, signals its importance by pointing at it. His gesture is underlined by the contrast of his red sleeve against the bright yellow fabric of the curtain. Eugène and Michel straddle a rifle, which appears to have been discarded while the boys stop to admire the sword. Michel's gaze, whose body interlinks with Eugène's—arm around shoulder and crossed feet between his younger brother's legs—leads to the older brother and the oversized sword. Joseph stands isolated against a balustrade with a large flat plain and a river behind him.

Linda Nochlin and Ann Sutherland Harris included this work in their groundbreaking 1976–1977 exhibition, *Women Artists, 1550–1950*, and it was also reproduced by *Apollo* Magazine in its review of the show (though not discussed).[2] Harris and Nochlin, Nancy Heller, Margaret Barlow, and Jordi Vigue include reproductions of this painting in their surveys of women artists, while numerous other scholars include Godefroid more generally as one of several female artists and instructors.[3] But Harris and Nochlin's catalog essay remains so far the most extensive published analysis of this painting, which they interpret with a primary emphasis on the masculine, paternal, and martial elements. The rifle and sword are read as symbolic of Marshal Ney's progression from hussar to marshal. This sword may have been a gift to Ney from Napoleon at the time of his wedding to Aglaé Auguié, the boys' mother, and has been read as a reference to martial duty, portending future responsibilities in the public sphere and connecting all of the boys to the adult male homosocial world of combat. The exchange of glances from youngest to middle to oldest boy helps to encode this future, as do the presence of the globe, books, and papers, all which suggest that beyond fantasy play, the boys are being educated for a life engaged in politics and the law. These objects, like the weapons, belong to an iconographic tradition in male portraiture showing their grooming for leadership.[4]

Figure 1. Marie-Éléonore Godefroid, *The Sons of Marshal Ney*, 1810, oil on canvas (162 x 173 cm). Gemaeldegalerie, Staatliche Museen, Berlin (bpk, Berlin, Gemaeldegalerie, Joerg P. Anders, Art Resource, NY).

That the painting addresses fraternity, signaled in particular by the embrace of the two younger sons and the middle child's gaze towards his eldest brother, is clear. Both intimacy and distance between the boys is suggestive of the complicated relations of brothers. No doubt viewers in 1810 read the painting as illuminating these relationships and those between the boys and their imagined futures as men. They might have also imagined that Joseph, whose gaze is directed outside of the image, was looking at his father. He smiles more warmly than his brothers as he displays the sword, a symbol both of his possible future profession and that of his father. These series of bonds between males would also hint at the bond between Napoleon and the boys' father, Marshal Ney, a renowned soldier who had risen from being a cooper's son to becoming a great general and friend of the emperor.

Yet these circles of male relationships are only one set of meanings to be found in the painting.

One could also imagine that Joseph is gazing outside the picture frame at his mother, who was likely present when the boys posed for the painting. It is not hard to imagine Madame Ney's attendance at the initial sitting, as she knew Godefroid from their time together at Madame Campan's school. And the sword can be read as a reference to *her* union to Marshal Ney. Of course Joseph could also be looking at the artist herself. I introduce the presence of these two unseen women as a way of signaling *other* sorts of homosocial relations that lay behind this painting, that is, the "invisible" connections between women, which have been ignored, overlooked, or, perhaps simply forgotten. Indeed, both the boys' mother and their portraitist had connections that may have brought this commission into being. Their mother, Aglaé Auguié, was the niece, former ward, and student of Madame Jeanne Campan, the founder of the leading school for elite girls in France. Marie-Éléonore Godefroid, a single bourgeoise, was a former teacher at Madame Campan's school, but by 1805 had become a studio assistant to François Gérard, one of the most important painters in Napoleon's France. By considering the connections between Auguié, Campan, and Godefroid we can add depth to our understanding of a work typically treated as merely an example of proficient painting by a woman in the early nineteenth century, as only an illustration of children in this period, or as simply as a footnote to the drama of relations between men.

Godefroid Between Past and Present

For at least four decades, feminist art historians have worked to recuperate neglected women artists, contesting the myth that the art world was a male-only sphere. Their work has included surveys of women artists, anthologies that challenge the gendered structures of the discipline, as well as numerous articles, dissertations and monographs addressing individual women artists and patrons.[5] Despite the tremendous headway here, we continue to know little about women's activity in the art world in the last decades of the eighteenth century and opening of the nineteenth. Few women had the financial or artistic success of François Gérard, or Jean-Baptiste Isabey, and none had a career like Jacques-Louis David, an artist who has inspired substantial scholarship.[6] The relative lack of scholarly work on women's roles in the art world, whether in the studios of the famous or the lesser known artists of the day, not only hides women from view but it also narrows our collective historical understanding of the richness of lived experience, artistic production, and the workings of the art world more broadly.

In contemporary art historical practice, the art world is frequently presented as an all-male enclave of stars, with very few female participants. In *Emulation* (1995), for example, Thomas Crow explores and celebrates the relations between the male artists at work in Jacques-Louis David's circle, interpreting their paintings as revealing traces of their competitive and fraught relationships. In particular, their images of men served as the staging ground to express their charged, sometimes tortured emotional lives in David's atelier, which was, in Crow's words, "constructed away from the presence of women."[7] Though Crow enriches our understanding of the Davidian school, particularly in his analysis of the careers of Jean-Germain Drouais (who died young in 1788), Antoine-Jean Gros, Anne-Louis Girodet, and François Gérard—all among David's star students—he excludes women from this circle. This erasure of women from David's circle was noted in an important book review by Philippe Bordes in 1996 and challenged by Margaret Fields Denton in her research on Angélique Mongez, one of David's more successful female students and a rare female history painter.[8]

Abigail Solomon-Godeau's *Male Trouble* (1997) also provides an important corrective here with its grounding in psychoanalytic discourse and feminist criticism. She argues that a French Revolutionary crisis of masculinity arose out of an attempt to incorporate femininity while excluding actual female actors both from the political realm and from spheres of cultural production, including of course the visual arts. While her argument provides a compelling model explaining how art history's exclusivity has been reinforced, its project is different from helping to recover how female artists sought and received training, exhibited their work, and participated more generally in the art world. Solomon-Godeau's book is populated by a similar cast of characters as in Crow's, mostly male and mostly struggling with masculinity and its relation both to the public and private spheres. Though Solomon-Godeau criticizes the art historical "tendency to erase women artists altogether from the artistic scene," she nonetheless argues "the retrospective disappearance of those women artists who did (in whatever measure) participate in the life of the studios and did receive instruction from the master artist may reflect not only their marginality, but their irrelevance to" the relationships between male students and their male masters in the late eighteenth- and early nineteenth-century art world.[9] Crow treats this crisis as interpersonal while Solomon-Godeau views it as cultural and political, but both studies ignore or minimize women's active presence in the art world.

In this article, I propose that Godefroid was neither irrelevant to nor excluded from the Davidian school and the project of what Crow identifies as David's "advanced art." Although Godefroid did not train with David, all of the male artists she worked with did, including her brother, Ferdinand-

Nicolas, Isabey, and her teacher and patron Gérard. Her aesthetic, both in the works she created on her own, those she worked on within Gérard's studio, and those that she copied for Napoleon and for the restoration Bourbons, were deeply informed if not directly shaped by Davidian aesthetics. She even painted a copy of David's self-portrait for the museum at Versailles late in her career. In all of these ways, Godefroid's work can help challenge the view that the "advanced art" of Revolutionary and Napoleonic era was not simply a masculinist project, but also one only made by men.

Louis-Léopold Boilly's painting, *Gathering of Artists in the Studio of Isabey* (1798, Paris, Musée du Louvre)[10] epitomizes this imagined all male space in its depiction of a fashionable meeting of artists in Jean-Baptiste Isabey's studio. (fig. 2) This portrait gathers Isabey, Godefroid's teacher and colleague, and Gérard, her master, among their male peers. In the painting, Isabey, in red, and Gérard, seated in black, concentrate on the canvas perched on the easel. Around the room, Boilly has presented a collection of identifiable male artists and architects, actors, poets, and musicians.[11] In a frieze along the cornice, there are medallion portraits featuring famous painters from the past identified by name, *patrie*, and dates of birth and death. Boilly portrays all of these men as fashionable gentlemen of the late 1790s while simultaneously incorporating them into the age-old pantheon of "great artists." Scholars have interpreted this painting, on the one hand, as placing history painters at the pinnacle of the academic hierarchy and, on the other, as reordering this hierarchy based on contemporary artistic practices ultimately devaluing the status of history painting in relation to other more popular genres.[12] In the painting itself and in either reading, women are absent. This parallels Crow's depiction of a masculinist world that excluded actual female participants—unless we count the presence of females as decoration, such as the paintings and sculpture of ancient Greek women in the background and the bust of Minerva perched on a heater.[13]

Yet this painting—and many other visual works celebrating an idealized masculine world—should not be read as purely documentary. It was widely recognized, as historians have shown, that post-revolutionary Parisians did not view the art marketplace as an exclusively all-male sphere.[14] A variety of documentary and visual sources provide evidence of female participation. For example, substantial numbers of women were actively exhibiting in the open Salons and taking advantage of the dissolution of the Royal Academy, which had limited entry to all but four women at a time. Margaret Oppenheimer has found that after 1789 more women "began to appear among the copyists at the Louvre" and "to enroll in Iconography courses at the Muséum National d'Histoire Naturelle."[15] But perhaps even more impressive, she has shown that there was a steady and quite extraordinary increase in the number of

Figure 2. Louis-Léopold Boilly, *Gathering of Artists in the Studio of Isabey*, 1798, oil on canvas (71 x 110 cm). Louvre, Paris, France. (Réunion des Musées Nationaux, Art Resource, NY).

women participating in the Salons. The percentage of women exhibiting, in fact, increased by 1600 percent between 1789 and 1806, precisely when Godefroid began to exhibit her work.[16]

The growing number of women seeking training and professional positions had an impact on the visual portrayal of women as artists, too. Although again we must use caution when treating any painting as documentary, it is worth considering the many works that began depicting women working as artists, for example in a series of images by Hubert Robert, an older contemporary of Godefroid's. Robert was famously friends with Elisabeth Vigée-Lebrun and supported other female painters in their pursuit of artistic training—as in fact did many of the men pictured in Boilly's image.[17] In almost all of the versions of Robert's images of the to-be-renovated Louvre galleries, he portrays female artists, perhaps including members of the Louvre copyist staff.[18] These images, produced from the 1790s until his death, show men, women, and children walking, conversing, and participating in the making of art by copying the paintings and sculptures distributed throughout the Grande Galerie. In his 1796 *View of the Grande Galerie of the Louvre* (Paris, Musée du Louvre), Robert depicted a woman with a large drawing board leaning over her work; behind her another woman with a young girl stands

Figure 3. Hubert Robert, *View of the Grande Galerie of the Louvre*, 1801–1805, oil on canvas (37 x 46 cm). Louvre, Paris, France. (Erich Lessing, Art Resource, NY).

and observes her efforts. In Robert's representation of the Louvre, the gallery becomes a space for artistic practice, one engaged in by women and men, publicly and collectively. Between 1801 and 1805, Robert created another view of the Grande Galerie (Paris, Musée du Louvre), once again populated by male and female artists. (fig. 3) He duplicates the same works of art as in his 1796 *View*, but this time includes *more* female artists; one woman stands almost heroically on an elevated platform copying a painting hung across from her perch. On the column base next to her, another woman is drawing.

Other contemporary artists, including Constantin Bourgeois, similarly recorded women at work in the Louvre, for instance in his drawing of an exhibition at the Louvre in Year V (1797–8, Paris, Musée du Louvre). Here, we see a female artist sketching, but given her position seated in an embrasure, we are unable to see whether she is copying work on display, or perhaps capturing the milling crowd around her. Either way, Bourgeois and others in their portrayals of women at work in the galleries normalized the contemporary female artist.[19] There are even depictions of women in studio settings, including one by Vincenzo Camuccini, showing women and men in an atelier while a cadaver arrives in a crate in preparation for life study.[20] And women themselves actively represented their own artistic practice. Although little known today, there are numerous portraits of young female artists working at their craft either alone or in the company of other women or men that were produced by their female colleagues.[21]

Recognizing these sociological and representational changes that registered a rising number of women participating in the visual arts in the post-Revolutionary period alters our reading of Boilly's image of fashionable male artists consorting in a single-sex setting as a fantasy. On the one hand, gatherings like the one Boilly depicts may indeed have taken place; but on the other, they were, in their complete exclusion of female artists, atypical events in post-Revolutionary Paris. For example, François Gérard held a regular salon on Wednesday evenings, which his wife continued after his death until 1848; across the decades, one of Godefroid's regular tasks was to assist in the gatherings, and there is no evidence that Baronne Gérard and Godefroid were the only women present.[22] Whether male or not artists only socialized with other men in these Boilly-like events, they had significant contact with and dependence upon women in their daily lives. Women provided them with significant capital, connections, and even labor, more than either this image or current scholarship would suggest.

As another example, Jacques-Louis David's wife provided a steady source of wealth, plus he worked with women as students in the years before 1787 when teaching women was prohibited by the Academy. After its dissolution, however, he returned to teaching female students and serving them as a conduit to patronage, for instance in the case of Angélique Mongez.[23] Others who worked with female artists included Antoine-Jean Gros, who instructed Louise-Joséphine Sarazin de Belmont, and Sarazin de Belmont in turn commissioned a funerary monument dedicated to him from Félicie de Fauveau, a female sculptor.[24] Isabey taught Hortense de Beauharnais, the Empress Josephine's daughter, among others, both in and out of Madame Campan's school. François Gérard also had female students, including Elisabeth Chaudet (whose husband is seen in Boilly's *Studio*), Émilie Brongniart, whom he depicted in a portrait holding a porte-crayon shown in the Salon of 1795, and Louise Rose Julie Duvidal de Montferrier, described by Germaine Greer as both his and Godefroid's student.[25]

Most significant for this article, of course, is the role that Godefroid played in the contemporary art world. In terms of her support of men's artistic production, she served Gérard in numerous ways in his studio and his household. The volume of drawings, paintings, and letters that he produced fundamentally depended on her labor. In Gérard's studio, Godefroid found herself working in a preeminent space—artistically and politically—as he was one of Napoleon's chief portraitists and after 1817, the First Painter to Louis XVIII. In terms of her own position in the Davidian world, Godefroid was also a fully-fledged artist in her own right who exhibited her own commissions publicly in nineteen Salons between 1800 and 1847. Early in her career, in the first decade of the nineteenth century, she capitalized on her relationships with other females she knew from Madame Campan's Saint-Germain-en-Laye school, as they (or their relatives) commissioned her to produce paintings for them. These relationships with women made possible Godefroid's career as an independent artist, but also signaled the barriers to her full artistic independence.

Sketching Godefroid's Biography

It is difficult to trace the full extent of Marie-Éléonore Godefroid's artistic career given the scarcity of sources, but records from the nineteenth century and a recent article by Clotilde Schwab-Pourbaix help to situate Godefroid solidly in her milieu.[26] Our understanding of her professional life is enhanced by her many, although sometimes only marginal, appearances in others' biographies, memoirs, and literature about other artists and various elites of the period, including Madame Campan and the illustrious Juliette Recamier. Though generally only a bit player in the larger dramas of these more famous lives, she nonetheless shows up often enough that we can reconstruct a fair amount about not only her professional life, but also the intricacies of the social relations that animated the contemporary art world. Further, as a childless, unmarried, and financially struggling artist, she died with few possessions and no children to preserve and promote her legacy. As a result, absence haunts my account of Godefroid's life: significant biographical information is missing and most of her artistic production has been lost, mislaid, or misattributed.[27]

But we do know some things for certain: she was born in Paris in 1778, the granddaughter and daughter of royally appointed art restorers. She was trained as an artist, but also more generally in the *arts d'agrement*, eventually joining Madame Campan's first school at Saint-Germain-en-Laye as an instructor where young women from the Napoleonic elite were trained. While working at Madame Campan's, Godefroid publicly exhibited her paintings for the first time in the Salon of 1800 at the age of twenty-four, joining a growing contingent of female artists. Around 1805, Godefroid began to work with François Gérard and she appears to have joined his household by 1812, becoming a combination of studio and office assistant and companion for him, his wife, and their nephews.[28] At Gérard's studio, she is credited with a number of high-profile copies and models for the Gobelins tapestry factory. Gérard, unlike David, survived the political upheavals of the period and continued to receive imperial and royal commissions, including painting copies of portraits for the Musée historique planned for Versailles by Louis-Philippe.[29] Godefroid was no doubt a beneficiary of her mentor's political skills, for she too survived the many regime changes of the age. After Gérard's death in 1837, she completed one of his large and unfinished history paintings to mixed reviews. She also assisted his nephew in finalizing the painter's affairs and in writing his biography, and remained in the Gérard household with his widow where she continued to receive commissions, including one for a painting, *Notre-Dame du Rosaire*, destined for a church in Senegal, then a French colony.[30] Having witnessed several revolutions and successive governments, Godefroid died in 1849 in the cholera epidemic, months after Baronne Gérard's death.

Though Godefroid lived and worked with the political and artistic elite throughout her life, she herself never joined this elite, artistically, economically, or maritally. Because of her marginal status in this world, her connections to others were of vital importance in the building of her career. Because she never married and never achieved complete financial independence, her relationships with other women were essential for her personal and professional survival.[31] Like all other artists, she could only survive by making and maintaining networks of peers and patrons, but it was her set of relationships with other women that were most significant and valuable. And it was also her unusual background of having come from an artistic matriarchy and a childhood in female-headed households that perhaps prepared her for relying on other women for professional support.

Like many female artists, Marie-Éléonore Godefroid was the product of an artistic family, and like many artists of both sexes, her family might best be described as an example of the "rising bourgeoisie," a family who used their position as artisans and artists to raise their status. What is somewhat more unusual is that this modest artistic dynasty was founded by a matriarch, her grandmother Marie-Jacobe van Merle Godefroid (?-Paris 1775). Marie-Jacobe and her husband Ferdinand-Joseph Godefroid (Lille?-Paris 1741), settled in Paris, possibly from Antwerp in 1727 or 1728. Establishing themselves as picture dealers and cleaners, the Godefroids worked for major Parisian art collectors, including the prince de Carignan and the comtesse de Verrüe.[32] Ferdinand-Joseph was killed in a duel in 1741, leaving his wife with the care of their children. The widow Godefroid, as she would come to be known in the Academy's records, petitioned Charles-François Le Normand de Tournehem, the Directeur-Général des Bâtiments, to allow her to continue the business in support of her family, gaining a reputation for both her skill as a painting restorer and her tenacity.[33] She invented a technique for lifting paintings off of old supports and placing them onto new ones, for which she received the title of "Painting Restorer to the King," an exclusive privilege held by her family until her death in 1775. Her son and Marie-Éléonore's father, Joseph-Ferdinand-François Godefroid (1729–1788), trained as a painter, spending the years 1753–1759 as a pensioner at the academy in Rome. Upon his return to Paris, he opted to continue the painting restoration business that had been so successful, taking over after his mother's death in 1775. Thanks to her grandmother's establishment as the "restorer to the King" and her persistence, the family was given an apartment at the Louvre where Marie-Éléonore was raised until age ten. This is where she first encountered François Gérard, at the start of his career, but little else is known of her early artistic connections or education. We do know her older brother, a student of Jacques-Louis David and a friend of both Gérard and Girodet, encouraged her as an artist.[34]

When Godefroid's father died in 1788, the family was forced to leave their much-coveted lodgings and her mother was left as head of the family. Little is known of her mother beyond a nineteenth-century description casting her as a "humble bourgeoise, mais jolie, vive, intelligente."[35] She made sure to educate her daughter in social graces, music, and literature so that she could mingle and move up in society, surely with the aim of ensuring a good marriage.[36] French political upheavals may have dashed the family's hope for a match, but Godefroid's artistic training proved useful. By the 1790s, she was apparently sufficiently skilled to assist her brother, supplying him with drawings for his male students to copy at a boy's boarding school.[37] And these skills helped her land an appointment in Madame Campan's school, where she may have received further training from the artist Jean-Baptiste Isabey. Indeed, in the Salon livret from 1806 she is described (at the age of thirty) as an "élève de la maison de Mme. Campan," although she was also working as a "professer le (*sic*) dessin."[38]

What is significant here is that the Godefroid family was a family led by women—first, under the head of the "widow Godefroid" and later by Marie-Éléonore's mother after the death of her father. After his death, her training allowed her to work under the auspices of yet another professional woman at a girl's school. In other words, in Marie-Éléonore's experience, women's professional efforts and women's leadership were not only a part of daily life, but necessary for her survival.

As a young woman in a precarious economic and social position, Godefroid's relationship with a group of powerful and well-connected women allowed her to build a career. After the Godefroid family's eviction from the Louvre, they likely remained in Paris, though by 1795 they fled Paris, possibly for political reasons. A family friend, an officer in the National Guard stationed in Paris, apparently introduced the Godefroids to Madame Jeanne Campan in 1795 where Marie-Éléonore was hired to teach drawing and piano forte.[39] It was here that she encountered Madame Campan's nieces, Adèle and Aglaé Auguié (later the wife of Marshal Ney) as well as Hortense de Beauharnais, and her mother, Josephine Bonaparte, who appears to have later bought one of Godefroid's paintings.[40]

This was Madame Campan's first school and was named the Institution de l'Education de Saint-Germain-en-Laye.[41] Although she was a member of the nobility herself, Campan stated in her posthumously published *On the Education of Girls* (1823) that she provided training suitable for all young women, whatever their rank or wealth. She led daughters of the elite to focus on more substantial educational fare in addition to the *arts d'agrement*, with training in music, dance, and conversation, in preparation for elite marriages. Indeed, the making of marriages seems to have been one activity that played an important role in this institution, as exemplified by her own niece Aglaé Auguié being introduced to her future husband Marshal Ney by Josephine Bonaparte while at the school. Campan also accepted students whose status was less privileged, but focused their attention on a kind of pre-professional training in music and the arts to prepare them for employment as instructors. Although Campan recognized that for some women this was necessary, she also attempted to inculcate in her students a version of femininity that carefully balanced modesty with the need to function in public as perhaps a hostess or an instructor; like Napoleon, she discouraged women's overly public professional activity, even disapproving of women displaying their paintings at the Salon and elsewhere.[42]

In 1805, Napoleon opened several schools for the daughters of members of the Legion of Honor and placed Madame Campan in charge of one at Écouen, necessitating the closure of her first school. She invited Godefroid to move with her in her role as a drawing and music teacher. Godefroid turned down the offer. Arbaud claims she left Madame Campan ultimately because Écouen was too far from her home in Paris.[43] If we frame this decision in terms of Godefroid's professional aspirations, however, perhaps the issue was not one of leaving home but of leaving work.

Under Napoleon, the art world continued to change, and according to Sébastien Allard and Marie-Claude Chaudonneret, dependence on royal commissions shifted towards the development of an art market, where the Salons became places to sell one's work.[44] In the last decade of the eighteenth century and in the first decades of the nineteenth, the opening of Salons to artists outside the Academy saw a dramatic increase in women's participation, and with the changing art market and its decline in royal commissions, women's ability to show their work publicly was essential for their professional survival. Godefroid first exhibited in the Salon of 1800, while still employed at the school, even though this was just the type of activity Madame Campan disapproved of in her treatise on education and in her private correspondence with others. It is worth speculating that Godefroid's decision to leave Madame Campan's service had much to do with her desire both to exhibit her work publicly and to devote herself to painting full time.[45]

After her return to Paris, Godefroid worked for Gérard making copies of his portraits. Her relationship with Gérard was a long-standing one. It is not clear how they came to work together, but they were connected through several circumstances. Both had been together as children living at the Louvre. Gérard and her brother had built a close friendship first at their Louvre residence and then later in David's studio. Godefroid received additional training from Isabey, another close friend of Gérard's. She is generally known as Gérard's assistant, though this does not fully describe her professional activities. By her account, she produced over fifty full-length and bust-length portraits over her career for him.[46] In addition to working in the studio, Godefroid actually managed most of Gérard's correspondence, to the point of mimicking his handwriting, and she seconded the Gérards at social occasions. In 1812, Godefroid was invited to live with Gérard and his family and her friendship extended to Gérard's wife and to his nephews, who were raised in their home as well. After Gérard's death in 1837, Godefroid stayed on, cataloging his work with his nephew Henri, and living with his widow until her death.

Godefroid in the Studio: A Never-Married Female Artist

Marie-Éléonore Godefroid may have been what Melissa Hyde has called an "ordinary artist," but she was unusual in her status as a never-married female artist.[47] As in all other periods, most women at the turn of the nineteenth century married, with many of the remainder entering convents. About fourteen or fifteen percent of women in the late eighteenth and early nineteenth century remained unmarried, but these singlewomen rarely seem to have been able to become artists of Godefroid's note.[48] It is not clear how many women artists remained unmarried.[49] Some exceptional (married) female artists were the source of financial stability for their families, a few lived independently from their husbands on their own income, and others relied on family wealth to support their artistic career. But given her unusual status, it is worth asking what impact being single had on her status and her ability to work as an artist. Marie-Éléonore Godefroid was her sole source of support from what we can tell.[50] Apparently living and working on her own in Paris until 1812, her work may have provided her primary income. By 1812 she joined Gérard's household and she remained there until her death, having few possessions and no accumulated wealth. Working as both a studio assistant and a domestic servant—though perhaps framed in different terms by those involved—provided her the economic and emotional bonds that she may have lacked otherwise.[51]

Her choices to support herself align interestingly with those of unmarried bourgeois and noblewomen from earlier periods. According to Sharon Kettering, early modern French women who were married often worked in their husband's businesses, while widows often maintained their deceased husband's businesses, as Godefroid's own grandmother so successfully exemplifies. Widows and other singlewomen became school mistresses, governesses, and ladies' maids or they joined religious orders that allowed them to teach or serve the lay community in some way.[52] Noblewomen in need of supporting themselves financially had fewer options: marry, become a mistress, enter a convent, or enlist in household service. In Godefroid's case, she took a position in household service to the Gérards, but her role there was not one of servitude. Akin to the noblewomen Kettering has studied, she may have been able to acquire this position because of "special abilities"—in this case, she was a talented painter.[53] As an unmarried female artist, she was uniquely positioned to be able to join another household, but her single and female status also determined her position. Excluded from the training necessary to establish her own studio, she opted to work in that of a powerful male artist.

On the one hand, I am arguing that male-only networks—while they certainly existed—were not the only, or always most important, means of socialization for artists.[54] While art historians, for various reasons, have continued to focus on homosocial male networks without contextualizing these relations more broadly, a study of Marie-Éléonore Godefroid and her relations among women and men reminds us that the art world relied on both sexes for its capital, productivity, and social connections. The evidence suggests that male homosociality was more an ideal perhaps than a reality. But on the other, I am—perhaps paradoxically—arguing that truly homosocial female networks existed among women and were essential for the survival of artists like Godefroid. It is worth considering why and how that was so.

Whereas men could cross boundaries between public and private and had full access under Napoleon's regime to educational institutions, learned and artistic societies, state honors and benefits, not to mention property and economic exchange, women were barred from complete participation in these venues. Under Napoleon, as elite and aristocratic women, they lost their rank-based privileges from the *ancien regime*, and as the female sex in general, they lost the few rights they had gained temporarily during the French Revolution. Under Napeolonic law, they had few rights of full personhood, particularly as minors and wives. Because they were increasingly viewed as private creatures who should not participate fully in public spaces or mingle with men, same-sex private and familial relationships among women were vital for their social and professional development. Girls' schools, such as Madame Campan's, Josephine's breakfasts[55], visits to convents, and the recommending of female servants and employees among women without the involvement of men created a variety of spaces inhabited and controlled by women.[56] These spaces and settings allowed women to have access to other women without the intrusion of men, making these significant places for women to build personal and professional relationships. To be clear, it is not that women turned "naturally" to other women, but rather that women turned to each other because social conventions demanded that they socialize together.

These spaces and relations were not without tensions as they were cross cut by social rank, economic class, and marital status; sometimes we know that female artists found more support from male patrons and mentors than from other women. Nor are these women and their professional relations always easy to trace with absolute certainty, particularly in Godefroid's case as an ordinary artist and a childless woman. We do know, however, that these same-sex relations were vital for better-known female artists, and can presume that the importance of female patronage held true across ranks. Before the Revolution, for instance, Marie Antoinette supported Elisabeth Vigée-Le Brun's membership in the Royal Academy and she secured Anne Vallayer-Coster's lodgings in the Louvre. On both sides of the Revolution, the Comtesse d'Angiviller served as patron to numerous female artists, including Geneviève Brossard de Beaulieu (1755–c.1835) and Adélaïde Labille-Guiard. Josephine Bonaparte lent her support to many female artists, and in turn some of these women, including Vallayer-Coster tapped these homosocial relations to advance the cause of their male relations.[57]

In Godefroid's case, though little documentation survives revealing how she acquired her commissions and what her patrons expected, we can nevertheless triangulate relationships to see that her patrons and clients had either attended, taught at, or supported Madame Campan's school or were one or two degrees separated from those with direct connections to the school. These particular relationships with their linkage to Campan were especially prominent in the early 1800s for her as she forged her working relationship with Gérard and won his favor. For example, it seems possible that the success of the painting of the Ney sons could have led to the commission for another, acclaimed Godefroid portrait, the lost portrait of Queen Hortense and her sons shown at the Salon of 1812.[58] Aglaé Auguié, the mother of Ney's children, was Queen Hortense's lifelong friend and both were likely students of Godefroid's at Saint-Germain-en-Laye. It is possible that Hortense, who maintained an extensive correspondence with Augié and Campan, could have heard about, if not seen the portrait. We can read these paintings and the commissions that lead to them as a link back to relations among women who operated in different circles but whose lives intersected at significant moments.

Boys will be Boys

It is worth returning to Godefroid's *The Sons of Marshal Ney* (fig. 1) to reconsider its possible meanings in light of the context I have sketched above. This portrait, like all portraits, was designed in hopes of pleasing the patron and was reflective of the artist's style and aesthetic choices. But it was also a repository for social relations, including the broader relations between groups in this period and the more specific ones, identifiable between the artist, sitters, and matrons or patrons of the work. While this portrait has been read as reflecting an idealized partnership between Marshal Ney and Napoleon, alternate meanings can be generated if read from the perspective of the boys' mother. It is obvious, but necessary, to state that regardless of the title of the painting, these were the sons of both Neys and the connection to Godefroid arose from relations between Madame Ney and the artist. The work is not then evidence of only the male homosocial relations so visibly and obviously portrayed here, but also of matronage between women that introduced Godefroid into the Ney circle.

In the painting, the references that surround the boys and the company they keep—they are truly a "band of brothers"—depict them in preparation for their membership in adult male society. But perhaps the image also suggests a reference to the crisis in masculinity articulated by Solomon-Godeau. David's 1784 *Oath of the Horatii* (Paris, Musée du Louvre) pictured powerful male heroes clasping each other and saluting their father who presents them their swords; it also includes the slumped and despairing female relations in the lower right of the composition. This image has been interpreted as a celebration of the heroic public sphere envisioned as a pictorial *fraternité*, one that marginalized women.[59] The French Revolution did not result in David's masculinist ideal; instead, it reordered political structures that invoked a parallel crisis in the depiction of the heroic male form, which was captured by David's students of the 1790s and early 1800s with their depictions of dead, dying, or passive, yet physically beautiful male heroes. While their male bodies resembled David's depictions of men, their postures reflected those of the Horatii women.[60] For example, the now-lost posthumous portrait of Louis-Michel Lepeletier de Saint-Fargeau, painted by David with Gérard's assistance following the deputy's assassination on 20 January 1793, offers a particularly dramatic example of the heroic male in a state of feminized abjection (fig. 4).[61] While in fact Lepeletier was stabbed by a former royal bodyguard, David and Gérard transformed the murder weapon—almost mystically—into a sword of Damocles. As it hangs over Lepeletier's corpse, the sword visually evokes those of the Horatii brothers, thus simultaneously symbolizing both courage and sacrifice.[62] But Lepeletier's body does not echo that of the Horatii men. Rather, it recalls that of the Horatii sister in direct contrast with that of her father and brothers.

These iconic images by David and Gérard influenced nearly all artists who worked in the Parisian milieu, including Godefroid. She worked and socialized with them; she displayed her paintings alongside theirs at the Salons, and she, as an ordinary artist in pursuit of patrons and professional survival, was likely to reference their compositions and themes that so powerfully spoke to her contemporaries. Might we thus read Godefroid's portrayal of the young Ney boys as playfully commenting on the post-Revolutionary "crisis of masculinity" as much as invoking the idealized, heroic Horatii from two decades earlier? These are not young Horatii lifting their swords high: Marshal Ney's sword is too heavy for them to actually carry and thus remains sheathed and pointed downward. This image echoes David's many paintings of powerful men, but it undermines the visual assertion of the adult male body's unrestrained power. Indeed, these boys are sweet-faced, soft-limbed, and cherubic, dressed as was the fashion for elite male children.[63] While not overtly eroticized, as in Anne-Louis Girodet's celebrated *The Sleep of Endymion* (1791, Paris, Musée du Louvre) or David's *Death of Joseph Bara* (1794, Avignon, Musée Calvet), the boys' dress and pose reveal them for what they are – ephebes playing with the signs of virile masculinity that they themselves do not possess.[64] Even as the previous images, and perhaps this one as well, attempt to produce a visual field that excludes women, Godefroid's presence as the artist intrudes. As a painting by a woman artist necessarily working outside of the elevated arena of history painting—few women attempted to compete in this genre—a seemingly sweet and culturally compliant portrait of adored sons can be seen as possessing more ironic comments on male power and authority. With

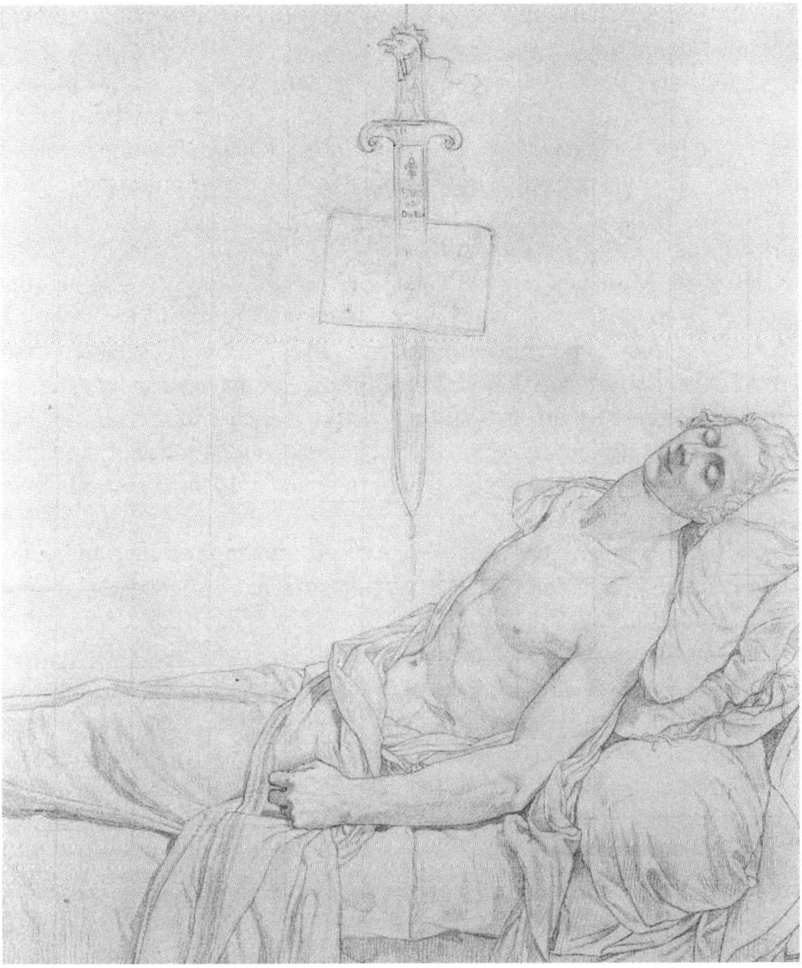

Figure 4. Anatole Devosges after Jacques-Louis David, *Le Peletier de Saint-Fargeau* (1760–1793) on his deathbed, crayon on paper (47.6 x 40 cm). Musée des Beaux-Arts, Dijon, France. (Réunion des Musées Nationaux, Art Resource, NY).

its portrayal of sheathed, heavy swords hanging downward and the boys' youthful dress, this painting is not, after all, fully committed to portraying boyhood or fraternity as all-powerful; indeed, the dramatic compositional division suggests metaphorical 'directions' for the development of future versions of masculinity. Godefroid's portrait challenges the boundaries of genres and gender: it is a portrait made by a marginal female artist masquerading as a scene of everyday life and which reflects a potentially subversive reading of iconic history paintings by a male artist at the pinnacle of the academic and artistic hierarchy.

Considering the limitations imposed on Godefroid as a female painter, really only able to practice as a portraitist and as a single woman entirely reliant on her connections, we can view these compositional and thematic choices in her Ney portrait as a sly commentary on those boundaries. Under the monarchy, history painting had been privileged, and David's *Oath of the Horatii* and his later *The Lictors Returning to Brutus the Bodies of his Sons* (1789, Paris, Musée du Louvre), both royal commissions, were seen as the premier examples of the genre. Under Napoleon's Empire, history painting was ousted from its preeminent position. Still important for Napoleon and later Louis XVIII, it was no longer uncontested as the most sought after or respectable genre for artists. The Ney portrait is not a history painting, but it is worth noting that it was made in the prestigious format of the "full-length portrait," as listed in the Salon *livret*. Such full-length portraits were more valuable and significant than smaller formats. Compared to a straight portrait, these full-length images demanded artistic ingenuity and skill, posing figures in a complex scene, with hands and feet occupied in a realistic and meaningful way. Godefroid's Ney portrait was innovative, combining the endearing sensibility of a genre scene with a more traditional depiction of likeness while also invoking the magisterial historical tradition of bodies in space doing interesting and meaningful things. At the same time, during the Directory and under Napoleon, portraits were politically safe—they could be read in a straightforward representational way and they no longer were associated with and commissioned by primarily the aristocracy. They depicted in the post-revolutionary world a seemingly apolitical space as they were set in private and thus valued as pure, virtuous, familial, and natural. Such transformations allowed, according to Philippe Bordes, "critics [to] t[ake] the genre of portraiture more seriously than before."[65]

It is into this post-Revolutionary context that female artists, including Godefroid, launched their careers as portraitists, and did so in a highly acceptable way. For female artists, this provided an avenue for them to bridge their positions from within the newly reified private sphere, reconstituted in the Napoleonic code, to the public space of the Salons. Female artists could "naturally" present images of mothers, fathers, and children without raising accusations of the loss of modesty.[66] Godefroid's painting of the Ney brothers drew the notice of Charles Landon, a leading art critic of the early nineteenth century, who did not say much about the portrait itself, but acknowledged her as a one of the "mesdames" exhibiting noteworthy portraits. For Landon, Godefroid's work stood out amongst an ever-growing field of portraitists, male and female, in the Salon.[67] This was significant notice in the rapidly growing marketplace for art. No longer was government support guaranteed, even for the most well-known, well-trained artists, and competition for patronage, clients, and sales diversified the arena for commissions, particularly for those on the cheaper end of the scale. While women had historically been mostly excluded from training as history painters, they were encouraged to pursue portraiture for a variety of reasons. Portraiture, especially of women and children, was regarded as an appropriate (if not unproblematic) arena for female artists to specialize in since it was frequently seen as mimetic, mechanical, and could be produced and frequently was presented in the private sphere.[68] Yet, one aspect of the Ney portrait is that it engages larger questions and issues within the public sphere by adapting and borrowing elements from paintings of men by male artists which have since been read as exemplary of masculinity and its associated crisis in this era. And it is in this sense, though we are looking at a portrait of boys at play, we are also looking at an artist fashioning a place for herself among a large, competitive field of painters, women and men alike.

Godefroid's portrait references the public world of men that these boys were expected to grow into; she herself had one foot in and one foot out of this world. We could also set this image into the context of domesticity and the education of children; as a woman it might be presumed that Godefroid depicts a "feminine" world. To see this as reflecting a woman's experience assimilates all women to a domestic life concerned with motherhood and child-rearing—something not in Godefroid's personal experience—reinforcing a sense of discrete arenas of male and female action. It is more useful to see this image negotiating the overlapping of so-called "masculine" and "feminine" spheres, the public and the private, the political and the domestic.

In the creation of this portrait, the Ney children met the gaze of a woman who returned what I can only imagine was a steady gaze back. This carefully wrought composition indicates that Marie-Éléonore Godefroid was an accomplished painter and draughtswoman. This is a highly finished and even witty portrait of young boys growing up in the context of the Napoleonic empire. It draws on an established tradition of heroic male representation, produced by Godefroid's male peers, while also nodding to newer ideas about childhood and educational development. The sword carries additional significance. It was a wedding gift from Napoleon, who had encouraged the match between Ney and Josephine's daughter's friend and schoolmate. As a wedding gift, it is an example of a bond between men cemented with a woman as object. Yet this portrait likely came about because of the relationship between two women, Godefroid and Madame Ney. While there are few extant works that can be securely identified as Godefroid's, the remnants of her oeuvre lead us back to her relations with women.[69] Godefroid may have gained this commission in part through her association with Gérard, but it seems just as likely that this commission encodes a parallel history of relations between women.

Marie-Éléonore Godefroid's oeuvre is extremely challenging to identify definitively, not least because evaluating her work—like that of many artists—as the expression of a single individual is nearly impossible. Like so many "ordinary" artists of both sexes, she worked for and with others.[70] Clearly, Godefroid's relationships with men were essential in the creation of her career, but her relations *between* women ensured her professional survival and the possibility that she would even enter the historical record, however fragmentary that history may ultimately be. Women's social and professional networks are often ignored, perhaps because they are seen as peripheral or only duplicative of relations between male artists. In fact, however, they provide significant information, not only in the uncovering of the artistic careers and experiences of female artists, but also in the illumination of the late eighteenth- and early nineteenth-century art world with its intricate networks of kin, friends, employers, colleagues, and patrons.

NOTES

I would like to thank *SECC* editor Lisa Cody and the anonymous readers for their thoughtful comments on an earlier draft of this essay. In addition, Heidi Strobel, Amber Ludwig, and my Ithaca College research assistants provided invaluable feedback and support.

1. The painting is listed as No. 379 in the Salon *Livret* of 1810, page 47. See Pierre Sanchez and Xavier Seydoux, *Les catalogues des Salons* (Paris: Echelle de Jacob, 1999), 1: 185.

2. Ann Sutherland Harris and Linda Nochlin, *Women Artists, 1550–1950* (Los Angeles: Los Angeles Museum of Art with Alfred A. Knopf, 1976), 215–16, (color plate 85); Mahonri Sharp Young, "The Women," *Apollo Magazine* 105 (January 1977): 57–60.

3. Nancy Heller, *Women Artists: An Illustrated History* (New York: Abbeville Press, 1987), 82–83; Margaret Barlow, *Women Artists* (New York: Hugh Lauter Levin Associates, 1999), 42, 51; Jordi Vigue, *Great Women Masters of Art* (New York: Watson-Guptil, 2002), 183–86; Margaret Oppenheimer, "Women Artists in Paris, 1791–1814" (Ph.D. Diss., New York University, 1996), 187–89; Charlotte Yeldham, *Women Artists in Nineteenth-Century France and England* (New York: Garland, 1984), 1: 241, 248; Germaine Greer, *The Obstacle Race: The Fortunes of*

Women Painters and their Work (London: Martin Secker and Warburg, 1979), 290; Melissa Hyde, "Women in the Visual Arts in the Age of Marie Antoinette," in Eik Kahng and Marianne Roland Michel, eds., *Anne Vallayer-Coster: Painter to the Court of Marie-Antoinette* (New Haven: Yale University Press, 2002), 75–94, 91, n40, mention Godefroid as an example of a female artist and teacher.

4. *Portrait of the Dauphin* by Louis Tocqué (1737, Paris, Musée du Louvre) has the scattered papers and books, elaborate setting with drapery, and distant sky-view, as well as portraits of men at desks; compare also David's *The Emperor Napoleon in His Study at the Tuileries* (1812, Washington, D.C., National Gallery of Art).

5. For key relevant examples here, see Griselda Pollock and Roszika Parker, *Old Mistresses: Women, Art, and Ideology* (London: Routledge & Kegan Paul, 1981); the three volumes of essays edited by Mary Garrard and Norma Broude: *Feminism and Art History: Questioning the Litany* (New York: Harper and Row, 1982), *The Expanding Discourse: Feminism and Art History* (New York: Icon Editions, 1992), and *Reclaiming Female Agency: Feminist Art History after Postmodernism* (Berkeley: University of California Press, 2005); see also *Women, Art and the Politics of Identity in Eighteenth-Century Europe*, ed. Melissa Hyde and Jennifer Milam (Burlington, VT: Ashgate Press, 2003); Mary Sheriff, *The Exceptional Woman: Elisabeth Vigée-Lebrun and the Cultural Politics of Art* (Chicago: University of Chicago Press, 1996); Laura Auricchio, *Adélaïde Labille-Guiard: Artist in the Age of Revolution* (Los Angeles: J. Paul Getty Museum, 2009); *Anne Vallayer-Coster, Painter to the Court of Marie-Antoinette,* ed. Eik Kahng (New Haven: Yale University Press: 2002); Gen Doy, *Women and Visual Culture in Nineteenth-Century France 1800–1852* (London: Leicester University Press, 1998); Gen Doy, "Hidden from Histories: Women History Painters in Early Nineteenth-Century France," in Rafael Cardoso Denis and Colin Trodd, eds., *Art and the Academy in the Nineteenth Century*, (Manchester: Manchester University Press, 2000), 71–85.

6. For recent work on Jacques-Louis David's male students, see Sylvain Bellenger, ed., *Girodet, 1767–1824* (Paris: Gallimard, 2005); David O'Brien, *After the Revolution: Antoine-Jean Gros, Painting and Propaganda Under Napoleon* (University Park, PA: Pennsylvania State University Press, 2006); Sébastien Allard and Marie-Claude Chaudonneret, *Le Suicide de Gros: Les Peintres de l'Empire et la Génération Romantique* (Paris: Gourcuff Gradenigo, 2010). There have been no recent treatments of François Gérard, so we must continue to rely on Charles Lenormant's 1842 biography, *François Gérard, Peintre d'Histoire* (Paris: Imprimerie d'A. René et Compagnie, 1842, 1847) and the materials that Godefroid assisted in collecting, edited by his nephew, Henri Gérard, *Lettres adressées au baron François Gérard, peintre d'histoire* (Paris: Impr. De A. Quantin, 1888).

7. Thomas Crow, *Emulation: Making Artists for Revolutionary France* (New Haven: Yale University Press, 1995), 2.

8. Bordes notes that in 1793, David compared a portrait by himself unfavorably with one by Vigée-Lebrun, notably using a gendered comparison: hers was masculine, his feminine. He also followed her lead of painting on a wooden support instead of canvas. Bordes, *Jacques-Louis David: Empire to Exile* (New Haven: Yale University Press, 2005), 142. See also Philippe Bordes "Consolidating the Canon," *Oxford Art Journal* 19:2 (1996): 107–14 for his review of Crow's *Emulation*. Margaret Fields Denton, "A Woman's Place: The Gendering of Genres in Post-Revolutionary French Painting," *Art History* 12:2 (June 1998): 219–46; for another critique of Crow's exclusion of female artists, see Doy, *Women and Visual Culture.*

9. Abigail Solomon-Godeau, *Male Trouble: A Crisis in Representation* (London: Thames & Hudson, 1997), 51–52.

10. Musée des Beaux-Arts de Lille, *Boilly, 1761–1845: Un Grand Peinture Français de la Révolution à la Restauration,* Annie Scottez-De Wambrechies and Sylvain Lavissière, eds. (Lille: Musée des Beaux-Arts de Lille, 1989); Susan Siegfried, *The Art of Louis-Léopold Boilly: Modern Life in Napoleonic France* (New Haven: Yale University Press, 1995), esp. 95–107.

11. *Boilly, 1761–1845: Un Grand Peinture Français de la Révolution à la Restauration,* Annie Scottez-De Wambrechies and Sylvain Lavissière, eds. (Lille: Musée des Beaux-Arts de Lille, 1989), esp. Sylvain Lavissière, "L'Atelier d'Isabey: un panthéon de l'amitié," 52–63; Siegfried, *The Art of Louis-Léopold Boilly,* 95–107.

12. Anthony Halliday, *Facing the Public: Portraiture in the Aftermath of the French Revolution* (Manchester: Manchester University Press, 2000), 141.

13. In at least two of the preliminary sketches for this scene, a small, unidentified girl appears. It is not clear who she is, but she was excluded from the final painting; see Lavissière, "L'Atelier," (figures 18, 19), 62–63. Compare these images with Boilly's *A Sculptor's Studio, Picture of a Family* (1804, Paris, Musée des Arts Décoratifs), which shows Houdon and his family and thus shifts the studio into the private, domestic space and incorporates female family members. On the gendered meanings of this painting, see Siegfried, *The Art of Louis-Léopold Boilly*, 104–05; Halliday, *Facing the Public*, 141; Ewa Lajer-Burchharth, *Necklines: The Art of Jacques-Louis David after the Terror* (New Haven: Yale University Press, 1999), 213–16.

14. Before the Revolution, women exhibited at venues outside the traditional Salons, including the Exposition de la Jeunesse, the Académie de Saint-Luc (until it was suppressed in 1776), and the Salon de la Correspondance (1779–1787); Oppenheimer, "Women Artists," 8–11.

15. Oppenheimer, "Women Artists," 16.

16. Oppenheimer, "Women Artists," 2.

17. Paula Radisich, "Que peut définir les femmes?: Vigée-Lebrun's Portraits of an Artist," *Eighteenth-Century Studies* 25:4 (Summer, 1992): 441–67, esp. 452.

18. Paula Radisich, *Hubert Robert: Painted Spaces of the Enlightenment* (Cambridge: Cambridge University Press, 1998); Nina Dubin, *Futures & Ruins: Eighteenth-Century Paris and the Art of Hubert Robert* (Los Angeles: Getty Research Institute, 2010).

19. Andrew McClellan, *Inventing the Louvre: Art, Politics, and the Origins of the Modern Museum in Eighteenth-Century Paris* (Cambridge: Cambridge University Press, 1994), (figure 47), 128.

20. On Camuccini's image, see Margaret Oppenheimer, "'The Charming Spectacle of a Cadaver': Anatomical and Life Study by Women Artists in Paris, 1775–1815," *Nineteenth-Century Art Worldwide: A Journal of Nineteenth-Century Visual Culture* 6.1 (Spring 2007), *http://www.19thc-artworldwide.org/index.php/spring07/142-qthe-charming-spectacle-of-a-cadaverq-anatomical-and-life-study-by-women-artists-in-paris-17751815.*

21. For example, see Adrienne Marie Louise Grandpierre-Deverzy, *Intérieur d'un atelier de peinture* (1822, Paris, Musée Marmottan) and Marie Bashkirteff, *L'Académie Julien* (1881, St. Petersburg, Hermitage), both in Yeldham, *Women Artists*, 235–36. Also see, Louise-Rose Julie Duvidal de Montferrier, *The Drawing Class in Edinburgh 1830, including Mademoiselle, afterwards the Duchess of Parma, the artist, Duchesse de Gontout, and the Duchesse d'Angoulême*, which shows a male artist examining the work of a young female artist. Duvidal de Montferrier had been a student at Campan's school and was apparently connected to Godefroid and Gérard as a student. See Greer, *The Obstacle Race*, 290, for illustration and information.

22. Gérard, *Lettres addressées*, 20–22; 30–33.

23. Denton, "A Woman's Place," 242.

24. Allard and Chaudonneret, *Le Suicide de Gros*, 20, 23.

25. Halliday, *Facing the Public,* 53, 70; Greer, *The Obstacle Race,* 290.

26. Four sources survive that provide most of my information about Godefroid. A short pamphlet by Sainte Vallière, "Marie-Éléonore Godefroid, Artiste-Peintre" (Paris: Imp. De Mme de Lacombe, 1847); Louis Arbaud's more extensive two-part article, "Marie-Éléonore Godefroy," *Gazette des Beaux-Arts* XI, Deuxième série (1869), volume 1, Part 1, 38–52 and volume 2, Part 2, 512–522. Henri Gérard, *Lettres adressées*; Clothilde Schwab-Pourbaix, "Marie-Éléonore Godefroid et ses portraits conservés au musée national des châteaux de Versailles et de Trianon," *La Revue des Musées de France* 5 (Dec. 2008): 63–71.

27. Schwab-Pourbaix has found that Godefroid had few possessions when she died; "Marie-Éléonore Godefroid," 70, fn 66.

28 In the Salon *livret* from 1812, she lists Gérard's address as her own for the first time: 6, rue Bonaparte. Sanchez and Seydoux, 1: 45. This date corresponds with a degenerative illness that Gérard developed in 1812. It should also be noted that between 1812 until 1819 Godefroid does not appear to have exhibited at the Salon,

perhaps due to increased domestic responsibilities; Lenormant, 50–56. Although only speculation at this point, it seems possible that Baronne Gérard invited her to join the family, and, after Gérard's death, to remain with her. Many of Gérard's epistolary correspondents greeted him, his wife—and Godefroid—who was apparently seen as part of the artist's intimate circle.

29. Schwab-Pourbaix, "Marie-Éléonore Godefroid," 64–65.

30. Gérard, *Lettres adressées*, 23; Schwab-Pourbaix, "Marie-Éléonore Godefroid," 68; the painting is now untraced.

31. Eve Kosofosky Sedgwick, *Between Men: English Literature and Male Homosocial Desire* (New York: Columbia University Press, 1985); Margaret Hunt has offered important nuanced revisions particularly to our understanding of women's homosocial relations in *Women in Eighteenth-Century Europe* (Harlow, UK: Pearson Education Limited, 2010).

32. Lawrence and Magdalena Kasman, "Jeanne-Baptiste d'Albert de Luynes, Comtesse de Verrue (1670–1736): An Art Collector in Eighteenth-Century Paris," in *Women and Art in Early Modern Europe: Patrons, Collectors, and Connoisseurs*, ed. Cynthia Lawrence (University Park, PA: Pennsylvania State University Press, 1997), 207–26; 218.

33. For the "widow Godefroid," see Andrew McClellan, *Inventing the Louvre: Art, Politics, and the Origins of the Modern Museum in Eighteenth-Century Paris* (Berkeley: University of California Press, 1994), esp. 24–27.

34. Oppenheimer, "Women Artists," 187; Arbaud, "Marie-Éléonore Godefroy," 43; Gérard, *Lettres addressees*, 22.

35. Schwab-Pourbaix gives her first name as Marie-Madeleine; Schwab-Pourbaix, "Marie-Éléonore Godefroid," 70. Arbaud identifies her family name as Ganneron from near Saint-Germain-l'Auxerrois; Arbaud, "Marie-Éléonore Godefroy," 40.

36. Godefroid also received musical training with Étienne Nicolas Méhul, a composer and friend of her father's; Gérard, *Lettres addressees*, 22; Arbaud, "Marie-Éléonore Godefroy," 40.

37. Arbaud, "Marie-Éléonore Godefroy," 44.

38. Salon *livret* of 1806, 41, reproduced in Sanchez and Seydoux, *Les catalogues des Salons,* 1: 114.

39. Arbaud, "Marie-Éléonore Godefroy," 44–45; Schwab-Pourbaix, "Marie-Éléonore Godefroid," 63–64.

40. Madame Campan's nieces came to live with her the year of their mother's 1789 suicide; J. Lucas-Dubreton, *Le Maréchal Ney, 1769–1815* (Paris: Librairie Arthème Fayard, 1941), 32–33; on Josephine's purchase of work by Godefroid and other women, including Angélique Mongez (1775–1855), Henriette Lorimer (c.1775–1854), and Jeanne Elisabeth Chaudet (1767–1832) whose husband is pictured in Boilly's group portrait, see Eleanor Delorme, "Josephine as Patroness of the Arts," *The Magazine Antiques* 162.3 (1971): 132–41. Delorme, unfortunately, does not include information about either specific paintings or her sources.

41. Catherine Montfort and J. Terrie Quintana, "Madame Campan's *Institution de Education*: A Revolution in the Education of Women," *Australian Journal of French Studies* 331.1 (1996): 141–57; Rebecca Rogers, "Competing Visions of Girls' Secondary Education in Post-Revolutionary France," *History of Education Quarterly* 34.2 (Summer 1994): 147–70; Laura Auricchio, "The Laws of Bienséance and the Gendering of Emulation in Eighteenth-Century French Art Education," *Eighteenth-Century Studies* 36.2 (Winter 2003): 231–40.

42. Arbaud, "Marie-Éléonore Godefroid," 50–51; sources indicate that Godefroid first exhibited her own work at the Salon of 1800, but the first public notice of her work appeared in the 1806 livret.

43. Arbaud, "Marie-Éléonore Godefroid," 48–49.

44. Allard and Chaudonneret, *Le Suicide de Gros,* 114.

45. Oppenheimer, "Women Artists," 188.

46. Arbaud, "Marie-Éléonore Godefroid," 49.

47. Hyde describes "ordinary artists" as women and men whose careers "might not have been on par with the extraordinary ones" but who were active, talented, and even acknowledged by their peers; Hyde, "Women and the Visual Arts in the Age of Marie Antoinette," 78.

48. Christine Adams, "A Choice Not to Wed? Unmarried Women in Eighteenth-Century France," *Journal of Social History* 29.4 (Summer, 1996): 883–94, 883. Cécile Dauphin, "Single Women," in Geneviève Fraisse and Michelle Perrot, eds., *A History of Women in the West* (Cambridge: Belknap/Harvard University Press, 1993), 427–42. Michèlle Bordeaux, Arlette Farge, and Christiane Klapisch-Zuber, eds., *Madame ou Mademoiselle? Itinéraires de la solitude féminine, XVIIIe–XXe siècles* (Paris: Montalba, 1984). Judith Bennett and Amy Froide, eds., *Singlewomen in the European Past, 1250–1800* (Philadelphia: University of Pennsylvania Press, 1999), esp. their intro. (1–37) and Maryanne Kowalski's "Singlewomen in Medieval and Early Modern Europe: The Demographic Experience," 38–81.

49. For comparisons with female writers, who tended to never marry or to wait until widowhood to begin their active publishing life, see Christine Théré, "Economic Publishing and Authors, 1566–1789," in *Studies in the History of French Political Economy: From Bodin to Walras*, ed. G. Faccarelle (London: Routledge, 1998), 1–56; female authors tended "to come from privileged backgrounds and to live in Paris," according to Théré, "Women and Birth Control in Eighteenth-Century France," in *Eighteenth-Century Studies* 32.4 (Summer 1999): 552–64.

50. It is unclear what happened to her brother or his career beyond remarks in biographical accounts that describe him as one of David's students and a teacher at a boy's school. He does not appear in artist's dictionaries, though Marie-Éléonore does, suggesting that he may not have survived the Revolution.

51. This arrangement was most likely contracted with François Gérard; relations between women come in to play as Godefroid had to build a relationship with

Gérard's wife, one that ultimately survived the artist's death. Celibate men and women were preferred for service in noble households; Kettering, "Household Service of Early Modern French Noblewomen," *French Historical Studies* 20:1 (Winter 1997): 55–85, 66 n50.

52. Kettering, *Careers*, 66.

53. Kettering, *Careers*, 62.

54. I am distinguishing here between training, which would have taken place in primarily all-male enclaves and socialization, which would have included salons, Salons, and other forms of patronage-building exercises.

55. Steven D. Kale, "Women, Salons, and the State in the Aftermath of the French Revolution, "*Journal of Women's History*, 13.4 (Winter 2002): 54–80; Kale describes these as opportunities for young women of the court to refine their manners "free of the intimidating presence of men"(62).

56. Kettering, "Household Service," 57.

57. On Marie-Antoinette's support of Vigée-Le Brun's, see Sheriff, *The Exceptional Woman*, 74–78; on her support of Vallayer-Coster, see Roland Michel, "Vallayer in Her Time," *Anne Vallayer-Coster*, 19; for a useful list of pre- and post-revolutionary examples of women artists who sought and received support from elite women and the role of the Comtesse and Comte d'Angiviller, see Hyde, "Women and the Visual Arts," 81, and on Vallayer-Coster's tapping connections for her nephew, n77.

58. In addition, she appears to have received another commission for a portrait of children. In 1812, she also exhibited "Portraits des enfants de S. Exc. M.gr le duc de Rovigo," listed as 419 in the Salon. The locations of both paintings are unknown. See Sanchez and Seydoux, *Les catalogues des Salons,* 1: 223.

59. See Joan Landes: "However unbearable the consequences, he must be made to see the duty of men, for unlike the women he will assume his place as a citizen among men," in *Women and the Public Sphere in the Age of Revolution* (Ithaca: Cornell University Press, 1988), 152–58, 158. Godefroid herself may be seen to take the Horatti boy's position in the production of this portrait, not as a future citizen but as a marginal witness who straddles public and private. For Solomon-Godeau, it can also be read as "testimonial to an internalized division inhabiting the patriarchal Imaginary," one that threatens to destabilize "the integrity and unity of the male subject," thus requiring the production of an alternative, feminized masculinity to guard against the threat of sexual difference; Solomon-Godeau, *Male Trouble*, 96.

60. Solomon-Godeau, *Male Trouble*, 63. Solomon-Godeau discusses the range of idealized male nudes, from ephebic to virile, as a way to "figure sexual difference in a same-sex system -- sexual difference without women." The crisis she analyzes is the shift from pre-Revolutionary to post-Revolutionary formations of masculinity, one in which the beautiful male nude is ultimately displaced by that of the female nude.

61. Although David's final drawing and painting no longer exist, a preparatory drawing for an engraving after the painting, by Anatole Desvosges, does survive at the Musée des Beaux-Arts in Dijon and is the image reproduced here. See Robert Simon, "David's Martyr-Portrait of Le Peletier de Saint-Fargeau and the Conundrums of Revolutionary Representations," *Art History* 14.4 (December 1991): 459–87; Lajer-Burchharth, *Necklines*; Crow, *Emulation*, figure 115 at 118.

62. Crow, *Emulation,* 156–59.

63. The two elder sons are dressed like Napoleon's nephews in Louis Ducis's *The Emperor Napoleon on the Terrace of Saint-Cloud* (1800, Versailles) and similar to the boy in François Gérard's *Hortense, Queen of Holland, with her Son* (1806, Fontainebleau). The youngest is in a similar costume to the seated Lucien in Gérard's *Portrait of Caroline Murat, Queen of Naples, accompanied by her four children*, shown in the Salon of 1808 (Fontainebleau).

64. Solomon-Godeau, *Male Trouble*, 136–139. Solomon-Godeau cites Alex Potts and his discussion of the Bara painting, which reads as "an appropriation of the femininity elsewhere banished from political and cultural domains." (138).

65. According to Bordes, "this change benefited relatively minor draftsmen and miniaturists like Jean-Baptiste Isabey and Jean-Baptiste Jacques Augustin, while history painters like Anne-Louis Girodet, François Gérard, and David promoted themselves as serious artists through their portraits." Bordes, *Jacques-Louis David: Empire to Exile*, 128.

66. See Denton, "Gendering of Genres," 228, and Sheriff, *The Exceptional Woman*, 43–52, for a discussion of Vigée-Lebrun's self-portraits as a mother.

67. In the 1810 issue of the *Annales du musée et de l'école moderne des beaux-arts*, Landon wrote "Si les productions du premier ordre, celles que l'on peut ranger parmi les morceaux vraiment classiques, sont extrêmement rares aux expositions annuelles, on y remarques du moins, et notamment à celle de 1810, un grand nombre des tableaux de divers genres, intéressans par le choix du sujet, par la grace de la composition, l'agrément du pinceau ou la légèreté du coloris.... Parmi les autres portraits peints à l'huile, soit en pied soit en buste, qui abondent cette année au Salon, on a pu remarquer encore ceux de MM. Barbier-Walbonne, Berthon, Bouchet, Riesner; des mesdames Auzou, Benoît, Capet, Charpentier, Chaudet, de Romance, Godefroy (*sic*), Lorimier, etc., etc." "Salon of 1810," *Annales du musée et de l'école moderne des beaux-arts* (Paris: Bossande et Masson; London: Longman, Hurst, Rees, Orme et Brown, 1810), 97–98.

68. Angela Rosenthal, "She's Got the Look! Eighteenth-Century Female Portrait Painters and the Psychology of a Potentially 'Dangerous Employment,'" in *Portraiture: Facing the Subject*, ed. Joanna Woodall (Manchester: Manchester University Press, 1997), 147–66.

69. Other paintings by Godefroid that function similarly include portraits of Queen Hortense (1801 and 1812), Madame de Staël for Juliette Recamier (1817),

Princesses Louise and Marie d'Orléans (1819), Madame Vigano (shown in the Salons of 1839 and 1842 and produced as a print), and Victor Hugo's father, *Bernard-François Balzac, né Balssa*, in the collection of the Institut de France, which also directs us to Godefroid's student who was Hugo's sister-in-law.

70. If we consider Godefroid's work for Gérard, we might ask whether the oeuvre of François Gérard was, indeed, fully "his." Crow has demonstrated how the work of David can be read as a record of his relations with his male students—Drouais, Girodet, Gros, Gérard among others. In this case, Godefroid's efforts for Gérard do not reflect homosocial bonding, but surely Gérard's training in David's studio must have had an effect on his practice and could provide similar ground for further study.

William Tell's Atlantic Travels in the Revolutionary Era[1]

MARC H. LERNER

"The story of William Tell has been told in various ways; it has been dramatized in almost every country in Europe where Liberty dare raise her head." So wrote William Hewetson in his 1810 translator's preface to Florian's *William Tell, or Swisserland delivered.*[2] As Hewetson explained, the character of Tell, a legendary Swiss alpine hero purportedly from the early fourteenth century, was used in a variety of locations to comment on local society and contemporary political culture, including moments of rebellion and revolution. Tell's role during the long eighteenth century is especially striking in its flexibility and ability to articulate divergent political arguments. During the Age of Revolution Tell helped to define a rights–based political culture, republican ideals, and political revolt as legitimate, but he also served to remind British audiences of virtue, loyalty, and devotion to the commonweal.[3] The William Tell story was more than simply a reflection of the often jagged and conflicted development of political culture over the long eighteenth century, it was also, in itself, a vehicle for making arguments. The Tell legend was more than a symbol or a parable, it was a seemingly living story that inspired ordinary people to take political action, sometimes in extraordinary ways by comparing themselves to, dressing as, and naming themselves after William Tell.

This article and the larger book project to which it belongs reflect two trends in eighteenth-century studies: first, the focus on the international context of the period with its transnational cultural and political exchanges, and, second, the emphasis on culture as a means to understand the emergent political ideals, nationalism, and revolutionary politics. In my work I argue that far from understanding a revolution in France as independent and isolated, we grasp its nature by exploring how it was shaped by and helped to form transnational intellectual and cultural trends.[4] The transitions and revolutions across the eighteenth-century Euro-Atlantic world must furthermore be understood as not only an intellectual transformation, but also as practice-driven developments.[5] Cultural trends and practices are not just reflections, but also motors of political transformation; history is made by objects, rituals and performances.[6] In addition to my emphasis on transnational exchange and culture as an engine of change, my project expands the parameters of the long eighteenth century, suggesting that the 1848 Revolutions were fundamentally shaped by eighteenth-century cultural developments, which, in turn, were shaped by cultural icons, including the figure of William Tell.

Known widely throughout Europe, North America and Latin America, the Tell story has long been open to multiple interpretations and available to make varied political statements. Its flexibility and ultimately ambivalent political meaning make the reiterations of the Tell story particularly revealing in the eighteenth century. After an introduction discussing the historical origins and uses of the story in Switzerland, this article focuses on a series of specific, intertwined versions of the Tell story that appeared in France and Britain from the mid-eighteenth century to the early nineenth century: Antoine-Marin Lemierre's *Guillaume Tell* of 1766, Michel-Jean Sedaine and André Grétry's 1791 comic opera, rewritten by Jean-Baptiste Pelissier in 1828 , Jean-Pierre Claris de Florian's 1794–1801 epic poem with its English translation, first published in 1810, and James Sheridan Knowles's 1825 five-act play.[7] Of course, this is not a comprehensive catalog of revolutionary era Tell stories as I have excluded or only briefly mention many, including most obviously Friedrich Schiller's 1804 classic play and Gioachino Rossini's 1829 famous opera, first performed in Paris. The four I do examine, however, exemplify the legend's malleability and polyvalent political meanings in the Atlantic World. Furthermore, Grétry's opera (rewritten by Pelissier and based partly on Lemierre's play) and Knowles's version (based partly on Florian's epic) were both performed on the Paris stage in the summer of 1828.

Historical Origins in Switzerland

Modern scholars have followed several paths through oral and written culture and across genres to trace Tell's lineage. In Switzerland, Wilhelm Tell was placed in the fourteenth-century past as part of a Swiss foundational myth. The first full Swiss recording of the Tell story appeared in the *White Book of Sarnen*, one of the early humanist chronicles, in the 1470s. Popular folk songs followed not long after, or, perhaps more accurately, were first recorded soon after. The authors of the *White Book of Sarnen*, "Das Lied von der Entstehung der Eidgenossenschaft" (1477), and festival plays based their telling of the story on older local traditions.[8] The *White Book of Sarnen* was possibly a copy of a now lost, older chronicle, which, in fact, made little impact because it was buried in cantonal archives until the nineteenth century.[9] It was the early sixteenth century chronicles by Petermann Etterlin and Heinrich Brennwald that made the story available. These chronicles were so successful that by 1514 it was no longer necessary to go into all of the details of the Tell story while referencing the events.[10]

As a *performance*, the Tell story was probably first presented in the early sixteenth century about two hundred years after the events it purported to describe. In 1512, for example, a popular festival play was written and performed in the canton of Uri.[11] This version had its roots in local oral traditions of popular songs and Swiss foundational myths. This 1512 performed version, known as the *Urner Tellspiel*, was one of several *Tellenspiele*—festival productions—that were performed regularly in the Swiss republics and was published by Augustin Fries in the 1530s and then distributed throughout the Swiss Confederation.[12] It was at this point in the 1530s and 1540s that the William Tell narrative became particularly popular.[13]

Later in the sixteenth century, Tschudi's *Chronicon Helveticum*, well known, though unpublished until the eighteenth century, and the published works of Josias Simmler codified elements of the story for both Swiss and European intellectuals. In all, there were at least eight different versions of the Tell story between 1470–1580, including chronicles and plays, and seventeen different versions of the *Tellenlied* before 1700. [14] These three forms do not cover a vast amount of symbolic material culture: statues, medals, monuments, stained glass, engraved cups, woodcuts, paintings and other sources such as pamphlets that followed the early renderings of the tale.[15]

Most of the versions of the Tell story share the same basic premise: William Tell, a simple Burger of the mountainous Swiss canton of Uri, was oppressed (directly or indirectly) by the tyrannical bailiff Gessler. In some versions, Gessler is a local aristocrat, whereas in others he represents Habsburg claims to the area; in all versions, however, he threatens Tell's (and Swiss) liberty. Tell refuses to bow down before the symbols of tyrannical authority (usually a hat) and thus is detained by Gessler, the personification of that authority. Gessler then capriciously forces Tell, an expert marksman, to shoot an apple off of his own son's head. Tell is, of course, successful, but in many versions Tell is further detained because a second arrow is discovered, which Tell admitted was meant for Gessler in case Tell's son had been harmed. Tell is once again enchained, but stages a daring escape in the midst of a spectacular storm. Tell then takes his revenge on Gessler and kills him. In the end Gessler pays the price for his tyrannical actions and Tell's victory over Gessler leads to the independence of the Swiss Cantons.

There was not agreement, however, on some other important elements of the story. Did Tell personally plan and lead the overthrow of Gessler and the independence movement of the Swiss or did he merely protect his family and allow the natural Swiss leaders to assert their authority? In the fifteenth and sixteenth centuries, the Tell story became closely associated with another foundational myth in early modern Switzerland. This second story of the Oath of the Rütli Meadow explains the origins of the Swiss Confederation as a conscious effort by the collected people to form an eternal alliance of free people. Originally, the stories were separate, with the Rütli Oath story, for example, recorded earlier in 1420 without mention of Tell.[16] According to this second foundational legend one representative from each canton of Uri, Schwyz, and Unterwalden gathered together in the Rütli Meadow in the middle of Lake Lucerne to take an oath on behalf of their respective populations that guaranteed liberty, property, and mutual defense.[17] In some versions Tell is never mentioned with only Fürst, Stauffacher, and Melchtal taking the oath. In some later versions, however, Walter Fürst, the representative of Uri, is linked to Tell as his father-in-law or companion, or Tell himself takes the Rütli oath with Stauffacher of Schwyz and Melchtal of Unterwalden. As these stories are combined in the sixteenth century, together they state the claim that the citizens of the mountain cantons of Switzerland threw off tyrannical, aristocratic, and foreign rule while establishing their own freedom.[18] The dispute among the different versions is whether or not Tell participated in planning the rebellion (the Oath) that overthrew the illegitimate rulers of the Swiss Cantons.

In the sixteenth century the Tell stories, songs, and plays could be read in the context of the emerging state form of the Swiss Confederation. Swiss elites, freshly confident from victory in the 1499 Swabian War with Maximilian of Habsburg, sought to justify the legitimacy of the Swiss

Confederation.[19] The Swiss used their foundational myths to counter the claims of the Imperial nobility that the Swiss were lawless, un-Christian hooligans who violated the social order by illegally overthrowing their natural, legitimate rulers.[20] The Swiss used the foundational narratives of the William Tell and the Rütli Oath stories to legitimate the use of force against tyrannical government. In this interpretation, Tell, the father, was forced to commit the unnatural act of shooting at his son. It was not the Swiss who killed their natural rulers like the Emperor claimed, but the Habsburgs who demanded unnatural actions from their subjects.[21]

Almost immediately following the first recording of these narratives, groups made use of differing interpretations of the Tell Story and Rütli Oath. By the eighteenth century there were two important categories of political interpretation: reinforcing the status quo of the local authorities or supporting popular rebellion. The elite-written chronicles, for example, emphasized the importance of elite rule in the cantons of the Swiss Confederation. The chronicles did not record Tell's participation in the foundational oath at the Rütli meadow, the mythical birthplace of the Swiss Confederation. Instead, it was Fürst, a member of one of the leading families of Uri, who represented the canton at the oath that rejected foreign rule. Tell, the common citizen, did not plan the insurrection against the tyrant Gessler and his aristocratic allies. Tell is instead portrayed as acting in defense of his family and continuing to respect the authority of his natural rulers. Although Tell stood up to the tyrant Gessler, the chroniclers interpreted this only as a move to force out the representative of a foreign power and restore the legitimate rule of the native Swiss elite, those who organized the oath and led the insurrection.

The popular ballads, festival plays and even popular unrest during a peasants' uprising in the mid-seventeenth century, on the other hand, emphasized another interpretation of the Tell legend. According to versions of the Tell story with this different emphasis, Tell led a popular revolt of the oppressed alpine peasants against the aristocratic tyrant Gessler.[22] Tell, in these versions, organized and led a clandestine plot that overwhelmed symbols of feudal and aristocratic rule in his efforts to restore an almost democratic freedom to the Swiss republics. According to this interpretation, Tell is not simply acting in defense of his family and property, but he leads a massive resistance movement and liberates all of Switzerland.[23]

Usually, the reception of the story was through one of these two categories: supporting the elite leadership of the Swiss republics or arguing for more popular input into politics. During the seventeenth century the image of Tell became increasingly bound up with peasant uprisings and even targeted the Swiss authorities, who began to fear the popular interpretation, as exemplified by an incident at the end of the 1653 *Bauernkrieg* (Peasant War).[24] After the rebellion had been crushed in Luzern, three peasants retaliated by killing a high-ranking member of the Luzern elite. What distinguished this action was that they committed this political assassination while dressed as William Tell and his confederates, a clear allegory for all observers. Pressing the point further, on the next day the three went to Mass, while still in costume. The public nature of this display, including their showing the murder weapon to all who were there, made a clear declaration that the three believed they were free from sin and God had approved their resistance, just as Tell's actions had been approved. The Tell song from the 1653 war was banned immediately, but the elite authorities could not wipe out the memory of the 1653 song or war.[25]

The more radical interpretations of the legend saw Tell deal with the tyrant Gessler (who was portrayed as both foreign and aristocratic) and lead a popular insurrection against the other aristocrats. The elitist versions provided more support to the status quo regime in Switzerland and elsewhere by painting the whole episode as the Swiss rallying behind their natural leaders—the native oligarchic elite—in order to expel the foreigners. The figure of Tell therefore represented an ongoing proxy battle during the long eighteenth century between those who saw true liberty as self-rule, free from the intervention of foreigners, and those who saw liberty as an egalitarian principle. By the eighteenth century, the Swiss elite had lost so much control over the story's interpretation that they downplayed the William Tell legend as much as possible. Several historians go so far as to claim that Tell was "half-forgotten" in Switzerland.[26]

Throughout the *ancien regime* oligarchic leaders of many Swiss cantons tried to cut out the democratic and revolutionary elements of the story, but radicals, such as Samuel Henzi and J. J. Bodmer, did not forget the popular aspects, and, in fact, embraced the narrative.[27] They mobilized Tell, an already fully accepted foundation myth, to justify an alternative vision of the Confederation, not just the elitist status quo.[28] In 1748 Samuel Henzi of Bern began to discuss with Bodmer his ideas for a new Tell play that emphasized the social unrest aspect of the story and popular participation. However, in 1749 Henzi was executed for plotting the overthrow of Bern's aristocratic regime. In the months of preparation for the plot, he was heavily engaged with the Tell material.[29] Perhaps he had seen the narrative as model for action just like the three peasant Tell actors of 1653.

In 1762 Henzi's manuscript play was anonymously finished and published in Paris.[30] Perhaps not unrelated to this publication, in 1762 Bodmer also wrote his own Tell drama, a play that stands as the first Tell drama of the eighteenth century written in the German language.[31] Bodmer's *The just Oath-taking* was a five-act play, which included a scene of the *Rütli Schwur*, but it continued to attempt to link Tell's personal act against an aristocrat with the cause of the entire Swiss people. Bodmer's manuscript was not published at first, but was clearly known, at least, to a small circle around Bodmer.[32] Bodmer and his students hoped to undermine the patrician dominated society, in part, by challenging the Chronicles' claims of the Swiss Confederation's aristocratic origins.[33] This radical circle in Zurich emphasized the notion of Tell overthrowing an unjust provincial administrator (rather than simply a foreign tyrant), while at the same time seeking to improve government practices. Taken together these projects seriously threatened the ruling oligarchic Swiss governments.

In that same year of 1762 the threat became explicit as Johann Caspar Lavater, one of Bodmer's students, confronted Felix Grebel, Landvogt of Grüningen, with his misrule and abuse of power. Even though Grebel was politically connected, Lavater, with the support of Johann Heinrich Füssli and Felix Hess, distributed a pamphlet that so publicized the issue that it forced the authorities to punish Grebel for his actions.[34] Bodmer's intellectual circle saw this episode as following the model of the original fathers of the confederation: virtuous sacrifice for the good of the collective.[35] Lavater had asked in his *Complaint*, "Should Zurich have no more Tells or Baumgartens?"[36] Lavater supported those descendents of Tell who were willing to stand against unjust arbitrary authority.

Lavater's actions brought some governmental reform and may have even convinced Bodmer to rewrite his play for publication in 1775. Bodmer's reworked *Schweizerischen Schauspiele* had a more radical agenda than its unpublished predecessor. Bodmer had transformed the single five-act play into four one-act plays.[37] The reworked version did not include a scene depicting the Rütli oath and thereby undermined claims of patrician leadership. Instead, Bodmer emphasized the character of Tell and a violent, popular rebellion became central to the narrative of opposing tyranny.[38] This popular aspect is exactly what the patrician elite of the Swiss republics tried to avoid.

The Tell Story Beyond Switzerland

The symbolically different interpretations also spread outside of Switzerland throughout the long eighteenth century. The Swiss oligarchs had no control over how the Tell story was interpreted outside of the Confederation. The widespread fame of the story, its varied interpretations, the existence of multiple versions of the story, and a lack of a single author or clearly recognized definitive text allowed many cultures to bend the story to their own needs across the political spectrum. In the seventeenth century images of Tell had already appeared in Dutch iconography.[39] In France, Swiss mercenaries introduced the Tell story.[40] Elsewhere, over the course of the next century, stories, plays, epics, operas, and their translations explicitly centered on William Tell were published in Belgium, the German states, Great Britain, Hungary, Ireland, Italy, Spain, the United States, and Latin America.[41]

From the mid-eighteenth century introduction of the character of William Tell into the Parisian cultural world, Tell served as a symbol against despotism outside of Switzerland as well as in Switzerland. In fact, for much of the second half of the eighteenth century the Tell legend was more vibrant in France than in Switzerland. In France, patriotic heroes, such as Tell (or Brutus), were used as national symbols, regardless of birthplace, and were used in literature, theater, and iconography to help to build a patriotic community and to contribute to civic education.

The 1762 anonymously finished play by Samuel Henzi, the executed Bernese radical, was the first published version of the Tell story in eighteenth-century Paris. It was, however, the 1766 performance of Antoine-Marin Lemierre's *Guillaume Tell* at the *Comédie Française* that thrust the Tell legend into the wider consciousness of French and Parisian cultural life.[42] Lemierre's text was explicitly anti-Habsburg; the author mentions Austria directly in Act I Scene 1 and Scene 2 as well as the Emperor Albert von Habsburg, all references that would have struck a note with an audience that disapproved of France's recent alliance with Austria. Lemierre's play also sides with the popular revolutionary version of the Tell story in which Tell explicitly leads the conspiracy against Gessler, not simply as an aggrieved father, but as citizen planning to overthrow the (admittedly foreign) regime with the help of his fellow republican citizen soldiers [Act V scene V]. This version follows the 1512 version of the festival play in which Tell leads an oath of the entire people to never tolerate tyrants, a particularly radical political message for a play produced during the monarchy of Louis XV and one that was unsurprisingly received poorly at the time.[43] Nonetheless, the *Comédie Française* revived the play multiple times over the next two decades, perhaps because the print version was quite popular with the European reading public from the start.[44] As a play, however, it was only in 1786 after some minor changes that Lemierre's stage version was well received.[45]

The William Tell story permeated the French cultural world beyond the theater, too, appearing in numerous Enlightenment texts, such as Louis de Jaucourt's 1765 entry in Diderot's *Encyclopédie*.[46] Tell was a natural figure for the *philosophes* to invoke as he epitomized the Enlightenment struggle to restore political virtue. The Abbé Raynal was so infatuated with Tell that he sought to build a monument to Tell on the Rütli Meadow, the mythical birthplace of the Swiss Confederation in Canton Uri. Raynal was not alone in his admiration—he was actually able to raise enough money to erect the planned 20 foot obelisk. The leaders of canton Uri, however, rejected the planned memorial because they viewed the monument as celebrating Raynal's vanity more than the virtuousness of the original confederates: "no stone monument was necessary," so long as one celebrates the "freedom of the Helvetians" and "feels oneself free." In addition, if that feeling "were to be lost in future generations, a monument to the Confederation would be useless."[47]

Many aspects of the Tell story resonated with Enlightenment thinkers and supporters of liberty, who sought not only to pursue progress and knowledge, but also to halt an encroaching degeneration and social corruption.[48] The character of Tell served as a hero who symbolized an older virtue and purity that had since been corrupted. Tell was not only the symbol of Swiss liberty in France, but he was also a model for a French path to greater freedom.[49] I would caution against categorizing this French support for greater liberty as some sort of pre–1789 revolutionary ideology. There was a growing republican discourse in late eighteenth-century France that sought reform and liberty, but did not advocate overthrowing the monarchy.[50] Many supporters of this republican discourse embraced the Tell story because the medieval world of Tell provided a link between the classical models of virtue found in the republics of Rome and Sparta and their own world.

The figure of Tell also had a recurring role during the French Revolution. In 1790, for example, the Oath of the Tennis Court was, in retrospect, widely compared to the Swiss founding oath on the Rütli meadow.[51] The revolutionary artist Jacques-Louis David saw Tell as a symbol of universal anti-despotism almost at the level of Lucius Junius Brutus, a well-established symbol of patriotism and republicanism.[52] David explicitly linked the figures of Tell and Brutus as embodiments of the battle against despotism in both the *Fête de la liberté* of 15 April 1792 and his unfinished work for the Paris Opera.[53] Contemporary accounts demonstrate that the implicit threat of a popular movement against tyrannical rulers was fully understood by observers.[54] In addition to David's frequent references to Tell, Lemierre's *Guillaume Tell* was revived and performed twelve times during the constitutional monarchy and another thirty-eight times before the Directory.[55] During the republic, a radical section of Paris named itself *la section de Guillaume Tell*, while in September of 1792, representatives introduced a bust of Brutus into the sitting room of the National Assembly, followed soon thereafter by one of Tell.[56]

In March of 1793, the Paris Commune voted to establish a free theater for the "instruction of the people" and that summer the National Convention ordered Parisian theaters to present only certifiably republican plays.[57] Perhaps it was the symbolic nature of Tell himself, as well as the themes of republican liberty and virtue, that encouraged the Convention to choose Lemierre's play as one of the three republican plays whose performances were to be subsidized by the government. On 2 August 1793 the National Convention decreed that Voltaire's *Brutus*, Marie-Joseph Chénier's *Caius Gracchus* and Lemierre's *Guillaume Tell* were to be performed for the public over the course of the following month: in the weeks leading up to the 5 September 1793 declaration that Terror was the order of the day, the Tell story was performed five times in Paris along with "other dramas which retrace[d] the glorious events of the revolution and the virtues of the defenders of liberty."[58]

Despite its apparent inherent virtues for the radical republic, Lemierre's play was a product of the old regime and therefore modified. In May 1794 it was even retitled *Les Sans-Culottes suisses*—which led to the implausible arrival of the *sans-culottes* in the Alps, accompanied by the strains of the *Marseillaise*.[59] Other oddities resulted from the revision of Lemierre's play. In its revolutionary presentations, the play changed Gessler's pivotal role, no longer directing him to force Tell to shoot at the apple on his son's head.[60] Perhaps excising Gessler's tyrannical demands from the production, as well as letting him drown instead of being killed by Tell, served to represent the impersonal justice and power of the sovereign people rather than the act of one man determining the fate of states, a message suitable for a republican collective.[61]

Not surprisingly, as the Revolution changed, so did the presentation and production of Tell. During the Revolution, it was not Lemierre's two versions that were most performed, but rather the comic opera *Guillaume Tell* by Sedaine and Grétry in which Tell, the supposed *sans-culotte* popular hero, had servants like the elite bourgeoisie or former aristocracy.[62] In the text of the opera itself, Tell's role was not entirely focused on leading the insurrection and only Gessler, the bureaucrat responsible to the distant Emperor, not the monarch, is blamed for any tyranny.[63] Though these portrayals of the Tell story may not be particularly radical or revolutionary, they certainly fit an opera composed throughout 1790 and premiered in 1791, under a constitutional monarchy in France. If the constitutional monarchy had any chance of success, the argument that the crisis of the Old Regime was initiated by ministerial despotism rather than royal despotism was essential to its foundation and the William Tell story, told in a particular way, fits into that template.

Grétry and Sedaine had both been successful under the Old Regime.[64] By 1790, both supported the constitutional monarchy, but Sedaine was suspected of supporting a return to the Old Regime. Although there is certainly no overwhelming evidence for this claim, the contemporaneous *Almanach général des spectacles* for 1791 did attack Sedaine for subverting his principles for monetary gain. Perhaps his libretto, composed in great haste, was a work of expediency.[65] If Sedaine and Grétry did compose Tell in order to prove their support for the revolution, they chose an excellent subject to rehabilitate themselves. This "democratic" subject was one of the rare medieval topics—Grétry's and Sedaine's comfort zone—that effectively supported any popular sovereignty.[66] Whatever their motivations, the revolutionary public embraced their work. The *Journal de Paris* described the audience's reaction on 11 April 1791: Sedaine's text "breathes hatred of oppression and love of liberty, all that had a connection with these two sentiments was applauded."[67] Charlton further comments on the later published version of the libretto that "to read Sedaine's prefatory material one would imagine that he was a fanatical republican and anti-monarchist."[68]

The distinction between Lemierre's version and Grétry's and Sedaine's version is not so easy to make, however. Lemierre's version had been singled out by the National Convention in 1793 as a worthy republican play, but it was also the product of the Old Regime, while Sedaine's libretto was actually written during the Revolution. Yet, the two texts were linked beyond their refusal to grant too much agency to the rebel Tell. Lemierre was a major source for Sedaine's libretto. In the published version Sedaine included a "prefatory note and a poem dedicated to the spirit of Antoine-Marin Lemierre" as Sedaine "took what he needed" from Lemierre's text.[69]

The argument that Grétry's and Sedaine's version was so distinct and represented the bourgeoisie while Lemierre's play was characteristic of the radical republic does not make all that much sense, especially when the same literature suggests that the opera reached the height of its popularity during the Terror, when one might expect the so-called bourgeois values to be less popular.[70] Futhermore, the opera's support for female political and military activity ran counter to "bourgeois" values and the explicit policy of the Convention to shut down all women's political clubs.[71] In this way, the opera was socially radical and espoused what perhaps should be considered *sans-culotte* values: a full commitment to revolution from every member of society.

This claim of distinct periods of popularity corresponding to specific political shifts also starts to collapse when examining the performance schedule of the opera and play during the Revolutionary decade. Both Lemierre's play and the Grétry opera had approximately the same percentage of their revolutionary performances during the radical republic, from 10 August 1792 until the end of the Terror.[72] Contrary to some other claims, the opera's production was not halted after 9 Thermidor. In fact, there were sixty-four performances after 9 Thermidor, while there were sixty-seven performances from its premiere in 1791 until the end of the Terror.[73] The performance schedule does not really support any conception of the opera as more or less popular during radical periods. The opera written by so-called constitutional monarchists was performed fifteen times from its premiere in 1791 to the 10 August overthrow of the monarchy and fifty-two times from 10 August 1792 until 9 Thermidor Year II. In conjunction with the sixty-four performances after the Terror, the evidence suggests a variable opera that could fit a variety of political contexts.

In the end Grétry's and Sedaine's *Tell* must be considered mixed in its message of popular revolution as Tell ultimately led the rebellion, but the role was thrust upon him and restricted.[74] The pastoral family scenes that dot the opera suggest some elements of the elitist defense of the status quo before the Revolution; Tell acts on behalf of his family as well as on the principle of targeting tyranny.[75] Both Lemierre's version and the opera support the defense of liberty, but the versions performed during the Revolution were sometimes hesitant in allowing all members of society as individuals to join that fight. The Jacobin attempt to republicanize the theater was unsuccessful since republican leaders could become the villain as well.[76] Perhaps at times, Sedaine's libretto could have given the Jacobins pause: "Arrogant sovereigns! in the bosom of indolence, enjoy the happy days that the fates allow you, and shepherds of a flock too great for you, fear the anger of a people aroused; let Tyranny expire at the feet of Reason."[77]

Florian's *Tell*

Another ambivalent Tell product associated with the Thermidor era was *Guillaume Tell ou La Suisse Libre* by Jean-Pierre Claris de Florian. This version was also a non-static version of the Tell story, an epic that supported multiple interpretations of Tell and the Revolution, both in France and elsewhere. Florian, was the grandson of a minor noble of the robe in Montpellier, who in 1788 was elected to the *Academie de Française* but, did not, as an aristocrat, sail unscathed through the revolutionary period. Florian was arrested during the Terror and it was in prison where he began his *Tell* epic, which thereby started as a product of the radical republic. In desperation at his plight Florian wrote to a deputy of the National Convention, an acquaintance of his, claiming to support the Revolution and begging for his release from prison. It was to this deputy that he sent a descriptive outline and completed first book of his version of the Tell story. He explains that his version demonstrated his loyalty to France and the revolution. "I have conceived of the plan of a work that I believe will be useful to public morals. I sing in my prison of the heroes of liberty."[78] In theory, this public instruction and improvement of public morality was exactly what the Committee of Public Safety and National Convention sought. Although Florian claimed that his work would serve the needs of the nation, he left the decision up to the representative of the people: "If you are not of opinion that the Poem may strengthen in the breasts of the youthful part of the French nation the love of the Republic, and the respect for simple manners, do not answer me; let me die here."[80]

In the first part of his text, Florian interprets Tell along popular democratic lines. We can see this by the fact that Tell is explicitly engaged in the popular rebellion against the tyrannical Gessler. Unlike in the earlier Swiss Chronicles, Tell leads the entire process of the oath taking and the subsequent popular rebellion. The elder statesman character of Walter Fürst is diminished to a colleague of Tell and responds to Tell's lead. This puts Florian's version within the framework of the revolutionary depiction of Tell as a popular liberator who planned the overthrow of the local nobility. Florian touches upon some important revolutionary signposts in his effort to demonstrate his loyalty and commitment to the revolutionary mission. He even refers to the sacred inalienable rights of nature embodied in the *Declaration of the Rights of Man and the Citizen.*

> Amis de la liberté, coeurs magnanimes, ames tendres, vous qui savez mourir pour votre indépendance, et qui ne voulez vivre que pour vos frères, prêtez l'oreille à mes accens. Venez entendre comment un seul homme, né dans un pays sauvage, au milieu d'un peuple courbé sous la verge d'un oppresseur, parvint par son courage à relever ce peuple abattu, à lui donner un nouvel être, à l'instruire enfin de ses droits; droits sacrés, inaliénables, que la nature avait révélés, mais dont l'ignorance et le despotisme firent si long-temps un secret.[81]

With these references to liberty, fraternity, and the sacred, inalienable rights of man, Florian might as well be discussing the French Revolution explicitly rather than in the guise of a Swiss context.

The classical republican discourse of pre-revolutionary and revolutionary France is also on display.[82] Florian emphasizes the importance of virtue and refers to the valor of the inhabitants of the three cantons at the center of "antique Helvétie," who sought to regain "les droits des hommes" that had been usurped. Continuing the revolutionary discourse, Florian in this introductory passage uses almost Rousseauian language:

> Leurs enfans, ignorans du mal, ... redoutant leur père, ne connaissaient d'autre bonheur, d'autre desir, d'autre espérance que de ressembler à l'homme de bien dont ils avaient reçu le jour; lui obéir et l'imiter formaient le cercle de leur vie. Ce peuple simple et vertueux, presque ignoré de l'univers, resté seul avec la nature, protégé par sa pauvreté, continuait d'être bon, et pourtant n'était point puni.[83]

Contemporary Swiss Patriots may have liked to claim that Florian was describing the still pure Swiss Confederation, but it is much more likely that he presented a vision of the French so-called Republic of Virtue. Tell is presented as a rustic peasant on the surface, but the implied connection with the poor, but honest, hardworking and virtuous *sans-culottes* is clear. Florian paints Tell as close as a character set in Alpine Switzerland can be to a *sans-culotte* (short of the revised version of Lemierre's play). Just as it was legitimate for Tell to lead the people in an uprising against Gessler, so too was it legitimate for the *sans-culottes* of Paris to overthrow the French despot.

After this initial, democratic section that Florian wrote, we do not know who wrote the rest of the text. The title page of the 1801 Paris edition labels *Guillaume Tell* as an "ouvrage Posthume" and translator, William Hewetson, attributed the completion and publication of Tell to a "bookseller of eminence" who had purchased all of Florian's papers and "published those works which Florian did not live to finish."[84] Book One of Florian's epic is a product of the radical Republic and reflects the values of the Republic of Virtue, but these principles do not remain throughout the text.

After the first part of Florian's epic there is a mixing of traditional categories of Tell interpretations, combining what I have identified as the "popular" interpretation and the "oligarchic" interpretation that resists full democracy.[85] On the one hand Florian's *Guillaume Tell* has Verner [Stauffacher] declare that "N'en doutez point, ces généreux peuples souffrent de la soif de l'indépendance; ils feront un jour, mon coeur le prédit, un même corps avec nous, une seule république redoutée et respectée de tous les rois de l'univers."[86] This emphasis on "une seule république" comes from the rhetoric of the revolutionary republic, one and indivisible. Of course, few self-respecting Swiss at the time would declare a need for a single unitary republic but this aspect of the text, which glorifies the single republic as a goal, is still in line with the radical mission of the 1794 French Republic.[87] Additionally, Tell's negative response to Verner's plan to lead the whole of Switzerland in revolt reflects a contemporary emphasis on the need for constant vigilance and the fear of plots.[88] These aspects fit with Florian's *premier livre* in terms of presenting an interpretation that fits with the radical republican worldview of Florian's jailers, to whom Florian is attempting to demonstrate his support.

Popular aspects are, however, toned down in the later parts of the posthumous publication, reflecting the Thermidorian and the Directory worldview that feared the full expression of equality and fraternity. The political philosophy of the Directory rejected the Jacobin ideology of the Terror and sought to create a moderate republican regime that could consolidate the gains of the revolutionary property owners.[89] Reflecting, this view, for example, in his closing speech, Florian's Tell warns against popular excesses. Although Tell endorses a broad understanding of liberty based on popular sovereignty of "all citizens at least twenty years of age" he declared the need to "Gardez-vous de l'ivresse de la victoire, gardez-vous sur-tout de l'idolâtrie pour ceux qui la remportèrent avec vous."[90] Furthermore, after supporting the popularly based election of magistrates, Tell implies a respect for the law and elected authorities.

> Elect a Landamman; let that ancient title, respected by our forefathers, become more so amongst us; let a council direct him and let him, in turn direct the council. Enact laws: without laws, what would you be? Liberty is but another name for submission to wise and prudent laws; without them, it would be licentiousness.[91]

This version fits the Directory (and even the Napoleonic regime) after Book One's presentation of the values of the radical republic. This speech allows for elections, but reinforces a notion of elite rule—allowing those who are trained to govern to do so. Tell himself has no desire other than to return to the status of fellow citizen so as to have "the right to fight in your ranks."[92]

This final republican, though not necessarily democratic, speech also demonstrates the persistence of a classical republican discourse into the mid 1790s, but does not demonstrate any particular loyalty to Robespierre's so-called Republic of Virtue.[93] Tell continued his final instructions by encouraging his listeners to "Gardez vos moeurs; qu'elles deviennent même plus austères: sans vertus point de liberté. Le républicain s'est placé, par ce nom, entre les anges et les hommes … Préparez-vous à soutenir ses efforts; préparez-vous aux batailles, ne comptez que sur Dieu et sur vos bras."[94] This focus on republican virtue, self-rule, and the reliance on God and one's own arms echoes a common theme throughout eighteenth-century discourse.[95]

Moreover, there are possible readings in Florian's work of outright hostility to the Terror, such as Tell's greeting to Verner in Schwyz: "Friend, it is finally the moment to deliver the *patrie* or end our unfortunate days."[96] It is not entirely clear if this sentiment placed in Tell's mouth is an expression of revolutionary anti-monarchical feeling or the expression of frustration with the period of the Terror. Perhaps the post-Thermidorian posthumous editors of Florian's work were suggesting that the figure of Tell and the revolution he led should just as well target the tyranny of the Committee of Public Safety as that of the old monarchy.

Because Florian died shortly after his release from prison in the aftermath of Robespierre's fall, he was easily made into a martyr of the overly aggressive radical Revolution. Like Thermidorian productions of Voltaire's *Brutus*, the editors of Florian's work try to paint the tyrant as Robespierre.[97] The publishers of Florian's work thereby suggest that Book One and its popular interpretation was only Florian's vain attempt to save himself. Each edition of *Guillaume Tell* begins with a short biographical sketch by L. F. Jauffret entitled "Vie de Florian." In this sketch Jauffret paints a picture of a sensitive poet cut down in the prime of life. He also casts doubt on the justice of Florian's arrest and subsequent prison term. In a further, obvious swipe at the Terror, the publishers include a poem by Jauffret, "Le Tombeau de Florian," which compares Robespierre to a new Nero who "dans sa rage inhumaine, immolait l'innocence avec impunite." Finally, "le peuple se lève et le tyran expire."[98] By shifting the target of the people rising against tyranny from the King to Robespierre, the editors shift the interpretation of the entirety of Florian's work. Tell evolves from a symbol against tyrannical monarchical rule to a symbol against the tyranny of Robespierre. This is part of the post-Thermidorian attempt to paint Robespierre as a ruthless despot and tyrant. This was done primarily to try to base the Directory regime on a legitimate foundation, but also it was a way for Convention members to excuse their own actions.[99]

Tell in the Anglo-American Atlantic World

Florian's epic also became extremely popular in the English-speaking world. Beginning with an 1805 translation, I have found twenty-one versions from at least five translators in the first fifty years of the nineteenth century. The English translators continued the process of turning Florian's *Guillaume*

Tell against the radical regime it started out supporting. Hewetson referred directly to the Terrorists by writing that Florian composed "his William Tell, the champion of Liberty, and sent it to be approved of by those *self-styled* sons of freedom who then deluged France with blood."[100] In addition to condemning the most radical phase of the French Revolution (and therefore the movement as a whole), the English translators absorbed Florian's text into British political culture by manipulating the translation for their own purposes.

In looking at the absorption of the translated text, there are several passages that demonstrate the ambiguity of Florian's *Tell* and its translation, especially after Book one. In several sections the English translations drive the process of reinterpretation even further. In the opening paragraph of his work, Florian refers to the courage of the rustic Tell, but the English translation refers to how a single man by his "individual courage raised this people, …" while the French text refers only to "son courage."[101] Hewetson goes beyond the letter of the French text to emphasize the individual. Another translated section of Florian's original text is when Tell explains to one of his compatriots that it is time to "délivrer la patrie."[102] The English versions add another wrinkle: "the hour at length arrived when we must deliver our country from its scourge or perish in the glorious cause of Liberty."[103] The addition of the word Liberty is a step in the making of Florian's epic a British text. In the context of the first book, this line, if included in the original French text, might have demonstrated support for the Terrorists' complete commitment to their conception of French liberty that was worth dying for in glorious battle, but the English text suggests otherwise. Here the translator or editors propose an alternative British conception of liberty that, as had Edmund Burke, argues against a false revolutionary sense of freedom and the "rights of man." In Burke's view liberty is not based on universal principles but rather on an entailed inheritance from ancestors, which in the British case, is the noble, ancient British constitution, a model of restraint and tradition.[104] According to this argument, true liberty existed in Britain, but never in Revolutionary France where "liberty" was nothing more than radicalism and fanaticism. The English translation's reference to the guillotine by raising the possibility that the country's "favorite patriots [might] perish disgracefully upon the scaffold" only emphasizes this claim.[105]

Perhaps Tell's final emphasis on moderate popular political participation explains why there were multiple English translations of Florian's poem and why the story was especially popular in Britain. The thinly veiled metaphor of Switzerland as an isolated mountainous "island" was certainly one way to discuss British ideals, but this anti-radical revolutionary viewpoint also appealed to the British opposition to French revolutionary excesses and justifies Britain's decades of warfare against France as virtuous and noble.

Although it was translated into English and repeatedly published in both Great Britain and the United States, Florian's version was not the only version in the English-speaking world. The popularity of Florian's poem is further evidenced by the impact the poem had on James Sheridan Knowles's theatrical versions from the 1820s. Like Florian's, Lemierre's, and Grétry's work, Knowles's play has a similar mixture of supporting a popular right to overthrow a tyrannical government, while also supporting elite representation or backing away from too much popular involvement in politics and democracy. Knowles's five-act play contained revolutionary elements, but he moderated radical politics. The gathered crowd in the final scene, for example, demanded that the defenders of the castle surrender William Tell; it did not demand the liberty of Switzerland, casting the event not as a planned mass rebellion but rather as a personal act of friendship.[106]

Evidence exists of a direct link between Florian's *Tell* and Knowles's version. Both Florian and Knowles have Tell's son, the eventual apple stand, leading a lost and terrified Gessler, the tyrant of Uri, through the mountain passes back to the safety of Altdorf, the canton's main town. Tell's son demonstrates the virtue of the entire Tell clan because he does this act of kindness without caring who Gessler is. Gessler is confused by such action and then angered by Tell's son when he speaks of virtue.[107] This device of children guiding Gessler to safety out of the mountains and his need to reassert control after his perceived humiliation, an act which leads to the apple shot in the village square, is an interesting addition to the story by Florian. He adds a girlfriend for Tell's son, but theirs is still a chaste, premarital, almost, adolescent relationship. The virtue of the young, who have no difficulties sleeping as innocents, comes shining through as opposed to the corruption of older rulers and the city (even if just a central village). Additionally, Tell's son is a model of behavior for young readers; the young should act virtuously and prepare to do what is right for their country. This enlarged role for the son echoes Florian's assertion to the National Convention that he hoped to improve the youth of France.[108]

Knowles explores moral instruction as well, which contemporary critics understood. Theater critic and literary editor, George Daniel praised the moral lessons taught by Knowles:

> Examples of patriotism and virtue are legitimate subjects for the stage … examples of human excellence cannot be too highly prized, or too generally known: and where can they be exhibited with greater and more universal effect than in the theatre? The noblest patriot that the world e'er saw was Brutus; there are others

> whose names cast glory over the page of history, and, among them, not the least illustrious is William Tell.[109]

Daniel becomes more specific in describing the proper lesson to be learned. The British "man of humble birth" should love freedom but not the dangerous systems based on principles. Daniel implies the need to respect one's intellectual (and social) betters:

> The character of William Tell is... the hardy mountaineer who has found the goddess Liberty a native of the woods. His love of freedom is more an impulse, than a system ... Such is William Tell- a man of humble birth, of mean education, of untutored manners; who, having little eloquence but that of truth, yet possessing a spirit honest, firm, and unconquerably brave, raised himself from an obscure yeoman to a distinguished patriot, and bequeathed to posterity a name which ...may rank among the proudest of antiquity.[110]

If there is a political message within these British versions of the Tell story, it is the emphasis on patriotism and the notion of the common good. Knowles's *Tell*, and presumably all British theater, could be used to better shape this common good, both politically and morally. As Daniel commented on Knowles's play, "it is not enough that a play shall be free from *political*, but from *moral* offence- that kings and ministers shall not be brought before a dramatic tribunal, but that decency and virtue shall be respected and maintained."[111]

Knowles's play, starring William Macready and written for a British audience, had success at Drury Lane in London in 1825. It was then produced in the British Atlantic world, Boston, New York, Philadelphia, Baltimore, and Dublin as expected for a popular play of the London stage.[112] In the United States, the response was lightning quick as well as enthusiastic. The play premiered in London in May and by 24 June 1825 reviews were available in American newspapers. Already in August, excerpts from Knowles's play were published for the American audience as were overviews of the legend to familiarize future theatergoers with the Tell story. In September, Knowles's play was in rehearsals in the new world and by October, it was already being performed in Boston and reached Baltimore by December. Although the enthusiastic and teary reception by the usually "staid" Boston audience attests to the power of Knowles's drama, the success of a British play in the United States is not surprising.[113] The audience for Knowles's play only grew in October 1826 when the first-string cast arrived and Macready assumed the role of Tell in New York. He then went on to perform in Boston and Baltimore with great success as well. Macready gained such renown that even the sale of Henry Inman's painting of the actor performing William Tell made national news.[114]

What is surprising is that on 4 July 1828, Macready's troupe also brought Tell back to Paris.[115] Parisian success for British plays was much rarer than in the United States. In fact, this was the first troupe to successfully introduce Shakespeare to a French audience.[116] Does a British play written by an Anglo-Irish author based on a revolutionary French text about a Swiss hero fighting for liberty impact its audience when performed in Paris on the Fourth of July? The same company of actors performed Hamlet on 14 July, a play (partly) about the overthrow of an illegitimate King who was the brother of the last legitimate King. Within weeks of these performances, Charles X, brother to Louis XVI, had passed a new censorship law to restrict revolutionary sentiment that appeared after previously loosened censorship regulations.[117]

After Rossini announced his intention in 1827 to write a grand opera based on the theme of William Tell, William Tell was in the air in Paris that summer of 1828, and there was some scrambling to cash in on the excitement.[118] Along with Knowles's play there were three French versions of the story performed as well: Jean-Baptiste Pelissier and Henri-Montan Berton rewrote Grétry's and Sedaine's opera, R. C. Guilbert de Pixérécourt presented a melodrama in imitation of Schiller's play and Xavier Dupeuty and Pierre de Villeneuve presented a vaudeville version of the story.[119] Although the rewriting of Grétry's and Sedaine's opera and the other Tell performances were commercial decisions, it was also a decision that resonated politically. For those looking for reform in the reactionary monarchy of Charles X, the William Tell story was ideal.

The new version of the Grétry opera fit particularly well; it featured a clear tyrannical villain in Gessler, who was guilty of obvious atrocities. Importantly, the populace did not form an insurrectionary mob, but they looked to old Mectal, the chief magistrate of the canton.[120] In Act III, the action culminated, Tell is a hero and shot Gessler, but old Mectal, the chief magistrate remained the authority figure. He designated his son as chief and it is young Mectal, not Tell, who took the oath and it is young Melctal who led the troops to overthrow Gessler's castle. Tell participates, he refuses to abandon his friends in the hour of need, but he does not plan the insurrection.[121] It is the Mectal family that exercised political authority, representing an elite-led restoration of proper government, not a popular insurrection.

This message of moderate, comfortable republicanism played in the United States as well. The New Orleans Opera Company toured the east coast with Grétry in its repertoire and it was performed at least thirty-two times in its revival in the United States.[122] Back in France, however, the moderate message might have been dangerous to Charles X. Within two years of the Paris debut of Knowles's *Tell*, and the refurbished Grétry opera (and within a year of the premiere of Rossini's *Tell*) the Bourbon monarchy had been replaced by the Orleans dynasty.

Correlation in this case has been mistaken for causation. Writing well after the events (in the 1860s), Fromental Halévy claimed that the cast of *Guillaume Tell*, inspired by Rossini's score, went directly from rehearsal to the barricades in 1830. Benjamin Walton has demonstrated, however, that there is not enough evidence to support the claim, though the legend has remained in circulation.[123] Simon Schama has declared that it was only with the 1830 Revolution in Paris that the "French Revolution" became transferable and that "memory … constructed political reality."[124] Thus it is plausible that the revolutionary elements of Rossini's *Tell* only emerged only after 1830, though linked to the idea of a French Revolution.

For the most part, the story of William Tell was a convenient, relatively safe vehicle for authors across the revolutionary world to make political statements.[125] The symbol could be imbued, however, with revolutionary meaning, reflecting the political culture of the period. This happened in eighteenth century Switzerland, revolutionary Paris, *Risorgimento* Italy and even newly independent Latin America as both Simon Bolivar and Benito Juarez were linked to the character of Tell. These examples demonstrate that the figure of Tell serves as a contested symbol in the long eighteenth century. I argue that these varied uses of the story of Tell reflect a rapidly changing political culture during a transformative period. The appeal of heroes did not diminish on either side of the political divide and the ambiguity of the Tell story allowed, at times, the character of William Tell to stand in for classical, oligarchic republican and democratic republican values as well as American patriotic values and Italian, German, British and French nationalist values. By looking at the various manipulations of the legend we can begin to get a sense of the assorted strains of revolutionary political thought and culture. Looking at the narrow prism of the Tell story is another example of how an examination of how cultural productions can teach us about the international revolutionary phenomenon in all of its varieties.

NOTES

1. Earlier versions of this article were presented at the Clark Library, CELLF (Sorbonne Paris IV), and ASECS 2010. Thank you to Peter Reed, Jenna Gibbs, Kathleen Wilson, Peter Reill, Stefania Tutino, Bob Maniquis, Shelly Charles, Sylvain Menant, Warren Roberts, Lisa Cody, two anonymous readers, and the members of the Mississippi 18th–19th century reading group for their comments.

2. William B. Hewetson in Jean Pierre Claris de Florian, *William Tell, or, Swisserland delivered* trans. William B. Hewetson. (Baltimore: Ph. H. Nicklin and Co., 1810), v.

3. For more on the creation of a rights-based political culture during this period, see Lynn Hunt, *Inventing Human Rights: A History* (New York and London: Norton, 2007); Jonathan Israel, *Enlightenment Contested: Philosophy, Modernity, and the Emancipation of Man 1670–1752* (Oxford: Oxford University Press, 2006), 3; Simon Schama, *Patriots and Liberators: Revolution in the Netherlands, 1780–1813* (New York: Vintage, 1992), 95.

4. See the growing chorus of calls for an emphasis on the global context, including Hunt, "The French Revolution in Global Context," in David Armitage and Sanjay Subrahmanyam, eds., *The Age of Revolutions in Global Context, c. 1760–1840* (Basingstoke: Palgrave Macmillan, 2010), 20–36; Hunt, "The Experience of Revolution," *French Historical Studies* 32 (2009): 671–87; Annie Jourdan, *La Révolution, une exception française?* (Paris: Flammarion, 2004).

5. Thomas Maissen, *Die Geburt der Republic: Staatsverständnis und Repräsentation in der frühneuzeitlichen Eidgenossenschaft* (Gottingen: Vandenhoeck & Ruprecht, 2006), 578–79; James Livesey, *Making Democracy in the French Revolution* (Cambridge, MA: Harvard University Press, 2001), 9.

6. See the broad historiographical tradition that deals with the cultural turn, for example, recently, Leora Auslander, *Cultural Revolutions: Everyday Life and Politics in Britain, North America, and France* (Berkeley and Los Angeles: University of California Press, 2009), 13.

7. A.M. Lemierre, *Guillaume Tell* (Paris: Vve Duchesne, 1770); André Ernest Modeste Grétry, *Guillaume Tell; opéra comique en trois actes* (Paroles by Sedaine) (Paris: J. Frey, 1791); Grétry, *William Tell, A Lyric Drama in Three Acts by M. Pelissier* trans. W.P.W. (Baltimore, 1831); Florian, *Guillaume Tell, ou la Suisse libre* (Paris: Guillement, 1801); Florian, *William Tell*; James Sheridan Knowles, *William Tell: a Play in five acts* (London: John Cumberland,1828).

8. Randolph C. Head, "William Tell and His Comrades: Association and Fraternity in the Propaganda of Fifteenth- and Sixteenth-Century Switzerland," *Journal of Modern History* 67 (Sept. 1995): 532.

9. Reto Tschan, "The Re-appropriation and Transformation of a National

Symbol: Wilhelm Tell, 1789–1895" (MA Thesis, University of British Columbia, 2000), 5.

10. Head, "William Tell and His Comrades," 532–33; Tschan, "Wilhelm Tell, 1789–1895," 5.

11. Oskar Eberle, ed., *Das alte Urner Spiel vom Tell Aus dem Jahre 1512* (Luzern, 1967). Head, "William Tell and His Comrades," 532.

12. Eberle, ed. *Das alter Urner Spiel vom Tell Aus dem Jahre 1512*, 3.

13. Hildegard Elisabeth Keller, "God's plan for the Swiss Confederation: Heinrich Bullinger, Jakob Ruf and their uses of historical myth in Reformation Zurich," in Randolph C. Head and Daniel Christensen, eds. *Orthodoxies and Heterdoxies in Early Modern German Culture: Order and Creativity, 1550–1750* (Leiden: Brill, 2007), 158.

14. Head, "William Tell and His Comrades," 527, 533; Rico Labhardt, *Wilhelm Tell als Patriot und Revolutionär, 1700–1800: Wandlungen der Tell-Tradition im Zeitalter des Absolutismus und der französischen Revolution* (Basel: Helbing & Lichtenhahn, 1947), 15–16; Wilfired Ebert, *Der Frohe Tanz der Gleichheit: Der Freiheitsbaum in der Schweiz, 1798–1892* (Zurich: Chronos, 1996), 46.

15. For images of some of this material culture from before the mid-eighteenth century see Lily Stunzi, ed., *Tell: Werden und Wandern eines Mythos*, 33–64.

16. Walter Dettwiler, *William Tell: Portrait of a Legend* (Zurich: Swiss National Museum, 1991), 7.

17. Ulrich Im Hof, *Mythos Schweiz: Identität–Nation–Geschichte, 1291–1991* (Zurich: Neue Zürcher Zeitung, 1991), 51 quoting *Das Weisse Buch von Sarnen.*

18. Franz Heinemann, *Tell-Iconographie: Wilhelm Tell und sein Apfelschuss im Lichte der bildenden Kunst eines halben Jahrtausends (15.–20. Jahrhundert)* (Luzern: Doleschal, 1902), 15.

19. Head, "William Tell and His Comrades," 534. Thomas Maissen (*Die Geburt der Republic*) warns that the Swiss did not fully conceive of their confederation as outside the Empire until after 1648.

20. For readings of Tell, in particular, in this period, see Head, "William Tell and His Comrades." For the general context see Oliver Zimmer, *A Contested Nation: History, Memory and Nationalism in Switzerland, 1761–1891* (Cambridge: Cambridge University Press, 2003), 20, 26–27 and Thomas A. Brady, Jr., *Turning Swiss: Cities and Empire, 1450–1550* (Cambridge: Cambridge University Press, 1985).

21. Head, "William Tell and His Comrades," 530–31.

22. See *Das alter Urner Spiel vom Tell Aus dem Jahre 1512.*

23. For this discussion of elite versus popular interpretations see Head, "William Tell and His Comrades"; Zimmer, *A Contested Nation*, 30–38; Labhardt, *Wilhelm Tell als Patriot und Revolutionär*, 26; Guy P. Marchal, "Die 'Alten Eidgenossen' im Wandel der Zeiten: Das Bild der frühen Eidgenossen im Tranditionsbewußtsein

und in der Indentitätsvorstellung der Schweizer vom 15. bis ins 20. Jahrhundert," in *Innerschweiz und frühe Eidgenossenschaft: Jubiläumsschrift 700 Jahre Eidgenossenschaft*, vol. 2, *Gesellschaft-Alltag-Geschichtsbild*, ed. Historischer Verein der Fünf Orte (Olten: Walter-Verlag, 1990), 323–32.

24. Marchal, "Die 'Alten Eidgenossen' im Wandel der Zeiten," 332; Andreas Suter, *Der schweizerische Bauernkrieg von 1653: politische Sozialgeschichte-Sozialgeschichte eines politischen Ereignisses* (Tubingen: Bibliotheca Academica Verlag, 1997); Zimmer, *A Contested Nation*, 35.

25. Zimmer, *A Contested Nation*, 37.

26. Jean-François Bergier, "Guillaume Tell révolutionnaire, ou le patriote ambigu," in *La Suisse & La Révolution Française: images, caricatures, pamphlets*, ed. Pierre Chessex (Lausanne: Éditions du Grand-Pont, 1989), 189; Heinemann, *Tell-Iconographie*, 39.

27. For the use of the figure of Tell by Bodmer's radical circle in Zurich, see Johann Jacob Bodmer, *Schweizerische Schauspiele*, ed. Debrunner (St. Ingbert: Röhrig Universitätsverlag, 1998), Daniel Tröhler, *Republikanismus und Pädagogik: Pestalozzi im historischen Kontext* (Bad Heilbrunn: Klinkhardt, 2006), 61–64, and Marc H. Lerner, "How the Swiss imagined republicanism and antiquity in the late 18th century," in Tristan Coignard, et al., eds., *Lumières et histoire / Enlightenment and History* (Paris: Honoré Champion, 2010), 294–99.

28. For more on Bodmer's use of a classical republicanism to undermine the hierarchical *ancien regime*, see Tröhler, *Republikanismus und Pädagogik* and Simone Zurbuchen, "Patriotismus und Nation: der schweizerische Republikanismus des 18. Jahrhunderts," in *Republikanische Tugend: Aussbildung eines Schweizer Nationalbewusstseins und Erziehung eines neuen Bürgers,* ed. Michael Böhler, et al. (Geneva: Slatkine, 2000).

29. Debrunner, "Nachwort," in Debrunner, ed. *Schweizerische Schauspiele,* 61.

30. *Grisler, ou l'ambition punie* (Paris, 1762).

31. Bodmer, *Die gerechte Zusammenschwörung*; Debrunner, "Die Schaubühne als eine Republikanische Anstalt betrachtet - Politisches Theater in der Schweiz (1748–1798)," in *Republikanische Tugend*, ed. Böhler, et al., 38.

32. Debrunner, "Politisches Theater in der Schweiz," 40; Debrunner, "Nachwort," 61–62.

33. Zurbuchen, "Patriotismus und Nation," 163–64.

34. Johann Caspar Lavater, *Der ungerechte Landvogd oder Klagen eines Patrioten* (1762).

35. Debrunner, "Nachwort," 64.

36. Lavater, *Der ungerecht Landvogd*, 6. "Solte Zürich keine Tellen, keine Baumgarten mehr haben?"

37. Debrunner, "Nachwort," 61–62.

38. Bodmer, *Schweizerische Schauspiele*; Debrunner, "Nachwort," 64.

39. For example, Stunzi, ed., *Tell*, 59.

40. Labhardt, *Wilhelm Tell als Patriot und Revolutionär*, 75.

41. This list, of course, does not encompass the wide variety of references to an apple shot, including Scandanavian Tales from the twelfth century (and possibly older), see "Toke of the Arrows" in Book X of the *The Danish History* written by Saxo Grammaticus trans. Oliver Elton (London, 1894), the English ballad of William of Cloudesly or a Persian Tale from 1175. See Alan Dundes, "The 1991 Archer Taylor Memorial Lecture, The Apple-Shot: Interpreting the Legend of William Tell," *Western Folklore* 50 (1991): 331–33.

42. Debrunner, "Nachwort," 61; Labhardt, *Wilhelm Tell als Patriot und Revolutionär*, 86–87; Labhardt, "Tells revolutionäre und patriotische Maskeraden," in Stunzi, ed., *Tell*, 95; Debrunner, "Politisches Theater in der Schweiz," 37. I refer to the 1770 version of Lemierre's play.

43. David Charlton, *Grétry and the Growth of Opéra-comique* (Cambridge: Cambridge University Press, 1986), 317; see *Das alte Urner Spiel vom Tell.*

44. According to *Les Spectacles de Paris ou Calendrier Historique & Chronologique des Théatres pour L'Année 1793* (Paris: Duchesne, 1793), Lemierre's *Guillaume Tell* was reprised in 1768, 1786 and 1790. Labhardt, *Wilhelm Tell als Patriot und Revolutionär*, (90) claims the tragedy was also performed in 1787 and seventeen times in all before the Revolution. The CESAR database (*calendrier électronique des spectacles sous l'ancien régime et sous la révolution*) lists only seven performances before the revolution.

45. Charlton, *Grétry*, 317, 362 (note 6). There were repeated printings in 1767, 1776 and 1783 from the Hague, Neuchâtel and Paris.

46. Fritz Ernst, *Wilhelm Tell: Blatter aus seiner Ruhmesgeschichte* (Zurich: Fretz and Wasmuth, 1936), 61–64; Albert Gier, "Guillaume Tell in French Opera: from Grétry to Rossini," in *Word and Music Studies: Essays in Honor of Steven Paul Scher on Cultural Identity and the Musical Stage,* ed. S. M. Lodato, Suzanne Aspden, Walter Bernhart (Amsterdam: Rodopi, 2002), 230. Louis, Chevalier de Jaucourt, "Suisse" in *The Encyclopedia*, volume 15.

47. Quoted in Labhardt, *Wilhelm Tell als Patriot und Revolutionär*, 72–73. See also Ernst, *Wilhelm Tell*, 70–71; Stunzi, ed., *Tell*, 85; Chessex, ed., *La Suisse & La Révolution Française*, 192; Willy Raeber, "Um ein untergegangenes Denkmal," *Zeitschrift für Schweizerische Archäologie und Kunstgeschichte* 8 (1946): 241–242.

48. For more on Enlightenment virtue, see Marisa Linton, *The Politics of Virtue in Enlightenment France* (Basingstoke: Palgrave Macmillan, 2001).

49. Labhardt, *Wilhelm Tell als Patriot und Revolutionär*, 80.

50. Keith Michael Baker, "Transformations of Classical Republicanism in Eighteenth-Century France," *JMH* 73 (2001). For more on this republican discourse in Switzerland, see Tröhler, *Republikanismus und Pädagogik*; Johnson Kent Wright, "Mably and Berne" *History of European Ideas* 33 (2007); Béla Kapossy, "Neo-

Roman Republicanism and Commercial Society: The Example of Eighteenth–century Berne," in *Republicanism: A Shared European Heritage* vol. 2, ed. Martin van Gelderen and Quentin Skinner (Cambridge: Cambridge University Press, 2002).

51. Labhardt, *Tell*, 101.

52. See Machiavelli, *Discourses*, Bk. 1, ch. 16, the reaction surrounding David's *The Lictors returning to Brutus the bodies of his sons*, Robert L. Herbert, *David, Voltaire,* Brutus *and the French Revolution: An Essay in Art and Politics* (New York: Viking Press, 1973) and Andries Raath and Shaun de Freitas, "Rebellion, Resistance, and A Swiss Brutus?" *The Historical Journal* 48 (2005): 1–26.

53. David's link between Brutus and Tell was not new. See the 1526 Graubunden example of Tell linked with Brutus and Lucretia in Head, "Tell and His Comrades," 534 and Raath and de Freitas demonstrating that Bollinger linked Brutus to Swiss politics, identity and democracy through oath taking (15–18).

54. Mona Ozouf, *Festivals and the French Revolution* trans. Alan Sheridan (Cambridge, MA: Harvard University Press, 1988), 67–68. Ozouf draws on the *Revolutions de Paris*.

55. CESAR database.

56. Herbert, *David, Voltaire,* Brutus *and the French Revolution*, 90, 101.

57. David A. Bell, *The Cult of the Nation: Inventing Nationalism, 1680–1800* (Cambridge, MA: Harvard University Press, 2001), 163.

58. Decree of 2 August quoted in Herbert, *Brutus and the French Revolution*, 145 note 102. Emmet Kennedy, Marie-Laurence Netter, James P. McGregor, and Mark V. Olsen, *Theatre, Opera, and Audiences in Revolutionary Paris: Analysis and Repertory* (Westport, CT: Greenwood Press, 1996), 394 references the original text *Archives Parlementaires de 1787 à 1860, Recueil complet des débats législatifs et politiques des chambres françaises,* première série (1787 à 1799), eds. J. Mavidal and E. Laurent, 82 (Paris: Librairie Dupont, 1867–1913), 70: 134–135; Labhardt, *Tell*, 111. For specific dates of performances see the CESAR database. Kennedy claims that the weak performance record demonstrates the failure of the Committee of Public Safety to republicanize the stage. Kennedy, et al., *Theatre*, 57.

59. James H. Johnson, "Revolutionary Audiences and the Impossible Imperatives of Fraternity," in Bryant T. Ragan and Elizabeth A. Williams, eds. *Re-creating Authority in Revolutionary France* (New Brunswick, NJ: Rutgers University Press, 1992); Labhardt, *Wilhelm Tell als Patriot und Revolutionär*, 111–12; Tell may have also been linked with the patriotic *Marseillaise* in revised versions of Sedaine and Grétry's 1791 comic opera about Tell. See Charlton, *Grétry*, 362 (note 3).

60. Emmet Kennedy, "Old Regime Tragedy and the Terror," in Kennedy et al., *Theatre*, 54; Lemierre, *Tell*, act IV scene II, 27.

61. For a related interpretation see Kennedy, "Old Regime Tragedy and the Terror," 55.

62. Grétry, *Guillaume Tell*. Kennedy, "Old Regime Tragedy and the Terror," 57.

The CESAR database records fifty-five total performances for Lemierre and 131 for Grétry's and Sedaine's opera.

63. Charlton, *Grétry*, 319; Gier, "Guillaume Tell in French Opera," 232.

64. Gier, "Guillaume Tell in French Opera," 231.

65. Charlton, *Grétry*, 318. Charlton cites the *Almanach* and Margaret Ann Rayner, "The Social and Literary Aspects of Sedaine's Dramatic Work," (PhD dissertation: University of London, 1960) for this claim.

66. Gier, "Guillaume Tell in French Opera," 231.

67. Quoted in Charlton, *Grétry*, 318.

68. Charlton, *Grétry*, 318.

69. Charlton, *Grétry*, 316–17.

70. Gier, "Guillaume Tell in French Opera," 232, 234. Twenty-six out of the fifty-five revolutionary performances of Lemierre's play were in 1794, which might drive the perception of radical. However, Grétry's opera was performed twenty-six times in 1794 as well. See CESAR database.

71. Tell's wife leads the women to the battlefield declaring a willingness to "die with you." Grétry, *Guillaume Tell*, Act III Scene VII. For the discussion surrounding the Convention's banning of female political societies on 30 October 1793, see Hunt, ed., *The French Revolution and Human Rights: A Brief Documentary History* (Boston: Bedford Books of St. Martin's Press, 1996), 135–138.

72. CESAR database. For Lemierre it was twenty-one out fifty-five total performances for 38.2% and for Grétry is was fifty-one out of 131 total performances for 38.9%. This method evaluates the link of each version to the most radical part of the Revolution within its own context of popularity. Since there were more total performances of Grétry's opera there is not much benefit to comparing absolute numbers.

73. See the CESAR database for a listing of all 131 (1791–1799) performances of Grétry's *Guillaume Tell*, Gier, "Guillaume Tell in French Opera," 234, and Charlton, *Grétry*, 324. Lemierre's play also had twenty-two of its fifty-five Revolutionary performances after the end of the Terror.

74. Charlton, *Grétry*, 316, 318–9. Tell's role was musically restricted as well.

75. See Act I Scene 1.

76. Kennedy, "Old Regime Tragedy and the Terror," 57–58.

77. Quoted and translated in Charlton, *Grétry*, 318.

78. Florian letter, quoted by Jauffret in Florian, *Guillaume Tell, ou la Suisse libre* (Paris: Guillement, 1801), 41.

79. Florain letter, quoted by Jauffret, in Florian, *Guillaume Tell*, 43.

80. Florain letter, quoted by Jauffret, Florian, *William Tell; or, Switzerland delivered* (1810), xxxiii.

81. Florian, *Guillaume Tell*, 73.

82. See Baker, "Transformations of Classical Republicanism;" Andrew Jainchill,

"The Constitution of the Year III and the Persistence of Classical Republicanism," *French Historical Studies* 26 (2003).

83. Florian, *Guillaume Tell*, 74–77.

84. Hewetson,in Florian, *William Tell*, vi.

85. See Labhardt, *Tell*, 126–7. In Labhardt's interpretation the whole epic is written by one author. Labhardt does not distinguish between 1790 democracy or 1794 revolutionary democracy, nor does he pay attention to how the editors of the posthumous work use the text. He emphasizes (126) that Florian writes in the style of the 1760s especially in Book I but does not explain the difference in styles (127).

86. Florian, *Guillaume Tell,* 155.

87. The unitary republic was in line with the mission of the post-Fructidor Directory as well. See Lerner, "The Helvetic Republic: An Ambivalent Reception of French Revolutionary Liberty," *French History* 18 (2004) and Thomas Poell, "The Unification of the Dutch State (1795–1813)," in O. Gelderblom (ed.), *The Political Economy of the Dutch Republic: Taxation, Government and Finance, c. 1500–1800* (Aldershot, UK: Ashgate, 2009).

88. Florian, *Guillaume Tell*, 154–55; for more on the issue of plots in the Revolution see Timothy Tackett, "Conspiracy Obsession in a Time of Revolution: French Elites and the Origins of the Terror, 1789–1792," *American Historical Review* 105 (2000).

89. For overviews on the nature of the Directory see Livesey, *Making Democracy in the French Revolution* and Howard Brown, *Ending the French Revolution: Violence, Justice, Repression* (Charlottesville, VA: University of Virginia Press, 2006).

90. Florian, *Guillaume Tell*, 202–03.

91. Florian, *Guillaume Tell*, 203; Florian, *William Tell*, 140–41.

92. Florian, *Guillaume Tell*, 204. See also Labhardt, *Tell*, 129. Labhardt labels this speech (inacurrately) as democratic. Although he admits that this speech represents the ideals of the men of 1789–90, he does not explicitly acknowledge the difference between the ideals of the early revolution and 1793–94.

93. See Jainchill, "The Constitution of the Year III and the Persistence of Classical Republicanism;" Jainchill, *Reimagining Politics after the Terror: The Republican Origins of French Liberalism* (Ithaca: Cornell University Press, 2008); Dan Edelstein, *The Terror of Natural Right: Republicanism, The Cult of Nature, and The French Revolution* (Chicago: University of Chicago Press, 2009).

94. Florian, *Guillaume Tell*, 203–04; see also, Rousseau, *Social Contract*, Bk. III ch. 4. "Where there a people of gods, it would govern itself democratically. So perfect a government is not suited to men."

95. For a discussion of these themes and overview of this literature see Lerner, *A Laboratory of Liberty: The Transformation of Political Culture in Republican Switzerland, 1750–1848* (Leiden: Brill, 2011), ch. 1.

96. Florian, *Guillaume Tell*, 143. "Ami, dit le héros à Verner, il est enfin venu l'instant qui doit délivrer la patrie ou terminer nos malheureux jours."

97. For Voltaire see Kennedy, "Old Regime Tragedy and the Terror," 53. See Sedaine's ambigious words quoted in Charlton, *Grétry*, 318.

98. Jauffret in Florian, *Guillaume Tell*, 49–50.

99. See William Doyle, *The Oxford History of the French Revolution* (Oxford: Oxford University Press, 1990), 281.

100. Hewetson, in Florian, *William Tell*, vi. Emphasis original.

101. Florian, *William Tell*, 39. Florian, *Guillaume Tell*, 73.

102. Florian, *Guillaume Tell*, 143.

103. Florian, *William Tell*, 100.

104. Burke, *Reflections on the Revolution in France*.

105. Florian, *William Tell*, 110; Florian, *Guillaume Tell*, 154–55.

106. Knowles, *William Tell*, Act V Scene IV, pp. 84–85. Knowles also had a three act version of his Tell play.

107. Florian, *Guillaume Tell,* 131–34; Florian, *William Tell*, 89–92; Knowles, *Tell*, III, I, pages 41–43.

108. Florian, quoted by Jauffret, in Florian, *Guillaume Tell*, 43.

109. Daniel in Knowles, *William Tell*, in *Cumberland's British Theater*, 5.

110. Daniel, in Knowles, *William Tell*, 6–7.

111. Daniel, in Knowles, *William Tell*, 5. Emphasis Original.

112. For Dublin, see "Unpublished Daybook from Royal Theater Abbey Street" Irish Royal Academy MS 12 S 17.

113. *Richmond Enquirer*, 24 June 1825; *Independent Chronicle & Boston Patriot*, 25 June 1825; *Rochester Telegraph*, 16 August 1825; *The Vermont Gazette*, 30 August 1825; *Independent Chronicle & Boston Patriot*, 12 Oct. 1825; *Baltimore Patriot*, 20 Dec. 1825; *Columbian Centinel American Federalist*, 15 Oct. 1825.

114. *Rhode-Island American and Providence Gazette*, 24 Oct. 1826; *Baltimore Patriot*, 03 Oct. 1826; *Louisiana Advertiser*, 13 Dec. 1826; *The Portsmouth Journal and Rockingham Gazette*, 12 January 1828; *Baltimore Patriot*, 25 January 1828. It was again news when it was resold in 1829. *Baltimore Patriot*, 31 August 1829; *Rhode Island American, Statesman and Providence Gazette*, 1 September 1829.

115. J.L. Borgerhoff, *Le Théatre Anglais A Paris sous la Restauration* (Paris: Librairie Hachette et Cie, 1913), 142–44. Macready's troupe performed Knowles's, *Tell* on 4 July, 7 July, 11 July and 16 July. Knowles, *William Tell, a tragedy in 5 acts*. Thanks to Emily Machen for her help in finding this version.

116. John Pemple, *Shakespeare goes to Paris: How the Bard Conquered France* (London: Continuum, 2005).

117. For reporting on the new law, see *Le Moniteur Universel,* 24 July, 1828. See also Gier, "Guillaume Tell in French Opera," 235.

118. Warren Roberts, *Discovering Rossini: Rossini and Post-Napoleonic Europe*

(Albany: State University of New York Press, under review), ch. 5.

119. R.C. Guilbert de Pixérécourt, *Guillaume Tell; mélodrame en six parties. Imité de Schiller* (Paris, 1828); Benjamin Walton, "Looking for Revolution in Rossini's *Guillaume Tell*," *Cambridge Opera Journal* 15: 2 (2003): 132; Gier, "Guillaume Tell in French Opera," 235; Charlton, *Grétry*, 324.

120. Grétry, *William Tell by Pelissier*, 6–7.

121. Grétry, *William Tell by Pelissier*, 15, 39–46.

122. *Baltimore Patriot*, 27 August 1831; Charlton, *Grétry*, 324. Knowles's *Tell* was referred to as a "patriotic play" as well. *American Mercury*, 20 December 1825.

123. Walton, "Looking for Revolution," 129–132.

124. Simon Schama, *Citizens: A Chronicle of the French Revolution* (New York: Knopf, 1989), 7.

125. Though productions of both Rossini and Schiller were transformed when produced in Austrian controlled territories in the 1820s and 30s. Rossini's opera shifted to Scotland and William Wallace while Schiller's Tell surrendered to the Habsburgs in Vienna in 1828. Philip Gossett, "Becoming a citizen: The chorus in *Risorgimento* opera," *Cambridge Opera Journal* 2 (1990): 50; *New Hampshire Sentinel*, 30 May 1828.

Civic Virtues in the Restless Polity: Sir Walter Scott's Fergusonian Vision of British Civil Society in Redgauntlet (1824)[1]

KATRIN BERNDT

What model of civil society did Sir Walter Scott base *Redgauntlet* (1824) upon? Did he promote moral progress as an end in itself? Which civic virtues did he consider as essential for the well-being of the polity? In this article I explore how Scott's novel can be understood anew as an allegorical representation of Adam Ferguson's philosophy as articulated in his *Essay on the History of Civil Society* (1767). In my discussion of the novel, I will identify Ferguson's rejection of the idea of moral progress; his consideration of the good polity as an "imperfect reality"[2] rather than as an anticipated, perfect future; and his veneration of civic virtues such as friendship, courage, civic passion and eloquence. I will challenge some of the conventional mainstays in Scott scholarship, particularly those that characterize his depiction of the Scottish nation as imbued with romanticized nostalgia. My analysis will show that Scott's conceptualization of the future of Scotland was pragmatic, sober, and inclusive, because it relied on the continuous engagement of her citizens.

Most critics position Sir Walter Scott as a writer who, in spite of his sympathies for Scottish passions and traditions, ultimately promoted the 1707 Union between Scotland and England as Great Britain rather than hewing to unilateral Scottish nationalism. As Duncan Forbes pointed out, Hanoverian Britain embodied the commercial, rational model of society that

Scottish Enlightenment philosophers such as David Hume and Adam Smith valorized—as did Walter Scott. This critical approach, introduced by Forbes's seminal essay on "The Rationalism of Sir Walter Scott" (1953), has been taken up by scholars who view Scott as accepting "the leading principle of conjectural history," based on the "law of the necessary progress of society through successive stages."[3] That is, Forbes and others situate Scott as belonging to what would later be called the Whig view of history, a positivist ideology that emphasized society's growing moral improvement, civility and tranquillity. This scholarly view has also emphasized the dualism in Scott's fiction between "sentimental Jacobitism and pragmatic Hanoverianism in which the former ultimately succumbs to the latter"[4] in a process referred to as the "cathartic assimilation"[5] of Scottish heritage into Hanoverian Britain.

For most of the twentieth century, Scott was also viewed as a novelist whose tales deliberately idealized Scottish history in order to provide both fictional reconciliation with, and nostalgic escapism to, a people who felt marginalized by the dominance of English culture. James Kerr described the use of romance as one of Walter Scott's "favorite tricks," which allowed him to "assimilate a violent past [by] transforming a bloody episode of British history into a series of sentimentalized pictures."[6] It is because of Scott's (successful) attempt to integrate fabulously amplified versions of Scotland's times of yore into Great Britain's national narrative that "cultural critics often have been simultaneously fascinated and appalled by the author's constructions of his native land," as they felt that his fictions have "trapped Scotland in its past."[7]

In the past two decades, literary criticism has begun to reappraise Scott's novels, particularly from a new historicist angle, which has stressed the impact of romance on the recreation of history.[8] Here, scholars have canvassed whether his fiction actually depicts (romanticized versions of) historical events, or merely renders the past and its fictional (re)invention useful for the present with recourse to the heightened imagery of the romance. According to Caroline McCracken-Flesher, Scott deserves to be reconsidered not only because he was more concerned about the future than the past, but also because his vision of Scotland was "not limited to any story of past or present, [but was] gesturing toward its realization in the ever opening tomorrow that is history."[9] In contrast to her positivistic recognition of Scott's formative embrace of Great Britain, Julian Meldon D'Arcy identifies a subversive agenda in his writing when he claims that Scott, in fact, promoted Scottish nationalism through an array of hidden subtexts.[10] Last but not least, scholars such as Ian Duncan and Penny Fielding have read Scott's oeuvre in the context of Edinburgh's literary culture in the pre-Victorian decades of the nineteenth century. They have taken into account Scottish (political and cultural) contributions to the British Empire, including the compensation that the increasing diversity of literary genres, several of which were inspired by regional narrative traditions, offered to those who still mourned the loss of national independence.[11]

In the following article, I would like to contest both the positivist and new revisionist views. Though the conventional and more recent new historicist approaches differ at multiple points, both accept the alleged duality of political allegiance in Scott's fiction and his membership in a Whig (re)creation of the Scottish past. Primarily, I question the assumption that Scott accepted a Smithean notion of social progress, from which all further conclusions on the assimilation of Scottish traditions are eventually derived. As my starting point, I examine McCracken-Flesher's claim that Scott's potential significance for a post-Devolution Scotland lies in his narratives' imaginative formation of the Scottish nation as never completed. In particular, I will show that the continuing significance of Scott's fiction for a continually existing and evolving Scottish nation must be attributed to the influence of Adam Ferguson's philosophy on Scott's representations of civil society, civic virtue and the ideal polity. Of particular importance here is the need to distinguish Ferguson's concepts from those of his contemporaries David Hume and Adam Smith.

It is not entirely new to acknowledge Scott's admiration of Ferguson—Duncan Forbes himself explained Scott's interest in the state of society (rather than in heroic characters and their deeds[12]) with his appreciation of Ferguson's philosophy. Forbes also noted that Scott's depiction of happiness, like Ferguson's, "ar[ose] more from the pursuit, than from the attainment of any end,"[13] and was influenced by the philosopher's description of the constructive impact of conflict on the formation of individual character and, hence, civil society.[14] Nonetheless, Forbes's examination skirted several essentials of Ferguson's philosophy. Claiming that "Scott's stories do not hinge on psychological conflict, but on the contrast between different 'degrees of civilization' and 'states of society,'"[15] Forbes barely referred to Ferguson when he conjectured that

> [t]his contrast between Highland and Lowland, so sharply exhibited in eighteenth-century Scotland, the existence of a "barbarous state of society," a sociological museum, at Edinburgh's back door, and the eruption of the Highlands in 1745, must have been a most potent factor in the outburst of sociological speculation after 1750, speculation which centred round the idea of the progress of society from rudeness to refinement. Adam Ferguson, hailed by some as the founder of sociology, was a Highlander who settled down near Edinburgh.[16]

Indeed, he was. And in contrast to his Enlightenment colleagues, most notably Adam Smith, Ferguson did *not* consider commercial economy as a suitable means to purify personal interactions.[17] Furthermore, he neither believed in irreversible progress, nor assumed that economic development and greater wealth would lead to the attainment of happiness—quite the opposite: "Withdraw the occupations of men, terminate their desires, existence is a burden, and the iteration of memory is a torment."[18] According to Ferguson, man's "disposition to action" had to keep "pace with the variety of powers with which he [was] furnished"[19] because the "most animating occasions of human life, are calls to danger and hardship, not invitations to safety and ease[.]"[20] The satisfaction of material needs would hence fail to secure happiness, "that mysterious thing,"[21] which can only be obtained by a mind that remains actively engaged in the affairs of society. Ferguson also opposed the Smithean idea that an enhanced morality would naturally develop alongside economic advancement. Ferguson's opposition here was reflected in terminology itself: He distinguished between *rude* and *polished* nations rather than between *primitive* and *developed* societies. He was well aware of the fact that the epithet *polished* was usually bestowed by nations upon themselves, "even [by] the most barbarous, or the most corrupted," whenever they struggled to distinguish themselves from a foreign culture whose customs and traditions they perceived as strange.[22] Labels such as *polished* or *barbarous* hence signified national self-estimation rather than development (whether economic, civic, or other).

Moreover, Hume and Smith relied on self-interest to positively affect the progress of society, a notable contrast to Ferguson, for whom the interests of the community always had priority over the concerns of the individual. A citizen, he argued, can achieve happiness only in a community that binds his engagement in the pursuit of its well-being: "That is the most happy state, which is most beloved by its subjects; and they are the most happy men, whose hearts are engaged to a community, in which they find every object of generosity and zeal, and a scope to the exercise of every talent, and of every virtuous disposition."[23] Another distinction to Smith and Hume concerns their view of human relations, including friendship, which they regard as significant only for cultural and economic advancement, and which they believe are refined by commercial culture. Ferguson refuses to consider human interactions only as "subsequent effects of device or invention" because he appreciates "the love of society, friendship, and public affection, penetration, eloquence, and courage"[24] as the "original properties" of man.

Not unlike Rousseau, who believes that improvement in learning and civilized culture would corrupt what he conceptualizes as natural virtues and liberties of mankind, Ferguson suspected commercial culture to possibly undermine vigorous and virtuous politics and a healthy, engaged civil society. It is important here to distinguish between commercial economy and enlightened values such as education: Ferguson's attitude to Enlightenment civilization differs considerably from Rousseau's pessimistic stance, for Ferguson saw human potential realized rather than spoilt in civic institutions—as long as they would allow for vital engagement. His distrust refers to consumerism because of its promotion of self-interest, which he believes to be detrimental to the interests of the community. Ferguson also objected to Rousseau's emphasis on the individual, but considered every citizen first and foremost as part of his community[25]—like Walter Scott, incidentally, whose credentials as a writer derived, not least, from his depiction of characters as agents actively involved in the affairs of their culture.

An essential aspect of Ferguson's philosophy was the emphasis he placed on *conflict*. In contrast to his fellow philosophers Adam Smith and David Hume, he believed that "men who compete, fight, interact and rise to challenges"[26] were essential for a healthy civil society. He argued on the basis of personal experience: for more than a decade, Ferguson had served as chaplain of the 42nd regiment, which fought in the battle of Fontenoy in 1745. Sir Walter Scott himself related an episode which described how Ferguson entered a battle at the head of his column, "with a drawn broadsword in his hand," thus defying his commanding officer, who reminded him that as a chaplain, he was not supposed to join the fighting, with the words "D—n my commission!"[27] According to another source, his reply was less belligerent, but Ferguson definitely remained with his soldiers during combat and earned himself "unbounded ascendancy"[28] over them. The philosopher also supported the establishment of a Scottish militia and was one of the founding members of the Poker Club in 1762, a group of men of letters who agitated for this measure.[29]

To Ferguson, conflict was neither harmful nor should it be prevented. Smith sympathized with citizens whose "respect and reverence for that constitution or form of government which is actually established" would begin to wane "in times of public discontent, faction, and disorder," and he subtly encouraged opposition to a government that "appears plainly unable to maintain the public tranquillity."[30] He and Ferguson clearly approached the idea of conflict from different angles: while Smith approved of opposition only when civic institutions failed to work properly, Ferguson encouraged fighting and contention as central cornerstones of civil society. Hume shared Smith's preference for calm, refinement and decency—states of restraint which he expected to thrive in the age of commerce.[31] His idea of civil society required an unchallenged, established government, "whose sole basis is, not pure reason, but authority and precedent. Dissolve these ties, you break all the bonds of civil society[.]"[32] Ferguson discarded such tranquil elaborations: he argued that human nature was fundamentally, in the words of Fania Oz-Salzberger, "synonymous with playful, aggressive masculinity."[33] Her analysis of Ferguson's ideas of civic engagement helps to explain why his imagined civil society wants neither tranquillity, nor law-abiding obedience as ends in themselves. For Ferguson, conflict was merely one aspect of the human capacity for friendship and bonding.[34] In fact, he regarded conflict an essential and constructive means of civil participation because it necessarily precedes the formation of (public) opinion, and the reconciliation of particular interests:

> In free states, therefore, the wisest laws are never [...] dictated by the interest and spirit of any order of men: they are moved, they are opposed, or amended, by different hands; and come at last to express that medium and composition which contending parties have forced one another to adopt.[35]

According to Ferguson, man has to fully realize his potential in order to become an active citizen. To achieve this, he needs to experience, and try, his innate qualities in interaction—which includes opposition and struggle—with fellow citizens.[36] Conflict is hence a form of public engagement, and therefore, it has *constructive* rather than destructive potential.

Ferguson was also concerned with the compatibility of virtue and the pursuit of wealth and happiness, an attainment which he saw realized in Highland culture where "communal bonds and public virtue"[37] were correlated. He promoted a model of citizenship which was "civically engaged and other-regarding and therefore virtuous."[38] According to Oz-Salzberger,

> Ferguson's civil society is the polity itself. It [...] is not a political artifact projected into a dim future, but an imperfect reality [...] No philosophy can bring it about, and no system of laws can guarantee its upkeep without constant civic alertness. A good citizen must be restless, and a robust polity mildly turbulent.[39]

As explained above, Ferguson argued that the primary obligation of each citizen was neither to achieve particular political goals nor to pursue self-fulfilment, but rather to remain actively and constantly involved in the affairs of the polity. The "turbulence," or state of constant unrest, was a sign of vitality rather than a cause of concern because a good polity includes friendship as well as enmity. Both are crucial aspects of how interaction realizes human potential, for "he who has never struggled with his fellow-creatures, is a stranger to half the sentiments of mankind."[40] Moreover, what his contemporary Hume deemed as progress—the establishment of political society, and the administration of justice[41]—was, to Ferguson, also a demonstration of human capacities. In this vein, he reconciled the pursuit of public and private interests by locating both in the nature of man: Ferguson claimed that the affection man has for others and his involvement in the affairs of his community are genuine expressions of his natural character rather than results of the more refined conduct in civilized society.

Literary criticism has yet to connect Ferguson's concept of civil society as virtuous in its turbulence and restlessness to the themes allegorized in *Redgauntlet* by Sir Walter Scott. This 1824 work is the last of his novels to explore the theme of Jacobitism. Unlike *Waverley*, *Rob Roy* and *The Fair Maid of Perth*, which all feature Scottish characters in different periods of Scottish history, *Redgauntlet* introduces a young generation who is British first and English or Scottish second. Since Scott is the first author in English to portray characters as vital parts of their society, his depiction of *Redgauntlet*'s young generation as distinctly British is significant. The novel recognizes and integrates separatist distinctions in a way that highlights both the outdated character of Jacobite loyalties and the continuing relevance of Scottish heritage for the formation of the British nation.

In contrast to preceding novels such as *Waverley* (1814) and *Rob Roy* (1818), *Redgauntlet* also appears to disregard any idealizing fictionalization of history, Scott's signature feature that has been viewed with such critical suspicion. The novel narrates an entirely fictional, rather than fictionalized, episode of Scottish history. It imagines an anti-climactic closure to Jacobite struggle that spares the Young Pretender, and his supporters, the humiliation of an enforced surrender. In *Redgauntlet*, Jacobitism is not beaten in battle, but outmoded by the accruing loyalty to Britain as a nation—a phenomenon whose lack of ultimacy makes the glorification of the defeated party obsolete. Moreover, the novel's recourse to romanticist features fails to encourage what I would coin "*caledomania*,"[42] a concept that denominates the (usually foreign) enthusiasm for Scottish history and traditions that was stimulated, not least, by Scott's other *Waverley* novels, and the commercial romanticization of Scottish national symbols such as the tartan dress. In *Redgauntlet*, Scott instead portrays quite ordinary characters, a somewhat sober representation of political loyalties, and an ending whose happiness was denounced by Julian Meldon D'Arcy as proceeding from a merely reasonable (and therefore unromantic) partner choice.[43] Scott's plot progresses through a series of serendipitous turns rather than through the forces of destiny. Furthermore, the reader is not encouraged to develop affectionate sympathies for "the Whig and Union view of Scottish history."[44] It is because of such elements that D'Arcy pronounces the novel's portrayal of Hanoverian allegiance and commercial success to be the "negative undercurrent of the narrative"[45] which, in addition to its all-too "perfunctory plot resolution"[46] and "dissonant narrative elements"[47] renders the two main characters disagreeable and thus, subversively, sheds a negative light on the Enlightened rationalism it purports to advocate.

Redgauntlet is, I believe, neither a sentimental account of Scottish passions nor a deliberately ambivalent endorsement of Hanoverian Britain as such. Scott's allegiance does not entirely lack decisive partisanship, but he rejects narrow-minded dualities when he endorses a model of civil society where citizens engage in political actions because they are attached to their respective community and have its interests at heart.[48] The allegorical potential of the novel therefore lies in its representation of citizenship and civic virtues that, although taking into account, concomitantly reach beyond, the demands and conditions of its age. The text suggests that while particular regional loyalties indeed must be respected, they must not be allowed to disturb the present or, following McCracken-Flesher, future interpretations of historical legacies. The British Union in *Redgauntlet* is a political entity that is supported by the younger generation, which is clearly striving to combine the best of both worlds in an egalitarian manner. Therefore, binary oppositions such as feudalism vs. commercial society, Romanticism vs. Enlightenment, or Scottish vs. English loyalties are equally ill-suited for the recognition of the text as the compellingly anticipatory vision of Britishness that it exemplifies. To allude once more to Ferguson, the main characters in *Redgauntlet*—Alan, Darsie and Lilias—are united by being born around the time of the (definite historical) end of the Jacobite struggle and their "common ties of affection to the [present] state."[49] Moreover, they can be described as embracing "the public without hope of profit" for they possess "[c]andour, force, and elevation of mind [which] are the props of democracy; and virtue is the principle of conduct required to its preservation."[50] The younger generation in *Redgauntlet* very much displays these democratic virtues, as will be further discussed below.

The years surrounding Scott's conception of the novel were shaped by the debate about how to properly preserve Scotland's national heritage, which reached its peak with plans to erect a national monument on the east-end side of Edinburgh's Princes Street.[51] According to Ian Duncan, an article series published in *Blackwood's Magazine* devoted to the "controversy surrounding the Monument" captured the "new ideology of an imperial cultural nationalism," an ideology founded on the belief that "the empire's moral and political welfare requires the cultivation of its ancient national distinctions."[52] This discussion recalled another one of Ferguson's arguments in which he claimed that "the political competitiveness of small republics supplies the most favorable conditions for the exercise of patriotism."[53] Seen this way, regionalism was not an obstacle to the integration of different communities within a larger political organization, but rather provided a cohesive bond that binds, and hence positively enabled, citizens to maintain their public affection for the state. In this context, it should be noted that it was the very mobility and adventurousness of those Scottish men and women who moved to London and the rest of the British Empire in the eighteenth century that significantly contributed to an expanding sense of Britishness. Their idea of nationhood was "far more cosmopolitan and enlightened than provincial, xenophobic 'Englishness'"[54] and thus helped to extend the British Empire's perspective in general, as well. They, in addition to Scottish writers and Enlightenment philosophers, were fundamentally contributing to the forging of the British nation, thus producing an idea of Britishness which explicitly draws on Scottish identity.

From a new historicist point of view, Sir Walter Scott transformed facts into events with both *Waverley* and *Rob Roy*, two texts which offer the perspectives of English protagonists on decisive moments of Scottish history. Recourse to this cast of participating observers gives the depiction of Scotland an ethnographic appeal; it also provides the foil for the ideologically inspired struggle of loyalties in both novels. In contrast, *Redgauntlet* relegates political dissent to the realm of generational conflict between Darsie and his Jacobite uncle, the eponymous character. This way, diverging allegiances are shown as co-existing in one social unit, the family, rather than as disrupting it. The idea of a form of union whose strength, to an extent, proceeded from encompassing distinctive loyalties is well developed in the thematic and formal characteristics of Scott's *Redgauntlet*. The central motif which serves to convey the political vision of the text is friendship, which occasions the changing homodiegetic narrative perspectives of the two main characters, the friends Alan Fairford and Darsie Latimer, who happen to be of Scottish and English origin respectively. Their close bond offers a model of the way in which the younger generation can overcome the tensions of the past. In this way, the novel presents not romanticized versions of actual historical events but an entirely fictional ending to the Jacobite struggle that allows both sides to leave the ideological battlefield with their heads held high.

At the beginning of the novel, set in first half of the 1760s, neither Darsie nor Alan appears to be involved in the Jacobite cause at all. They have grown up together in Edinburgh to become close friends but now decide to embark on different paths in life, their separation marking the beginning of the narrative discourse. The first volume consists of the letters the friends exchange when Alan finishes his training as a lawyer in Edinburgh, while Darsie travels through the south of Scotland in an impetuous attempt to lead a life of romantic excitement. He fantasizes about getting involved in all sorts of adventures related to his mysterious past, about which he does not know anything other than he is a wealthy Englishman who would risk losing his income and security should he ever actually visit England. Fascinated with what is concealed from him and forbidden, Darsie is particularly drawn to the English shore, a desire which he does not hesitate to express in his letter to Alan:

> One thing, however, I have seen; and it was with pleasure the more indescribable, that I was debarred from treading the land which my eyes were permitted to gaze upon [...]. I have seen, in a word, the fruitful shores of merry England; merry England! of which I boast myself a native, and on which I gaze, even while raging tides and unstable quicksands divide us, with the filial affection of a dutiful son.[55]

Their exchange shows both young men to be at ease with their respective national identities, and Darsie in particular shows little restraint when sharing his yearning for his unknown, but native country with his Scottish friend. Clearly, he is not afraid that his enthusiastic longing for England will in any way offend Alan. In their epistles, Darsie and Alan discuss their separate heritages, albeit with a focus on issues particularly related to Scottish history. Since Darsie grew up in Edinburgh, the fact that he is more familiar with Scottish culture than with English habits is drawn not as somehow problematic, but as merely consequential. Neither of the friends seems to perceive his particular heritage as a burden or an obstacle to their relationship. It is their self-evident attitude towards their cultural background which highlights that Scott sees both England and Scotland on equal terms rather than treating them as oppositional and consequentially promoting the "fatalistic cultural nostalgia"[56] for which he was criticized. As McCracken-Flesher observes, Scott "appreciates the conjunction between nation and valuation across narration" and "recognizes [that] a tale ever in formation through its telling inevitably gestures toward realization in the future."[57] *Redgauntlet*, featuring a young, self-confident Scottish lawyer and his English friend on an equal, even intimate footing, gestures towards a reaffirmation of the Scottish nation as a part of the Union through its genuine intellectual and economic contributions to Hanoverian Britain. The novel clearly portrays Scotland as a valuable, but distinct entity rather than as a crushed culture that survives primarily through nostalgia. Moreover, the main characters embody the "playful masculinity"[58] appreciated by Ferguson, not least because neither of them seems to have any doubts that their society will offer them opportunities of engagement. Their bond endows them with optimistic self-assertion and bestows on them what Ferguson described as gratifications of the heart.[59]

It is significant too that friendship is portrayed as more important than either familial or national loyalties in the novel. According to Ferguson, friendship is not only one of the "original properties" of mankind; as a central disposition, it also lays "the foundation of [our] moral apprehension."[60] In society, man acts "from affections of kindness and friendship" and "even in the case of those to whom we do not habitually wish any positive good, we are still averse to be instruments of harm."[61] Ferguson's concept of friendship encompasses both individually selected friends and the ideal deportment among citizens, not least because men are "the keepers of their fellow-creatures: They have made the indications of candour and mutual affection the test of what is meritorious and amiable in the characters of men[.]"[62] In *Redgauntlet*, such concern for the well-being of others is a prominent characteristic of Alan and Darsie. Their mutual affection is expressed, for example, when Darsie refers to Alan as the "one kind heart to throb in unison with my own."[63] They celebrate their friendship in their epistolary exchange when they intentionally create entertaining tales of their experiences designed to please and enthral each other; when they tease one another for their quirks and recall reckless deeds from their childhood; and when Darsie quickly renounces his (admittedly superficial) admiration for "Greenmantle"[64] as soon as Alan shows signs of having developed a serious interest in the young woman:

> Tell me honestly; for however the recollection of her may haunt my own mind, my love for Alan Fairford surpasses the love of woman. I know, too, that when you *do* love, it will be to
> Love once and love no more.
> A deep-consuming passion, once kindled in a breast so steady as yours, would never be extinguished but with life.[65]

Darsie's intertextual reference to "surpass[ing] the love of woman" aligns their friendship with the relationship of the biblical David and Jonathan, and illustrates the homosocial bonding that Eve Kosofsky Sedgwick saw defining men's relationships in this period.[66]

The Christian connotation of amity is also present in the character of Joshua Geddes, a Quaker fisherman who exemplifies the values of loyal friendship and civil conduct. In his search for Darsie after the young man's disappearance, Geddes experiences repeated ridicule and jeering from characters such as the notorious Peter Pebbles, but continues to pursue his endeavour to find and rescue Darsie with unflinching courage.[67] His obstinacy reflects Ferguson's sentiment that benevolent actions are indeed "the first and principal constituent of human happiness."[68] When Redgauntlet arrests Geddes under false accusations, Joshua maintains his dignity under threat until his prosecutor is forced to show him proper "respect [for] the fidelity of [his] friendship."[69]

Another example of the Fergusonian ideal of a civically engaged citizenry can be seen when the friends' epistolary conversation reveals that Alan's father defended the Hanoverian regime in the uprising of 1745. A loyal Presbyterian who fought in the western regiment, he swiftly retreated when chased by several denizens of the Highlands, "with naked claymores, and heels as light as their fingers."[70] Darsie mocks old Fairford's apparent cowardice, but Alan vindicates his father's behavior:

> And yet you impeach my father's courage. I tell you he has enough courage to do what is right, and to spurn what is wrong – courage enough to defend a righteous cause with hand and purse, and to take the part of the poor man against his oppressor, without fear of the consequences to himself. This is civil courage, Darsie; and it is of little consequence to most men in this age and country, whether they ever possess military courage or no.[71]

Alan's response to Darsie's attempt at teasing him about his father's quick escape serves several purposes. First, Alan challenges his friend's limited definition of bravery when he insists on distinguishing between military and civil courage. Second, Alan not only concedes his father's civil courage but also portrays it as the more disinterested and hence noble form of bravery since it takes "the part of the poor man against his oppressor." Civil courage is aligned here with Ferguson's ideal of equality, a democratic property that the philosopher considered to be a civic virtue, which is informed by man's regard for the interests of others: "Courage [...] is most easily assumed, or is rather inseparable from that ardour of the mind, in society, friendship, or in public action, which makes us forget subjects of personal anxiety or fear, and attend chiefly to the object of our zeal or affection."[72] Third, their exchange characterizes the friends' different personalities in a way that unhinges the abovementioned dualities often associated with Scott's novels, for it is Darsie, the Englishman, who appears to have a somewhat medieval, chivalric idea of bravery, while Alan's concept of courage derives from more contemporary notions of civil society. The nostalgia for feudal values hence is embodied not by the Scottish character, but by his English friend. Darsie, however, has never had access to his native land; he harbours romanticist notions in lieu of an actual familiarity with his heritage. When he is given the opportunity to join a hopelessly romantic cause, he shows little inclination to actually put his fancies into practice.

It is an irony of fate that it is Darsie who will be confronted with the Jacobite allegiance of his paternal family. He renounces his chance to take part in the rebellion, because he is neither passionate about the Stuart monarchy nor convinced that a reinstalled Stuart king would serve the interests of contemporary society. He, like a Fergusonian, is not afraid to express his scepticism when confronted with his uncle Redgauntlet's demand that he joins his rebellious scheme:

> I trust [...] that I shall never be found indifferent to the call of [honour and patriotism]; but to answer them with effect – even were I convinced that they now sounded in my ear – I must see some reasonable hope of success in the desperate enterprize in which you would involve me. I look around me, and I see a settled government – an established authority – a born Briton on the throne – the very Highland mountaineers, upon whom alone the trust of the exiled family reposed, assembled into regiments, which act under the orders of the existing dynasty. France has been utterly dismayed by the tremendous lessons of the last war, and will hardly provoke another. All without and within the kingdom is adverse to encountering a hopeless struggle, and you alone, sir, seem willing to undertake a desperate enterprize.[73]

Darsie's reason illustrates Ferguson's declaration that a soldier's "point of honour, in free and uncorrupted states, is a zeal for the public; and war to [him] is an operation of passions, not the mere pursuit of a calling."[74] It is precisely this definition of military valour, which explains the complete failure of the fictional Jacobite uprising in the novel. While his followers may owe Charles Edward Stuart their loyalty, their formal allegiance has lost its passionate momentum, since they no longer believe that a rebellion would actually serve the well-being of the polity. Any adherence to past schemes, now against their better judgment, would amount to little more than ignominy—a "mere pursuit"[75] rather than a passionate goal worth fighting for. Twenty years after the battle of Culloden, even those clan chiefs and lairds who had rallied to the Young Pretender in 1745 have become landowners who are no longer interested in revolutionary activities that would endanger their status and property.[76] The temporal setting of the novel can thus be read as supporting the idea of a national British identity, which was to thrive on the common basis of industrialization and imperialism.[77] *Redgauntlet* portrays the Jacobite cause as a hopelessly pathetic and politically bankrupt endeavour that is bound to fail because the former rebels have integrated into British society so successfully that they failed to realize that their political loyalties have turned from idealism into pretension.[78]

The place where most of the events in *Redgauntlet* take place, the Solway Firth on the west coast, possesses a particular metaphorical significance, too. In his reckless attempt to get closer to the forbidden border, Darsie almost drowns in the Firth because he underestimates the dangers of the Solway tides. He is rescued by a man whose countenance proves to be just as unpredictable as the sea, and who later turns out to be the eponymous Redgauntlet, his uncle and a Jacobite who has not yet given up on the idea of a Stuart dynasty. However, the Solway Basin has been "[k]nown as the 'Debatable Lands' after the Scots invasion of 1296,"[79] and it was at Solway Moss where 3,000 English soldiers defeated 10,000 Scots in 1542—a disgrace which is reputed to have been responsible for the subsequent death of James V within a month of the battle, a death which left Scotland in the hands of one Mary Stuart, then a newborn baby.[80] The region is fraught with reminiscences, both of a Scottish past that has been tied to English history, and a Scottish identity that was formed in conflict with the English neighbour. Its significance encompasses not only its violent past, however; the constant movement and "unstable quicksands"[81] of the Solway tides also suggest the flexibility of boundaries of all kinds. In this way, the setting exemplifies the persistent challenge of change, the constant unrest and state of "turbulence" that has, and will continue to, dominate the affairs of society.

The concept of a polity in the state of permanent unrest can also be observed on the formal level of the text. According to James Kerr, *Redgauntlet* is crafted as a historical novel that relies considerably on metafictional instruments,[82] because Scott draws attention to "his own strategies of reemplotment" when he "shifts the emphasis of his writing [...] toward the process of making historical narrative."[83] In *Waverley* and *Rob Roy*, this strategy made "a violent past palatable to the reader of the present."[84] In *Redgauntlet*, fiction replaces the past; the act of historiographic construction is stressed when different narrative perspectives are not only used, but when the change from one perspective to another is explicitly addressed. For example, in an interpolation at the beginning of the second volume, the third-person narrator announces the subsequent shift from homodiegetic, epistolary technique to omniscient narration. Claiming that he used the first only because of its "great popularity," he hastens to add that "a genuine correspondence [. . .] can seldom be found to contain all in which it is necessary to instruct the reader for his full comprehension of the story."[85]

The narrator here questions the authority of the epistolary mode in order to justify his own appearance and assumption of narrative control, but the switch to omniscient, heterodiegetic narration soon proves to have been only temporary, for two chapters on the reader is informed that "the continuation of this history assumes, with the next division, a form somewhat different from direct narrative and epistolary correspondence, though partaking of the character of both."[86] The novel henceforth switches between Darsie's journal and third-person accounts of Alan's adventures in its attempt to convey historical information as well as knowledge of man. Always interested in comprehending people's motivation and purpose, Ferguson himself had stressed that in addition to an enumeration of "the events and the succession of princes that are recorded in the order of time, [...] we have to consider the] characteristics of the understanding and the heart, which alone, in every human transaction, render the story either engaging or useful."[87]

In its insistence on the illegitimacy of continued rebellion, *Redgauntlet* applies the Jacobite standards to the rebels themselves. Not only are the former supporters of the Jacobite rebellion—with the single exception of the eponymous Redgauntlet himself—no longer passionately engaged in Jacobite goals, but Redgauntlet's own value system is considerably questioned when it is revealed that he is collaborating with Christal Nixon, a base criminal, in order to achieve his aims. Redgauntlet's chivalric code of honor, based on his belief in the natural superiority of feudal nobility, does not allow for corruption on the basis of self-righteous pragmatism. That Redgauntlet has only contempt for the man who serves him, that he has associated himself with a person whom he despises for the sake of the cause, strikes the final moral blow to this very cause.[88] It is only consequent with regard to the political stance of the novel that it is Nixon's treason, revealed at the end of the novel, which terminates the remaining rebels' schemes, who swiftly change course to discuss how to retreat rather than how to continue their struggle.[89]

Ferguson's "original properties," i.e. democratic virtues such as "candour, eloquence and penetration," are also embodied in the character of Darsie's sister, Lilias, who displays superior perception and understanding while Darsie and, admittedly to lesser extent, Alan display verbal bravura. Darsie indulges in expressive elaborations of his adventures and in teasing Alan with unrivalled cascades of allusions, puns, references and ironic twists.[90] Alan scolds Darsie's at times exuberant profusion, but still appreciates his friend's efforts to entertain him. He returns Darsie's affection with revelations of more personal concerns and anxieties that also embody Ferguson's ideal of perception and communication.[91] Alan, as the more mature and sincere of the two friends, is guided by his respect for his father and his concern for Darsie, both feelings illustrating Ferguson's conception of love as "an affection which carries the attention of the mind beyond itself, and has a quality, which we call tenderness, that never can accompany the considerations of [selfish] interest."[92]

Lilias, meanwhile, completes the trio through her passionate rebellion against the Jacobite legacy of her family; her keen and insightful determination both politicises and outbalances Alan's reliable "public affection" and Darsie's enthusiastic "eloquence." Raised by her Jacobite uncle and educated in a Parisian convent, Lilias develops her own sense of civic selfhood in defiance of her family's tradition of Stuart loyalty. She describes herself beginning this journey in opposition to

> the doctrines of the Abbess, whom I hated so much for her severity [...] I felt a childish delight in setting her control at defiance, and contradicting in my secret soul all that I was openly obliged to listen to with reverence. Freedom of religious opinion brings on, I suppose, freedom of political creed; for I had no sooner renounced the Pope's infallibility, than I began to question the doctrine of hereditary and indefeasible right. In short, strange as it may seem, I came out of a Parisian convent, not indeed an instructed Whig and Protestant, but with as much inclination to be so as if I had been bred up, like you, within the presbyterian sound of Saint Giles's chimes.[93]

It is interesting that while the spirit of rebellion is shown to have survived—Lilias after all rejects her Stuart heritage of rebellion and Darsie refutes his father and uncle's political doctrine—these three young characters are presented as the citizens of the British Union who leave the sectarian conflicts of the past behind but retain respect for the allegiances of those who fought in them. In a gesture of familial loyalty, Lilias offers to join her uncle in his exile in France; her true prospects however, lie in her marriage to Alan, which will unite the friends as brothers. So, from the final scene of excited retreat, they emerge, "Darsie, his sister, and Fairford, drew together, and held each other by the hands, as those who, when a vessel is about to founder in the storm, determine to take their chance of life and death together."[94]

Redgauntlet offers, in contrast to Scott's earlier novels, not a sentimental recreation of an actual historical conflict, but instead a narrative of a rebellion which never took place. Read as an allegory of Adam Ferguson's conceptions of civil society and its most vital characteristics, Scott's novel represents a passionate defence of a British polity that would draw strength from its turbulence, from its permanent want, and from its both persistent and diverging regional loyalties. In its imaginative alternative closure to the

Jacobite struggle, the novel offers a reconciliatory ending when it alleges that it was the Young Pretender himself, Charles Edward Stuart, who disowned the Jacobite cause. In this way, the Jacobites are endowed with the historical agency to officially concede their defeat and to renounce their ambitions. *Redgauntlet* is preoccupied with propagating an idea of greater Britishness which not only supersedes the struggles and tensions of the past, but which also steps out of the historical context of its inception. Its reliance on what Ferguson believed to be the original dispositions of mankind, which endow citizens with the means and the will to engage in their polity, guarantees the continuation of the national narrative Scott struggled to create—a narrative which remains a source of meaning, as Darsie hastens to announce in one of his letters: "I may just hint to you, we are but yet on the verge of the adventure which it is my purpose to communicate."[95] In this vein, *Redgauntlet* does not assimilate archaic vestiges of a tribal culture. It promotes passionate participation in the civic affairs of a restless polity, and envisages Scotland as a vital component of "the ever opening tomorrow"[96] that is British history.

NOTES

1. An earlier version of this article was presented at the Institute for Advanced Studies in the Humanities (IASH), University of Edinburgh. I would like to thank Susan Manning, Mirjam Schaub and Andrew Wells for their comments on the manuscript.

2. Fania Oz-Salzberger, "Introduction," to Adam Ferguson, [1767] *An Essay on the History of Civil Society* (Cambridge: Cambridge University Press, 2007), vii–xxv; xx. All references to Ferguson are from this edition.

3. Duncan Forbes [1953], "The Rationalism of Sir Walter Scott," in *Critical Essays on Sir Walter Scott:* The Waverley Novels, ed. Harry E. Shaw (New York: G.K. Hall & Co., 1996); 83–97; 89.

4. Julian Meldon D'Arcy, *Subversive Scott. The Waverley Novels and Scottish Nationalism* (Reykjavík: University of Iceland Press, 2005), 24.

5. D'Arcy, *Subversive Scott,* 16.

6. James Kerr, "Fiction against History: Scott's *Redgauntlet* and the Power of Romance," *Texas Studies in Literature and Language* 29.3 (Fall 1987): 237–60; 237.

7. Caroline McCracken-Flesher, *Possible Scotlands* (Oxford: Oxford University Press, 2005), 5.

8. Bruce Beiderwell, "Scott's Redgauntlet as a Romance of Power," *Studies in Romanticism*, 28.2 (Summer 1989), 273–89; Joanne Wilkes, "Scott's Use of Scottish Family History in *Redgauntlet*," *Review of English Studies* 41.162 (1990): 200–11; Harry E. Shaw, "Is There a Problem with Historical Fiction (or with Scott's *Redgauntlet*)?" *Rethinking History* 9.2/3 (June/September 2005): 173–95.

9. McCracken-Flesher, *Possible Scotlands*, 164.

10. See, for example, D'Arcy, *Subversive Scott*, 52.

11. Ian Duncan, *Scott's Shadow. The Novel in Romantic Edinburgh* (Princeton: Princeton University Press, 2007), x; Penny Fielding, *Writing and Orality: Nationality, Culture, and Nineteenth-Century Scottish Fiction* (Oxford: Clarendon Press, 1996), 9.

12. Forbes, "The Rationalism of Sir Walter Scott," 92.

13. Ferguson, *Civil Society*, 51; see also Forbes, "The Rationalism of Sir Walter Scott," 86.

14. Forbes, "The Rationalism of Sir Walter Scott," 86.

15. Forbes, "The Rationalism of Sir Walter Scott," 92.

16. Forbes, "The Rationalism of Sir Walter Scott," 92.

17. Lisa Hill and Peter McCarthy, "Hume, Smith and Ferguson: Friendship in Commercial Society," in *The Challenge to Friendship in Modernity*, ed. Preston King and Heather Devere (London: Frank Cass, 2000): 33–49; 46.

18. Ferguson, *Civil Society*, 45.

19. Ferguson, *Civil Society*, 48.

20. Ferguson, *Civil Society*, 47.

21. Ferguson, *Civil Society*, 51.

22. "The term *polished*, if we may judge from its etymology, originally referred to the state of nations in respect to their laws and government. In its later applications, it refers no less to their proficiency in the liberal and mechanical arts, in literature, and in commerce. But whatever may be its application, it appears, that if there were a name still more respectable than this, every nation, even the most barbarous, or most corrupted, would assume it; and bestow its reverse where they conceived a dislike, or apprehended a difference." Ferguson, *Civil Society*, 195.

23. Ferguson, *Civil Society*, 59.

24. Ferguson, *Civil Society*, 93.

25. Ferguson, *Civil Society*, 59.

26. Oz-Salzberger, introduction, xviii.

27. Francis Espinasse, "Adam Ferguson," in *Dictionary of National Biography*, Vol. VI, ed Leslie Stephen and Sidney Lee (London: Smith, Elder & Co., 1908) 1201.

28. Espinasse, "Adam Ferguson, " 1201.

29. Lisa Hill, *The Passionate Society* (Dordrecht: Springer, 2006), 178; see also Richard Sher, "Adam Ferguson, Adam Smith, and the Problem of National Defense,"

in *Journal of Modern History* 61.2 (1989): 240–68, 259 and Adam Ferguson, *Biographical Sketch or Memoir of Lieutenant-Colonel Patrick Ferguson Originally Intended for the British Encyclopedia* (Edinburgh: John Moir, 1816), 10.

30. Adam Smith, [1759] *The Theory of Moral Sentiments*, Vol. 6, book 2, section 12, ed. D.D. Raphael and A.L. Macfie (Indianapolis: Liberty Classics, 1982), 231.

31. Hill and McCarthy, "Hume, Smith and Ferguson," 47.

32. David Hume, *Essays: Moral, Political and Literary*, II.xiv.5, ed. Eugene F. Miller (Indianapolis: Liberty Fund, 1987), 44. Further references to Hume are from this volume.

33. Oz-Salzberger, introduction, xviii.

34. Ferguson, *Civil Society*, 25.

35. Ferguson, *Civil Society*, 125.

36. Ferguson, *Civil Society*, 23.

37. Oz-Salzberger, introduction, xviii.

38. Lisa Hill, "Civil Society Theory: Ferguson," in *International Encyclopedia of Civil Society*, ed. Helmut K. Anheier and Stefan Toepler (Springer Publications: New York, 2009), 400–04; 400.

39. Oz-Salzberger, introduction, xix–xx.

40. Ferguson, *Civil Society*, 28.

41. David Hume, *Essays, Moral, Political, and Literary*, 37.

42. Following popular usage of the term anglomania, I use *caledomania* in order to denominate the (usually foreign) enthusiasm for Scottish history and traditions.

43. D'Arcy, *Subversive Scott*, 194.

44. D'Arcy, *Subversive Scott*, 194.

45. D'Arcy, *Subversive Scott*, 198.

46. D'Arcy, *Subversive Scott*, 193.

47. D'Arcy, *Subversive Scott*, 198.

48. See Ferguson, *Civil Society*, 59.

49. Ferguson, *Civil Society*, 67.

50. Ferguson, *Civil Society, 67.*

51. The memorial, envisaged as a replica of the Greek Parthenon that reminded of the denomination of Edinburgh as the "Athens of the North" was meant to commemorate the contribution of Scotland to the defeat of Napoleon at Trafalgar in 1805. Construction began in 1826 but had to be stopped after funds ran out in 1829. To this day, an unfinished monument can be seen close to Nelson's Monument on Calton Hill, a place which nevertheless became a popular destination for excursions.

52. Duncan, *Scott's Shadow*, 16.

53. Duncan, *Scott's Shadow*, 16.

54. Lisa Forman Cody, *Birthing the Nation: Sex, Science, and the Conception of Eighteenth-Century Britons* (Oxford: Oxford University Press, 2005), 159.

55. Sir Walter Scott, [1824] *Redgauntlet* (Edinburgh: Edinburgh University Press,

1997), 16.

56. Francis Russell Hart, *The Scottish Novel: A Critical Survey* (London: John Murray, 1978), 202.

57. McCracken-Flesher, *Possible Scotlands*, 19.

58. Oz-Salzberger, introduction, xviii.

59. Ferguson, *Civil Society*, 56.

60. Ferguson, *Civil Society*, 38.

61. Ferguson, *Civil Society*, 38.

62. Ferguson, *Civil Society*, 40.

63. Scott, *Redgauntlet*, 4.

64. "Greenmantle" is, in fact, Lilias Redgauntlet, Darsie's sister, which is revealed in the third part of the novel. See Scott, *Redgauntlet*, 297.

66. Scott, *Redgauntlet*, 113.

66. Old Testament; II Samuel 1:20. See also Eve Kosofsky Sedgwick, *Between Men. English Literature and Male Homosocial Desire* (New York: Columbia University Press, 1985). Rick Incorvati further developed the aspect of non-normative desire to identify Darsie as a conspicuously passive character who is acted upon rather than acting himself. According to Incorvati, Darsie already represents the homosexual disposition Foucault saw emerging only in the late nineteenth century. Rick Incorvati, "Darsie Latimer's 'Little Solidity,' or the Case for Homosexuality in Scott's *Redgauntlet*," *Romanticism on the Net* 36–37 (Nov. 2004–Feb. 2005), http://www.erudit.org/revue/ron/2004/v/n36-37/011140ar.htm

67. Scott, *Redgauntlet*, 327–34.

68. Ferguson, *Civil Society*, 55.

69. Scott, *Redgauntlet*, 342.

70. Scott, *Redgauntlet*, 34.

71. Scott, *Redgauntlet*, 34.

72. Ferguson, *Civil Society*, 56.

73. Scott, *Redgauntlet*, 317.

74. Ferguson, *Civil Society*, 144.

75. Ferguson, *Civil Society*, 144.

76. Christopher Harvie, "Revolution and the Rule of Law," in *The Oxford History of Britain*, ed. Kenneth O. Morgan (Oxford: Oxford University Press, 1999), 470–517; 475.

77. Christopher Harvie, *Scotland and Nationalism. Scottish Society and Politics 1707–1977* (London: George Allen and Unwin, 1977), 73.

78. See Nathan Uglow, "Redgauntlet," in *The Literary Encyclopedia*, 18 June 2002 (http://www.litencyc.com/php/sworks.php?rec=true&UID=2441, accessed 10 August 2009).

79. "The Solway Basin," in *The English Landscape*, ed. Bill Bryson (London: Profile Books, 2000), 416. Incidentally, it was Sir Walter Scott himself who brought

the concept of the "debatable lands" to a wider public, applying it to territories as well as to intellectual and political discussions. In this context, the denial of boundary means that the unexpected can happen. See also Claire Lamont and Michael Rossington, eds., *Romanticism's Debatable Lands* (Basingstoke: Palgrave 2007).

80. John Guy, "The Tudor Age," in *The Oxford History of Britain*, ed. Kenneth O. Morgan (Oxford: Oxford University Press, 1999), 292.

81. Sir Walter Scott, [1824] *Redgauntlet* (Edinburgh: Edinburgh University Press, 1997), 16.

82. Kerr, "Fiction against History," 254.

83. Kerr, "Fiction against History," 238.

84. Kerr, "Fiction against History," 238.

85. Scott, *Redgauntlet*, 125.

86. Scott, *Redgauntlet*, 143.

87. Ferguson, *Civil Society*, 78.

88. Scott, *Redgauntlet*, 359.

89. Scott, *Redgauntlet*, 371.

90. See, for example, Darsie's recollections of their childhood adventures in Scott, *Redgauntlet*, 14–15.

91. See, for example, Allan's charming acknowledgement of his self-conscious anticipation when he tries to arrange his office interiors in a way that would leave a favourable impression on his first client in Scott, *Redgauntlet*, 66.

92. Ferguson, *Civil Society*, 18.

93. Scott, *Redgauntlet*, 303.

94. Scott, *Redgauntlet*, 371.

95. Scott, *Redgauntlet*, 19 (emphasis in the original).

96. McCracken-Flesher, *Possible Scotlands*, 164.

Gulliver's Economized Body: Colonial Projects and the Lusus Naturae in the Travels

DANIELLE SPRATT

The subject of Ireland's economy pulses through Jonathan Swift's writings of the 1720s.[1] Appearing initially in *A Proposal for the Use of Irish Manufacture* (1720) and later in *The Drapier's Letters* (1724–5) and *A Modest Proposal* (1729), two common prescriptive refrains emerge as key components of Swift's economic theory. Through the proto-economists or "economic projectors" in these works, Swift argues that the Irish must first start consuming only their own products (whether Irish linens or Irish babies) in order to establish the second, long-term goal of economic and political freedom from England.[2] Amidst this decade-long concentration on Ireland's financial affairs, Swift also composed *Travels into Several Remote Nations* (1726). In fact, in 1725, Swift alternated between the composition of the *Travels* and *The Drapier's Letters*, which effectively united all of Ireland against Wood's halfpence patent, a dictate from England that threatened to devalue Ireland's existing currency. This concurrence of composition is most apparent in Book 3 of the *Travels*, which depicts the political resistance of the people of Lindalino, who unite to fight against the tyrannical acts of the king and his flying island of Laputa.[3] Functioning as a kind of allegorical wish-fulfillment for political and economic autonomy, the Lindalinians, "who had often complained of great oppressions, shut down the town gates, seized the governor, and with incredible speed and labour erected four large towers, one at every corner of the city.... The people were unanimous, and had laid in store of provisions," and they follow this behavior with "very bold demands, the redress of all their grievances, great immunities, their choice of their own governor, and other the like exorbitances."[4] In this passage, Swift sketches the central points that the Drapier emphasizes over the course of his seven Letters: joining together to be self-reliant and, ultimately, forging independence from an oppressive governmental body.

For readers aware of *A Modest Proposal*, Swift's economic preoccupation is also clear at the end of Book 4, in which Gulliver flays the hides of baby yahoos to craft sails for his canoe. This grotesque resourcefulness anticipates the modest proposer's plan to use all parts of Irish babies to resolve Ireland's rampant poverty.[5] In arguing for the fiscal soundness of consuming a "young healthy child well nursed... whether stewed, roasted, baked, or boiled," the proposer notes, "Those who are more thrifty (as I must confess the times require) may flay the carcass; the skin of which artificially dressed will make admirable gloves for ladies, and summer boots for fine gentlemen."[6] Although critics have attended to these sections of Books 3 and 4, they have underreported the significance to the *Travels* of Swift's economic discourse.[7] Much has been written on the general topic of Swift's economic thought, as well as on his concerns about the distinctive case of Ireland's colonial situation: it was a "kingdom" that was nevertheless subject to economic sanctions and political dictates from England.[8] Developing this line of inquiry, I suggest that by viewing Gulliver as an economic projector in line with the modest proposer and the Drapier we gain a fuller understanding of the particular economic and colonial concerns of the *Travels*. After all, Gulliver himself admits, "I had my self been a sort of projector in my younger days" (183). Constantly invoking England's colonial powers to justify himself and his travels, Gulliver exhibits a projector's preoccupation with the governmental and economic structures of the nations he visits.

Rather than focusing primarily on issues of domestic consumption, Gulliver's narration in the *Travels* depicts the creation, control, and circulation of commodities between both colonized and colonizing peoples and nations. These commodities are not, however, manufactured products. Echoing the logic of projectors like the seventeenth-century economist and Royal Society Fellow Sir William Petty and eighteenth-century economists such as Thomas Prior and Arthur Dobbs, the narrative logic of the *Travels* takes seriously the economic tenet that "people are the wealth of the nation." As in *A Modest Proposal*, the commodities are living and usually human bodies.[9] Consequently, the newly emergent field of demographics, including population control, is implicated in the economic plans Gulliver espouses. Gulliver's accounts of the inhabitants of the nations he explores focus on methods of populating or depopulating a given territory in order to control it: specifically, these schemes relate either to emigration or various ideas of reproductive control, namely breeding or extermination. The issue of Irish emigration in particular was a glaring example of how the combination of economic theory and colonial practice had failed to improve living conditions for people in Ireland. Coerced emigration and other plans of population control also indicate how economic theory has the capacity to turn humans into consumable goods that the government must buy, sell, manage, and move in order to sustain the colonial nation. "When persons are understood to be valuable in terms of their labour power," Charlotte Sussman argues, "rather than their regional or religious loyalties, in theory they become portable. ... The quantification of population leads to assumptions about the transportable nature of subaltern bodies. ... The portability then becomes the key to a kind of biological conquest."[10]

Swift depicts this underlying joint colonial-economic logic by inscribing it upon Gulliver's body, which is forcefully moved, scientifically examined, and sexually commodified throughout the *Travels*. Just as the bodies of Irish babies articulate the desperation of the Irish poor and the flaws of Irish people and projectors alike, Gulliver's body mirrors his own economic and scientific theories, ultimately making him both a culprit and a victim of colonial practices. Gulliver is thus the text's foremost example of what I call the "economized body": a body that, through both his and others' use of colonial and economic theory, becomes objectified, animalized, and ultimately ostracized, making him neither human nor animal but rather what the scientific projectors in Book 2 call *lusus naturae*: a "freak of nature."[11] Rendering the physical and mental effects of colonialism and economics on Gulliver's body underscores the moral lesson inherent to the *Travels*' message: to enact economic theory on whole populations for the sake of colonial aims is at once to brutalize the population and, in turn, to make the projector a monster. In the same way that *A Modest Proposal* exploits the solipsistic logic of domestic consumption, this particular Swiftian iteration of economic thought suggests that methods of population control and colonial planning in effect treat people as objects, as animals, or, worst of all, as liminal bodies that escape any sort of classification.

The relationship here between the human body and the animal body is no coincidence. In Swift's time, animals had come to serve a significant epistemological function that distinguished rational man from irrational beasts.[12] This "human/animal divide" emerged in the wake of Descartes, whose *je pense, donc je suis* created the binary of human/animal that has invoked "concepts of power and subordination"; in the eighteenth century, as Ingrid H. Tague has observed, "there was a longstanding tradition...of using comparisons between animals and slaves to consider power relations in human society."[13] The *Travels*, with its rational horses and servile, irrational yahoos, suggests that Swift was well aware of this spurious divide, and this awareness helps fuel his critique of economic and colonial logic from a broadly philosophical and moral standpoint.[14]

While these connotations of animals are at play in the *Travels*, the economic theory of Petty and other projectors also employed the metaphor of the animal. Swift knew about Petty and his work and explicitly revealed this awareness in Modest Proposal.[15] In addition to being acquainted with Petty's son Henry, Baron Shelbourne, Swift corresponded with Anne Petty, Lady Kerry; he also owned a 1699 edition of Petty's *Political Arithmetick*.[16] Beyond Swift's personal connections to Petty and his family, the political climate of the time made economic discourse commonplace. The 1720s saw a flurry of publications on economic theory in response to what Patrick Kelly identifies as three significant economic crises: the Mississippi crash and South Sea Bubble in 1720; the aforementioned halfpence patent controversy that resulted in Swift's *The Drapier's Letters*; and, as a result of harvest failure, some of the worst famines from 1727–1729.[17] To address these economic crises, Petty developed his system of "political arithmetick," essentially the fundamental methods of modern statistical analysis. According to Ian Hacking, Petty was the founder of modern economics and the foremost economic projector of his time, serving as a fellow of the Royal Society and as one of the founders of the Dublin Philosophical Society.[18]

Petty's related term, "political anatomy," uses the image of anatomized or dissected animals to suggest that, just as good surgeons know the crudest details about the bodies upon which they operate, so too do good rulers need to know all aspects of their nation to rule effectively. The government, Petty argues, must be able to divide and quantify all aspects of society, from the people to the land and all of its assets, from livestock and trade commodities to infrastructure. In *The Political Anatomy of Ireland* (composed 1672; 1st ed. 1691), which was reprinted in 1719, just seven years prior to Swift's publication of the *Travels*, Petty follows Francis Bacon's claim that there is "a judicious *Parallel* in many particulars, between the *Body Natural*, and *Body Politick*.... Now, because *Anatomy* is not only necessary in Physicians but laudable in every Philosophical person whatsoever; I therefore, who profess no Politicks, have, for my curiosity, at large attempted the first *Essay of Political Anatomy*."[19] Petty's theoretical framework for his economic writings, then, is to use the methods of anatomy to understand the whole country; in this way, he seems to be anthropomorphizing the nation of Ireland as a whole.

But Petty does not ultimately consider himself to be dissecting a humanized body politic. Instead, Petty figures Ireland as a simple animal, one that is best suited for his rudimentary tools. Linking Ireland and its inhabitants to a "common" dissected animal, he writes,

> Furthermore, as Students in Medicine, practice their inquiries upon cheap and common *Animals*, ... I have chosen *Ireland* as such a *Political Animal*, who is scarce Twenty years old; where the *Intrigue of State* is not very complicated, and with which I have been conversant from an *Embrion*.... 'Tis true, that curious *Dissections* cannot be made without variety of proper Instruments; whereas I have had only a commin *Knife* and a *Clout*.... However, my rude approaches being enough to find whereabout the Liver and Spleen, and Lungs lye, tho' not to discern the Lymphatick Vessels, the *Plexus*, *Choroidus*, the *Vovuli* of vessels within the Testicles.[20]

Petty's language here figures Ireland as a "cheap and common" male animal that cannot be fully explored at present: his political anatomy can work upon the simple elements of society, and find "the Liver and Spleen," but it cannot "discern the Lymphatick Vessels... within the Testicles." Ironically, although Petty's economic theories require controlling and capitalizing on the reproductive abilities of the people, he admits that this very system is incapable of addressing more complex elements of the body politic and the individual bodies of the people. Petty's figuration "ends up debasing the objects of attention"; his language here demonstrates how economic rhetoric can move quickly from measuring goods and objects using the Baconian terms of "number, weight, or measure" to measuring people in an abstract, objectified manner.[21] Suggestively, despite using an uncomplicated "animal," Petty finds that his tools and methods are not yet enough to understand the entire nation of Ireland.

The end of Book 1 of the *Travels* begins to emphasize how the colonial agenda uses economic thought to conflate humans with what seem to be more manageable, quantifiable animals. For example, in his preparation to leave Blefuscu at the end of his travels throughout Lilliput, Gulliver explains that along with provisions of food, he takes "six cows and two bulls alive, with as many ewes and rams, intending to carry them into my own country, to propagate the breed.... I would gladly have taken a dozen of the natives, but this was a thing the Emperor would by no means permit" (99). Gulliver's language here is telling: he equates transporting animals to transporting people, thereby reflecting a logic typical of scientific travelers of the time.

Clement Hawes notes, "following the precedent of Columbus, the practice of returning with a sampling of 'natives'—with or without their consent—became common among subsequent European explorers" including William Dampier.[22] Because Gulliver succeeds only in transporting animals, this plan at first seems to relate solely to a standard scientific practice. Nevertheless, this moment rehearses the basic structure for the majority of Gulliver's economic schemes and has at its heart these two components: exporting bodies and controlling their reproduction.

Book 2 famously reverses Gulliver's position of scientific and colonial power, tracing a series of humiliating and demoralizing incidents that revolve around his increasingly economized body. This bodily economization anticipates his problematic use of colonial-economic theory toward Book 2's end. While in Brobdignag, Gulliver's body opens him up to seemingly endless, humiliating altercations. In essence, as a diminutive body, he represents the colonized body that is at the mercy of a larger, more powerful colonial governor. Throughout his travels in Brobdignag, Gulliver is either threatened by or actually receives a humiliating array of physical injuries from small animals of all kinds (including a kite, a snail's shell, a mole's hole, birds, flies, rats, a cat, a frog, and a dog).[23] Perhaps most memorable, however, is Gulliver's interaction with a monkey once he is a resident of the royal court. Gulliver recounts,

> He took me up in his right forefoot, and held me as a nurse does a child she is going to suckle, just as I have seen the same sort of creature do with a kitten in Europe.... I have good reason to believe that he took me for a young one of his own species, by his often stroking my face very gently with his other paw... holding me like a baby in one of his fore paws, and feeding me with the other, by cramming into my mouth some victuals. (135)

The threat that the monkey poses to Gulliver's person is not simply physical; it also symbolizes the ways in which Gulliver understands—and begins to deny—his own humanity within the context of scientific, economic, and ultimately colonial logic. As the studies by Laura Brown, Donna Haraway, Erica Fudge, and others have shown, eighteenth-century people living in metropolitan cities encountered spectacular examples of exotic animals that vexed the seemingly standard distinction between human and animal.[24] Cultural encounters with animals such as monkeys and apes occurred on a frequent basis through traveling fairs, side shows, and exhibits, and scientists' seeking theoretical mastery of animals through dissection and classification. For example, Edward Tyson's infamous The *Orang-Outang, sive Homo Sylvestris* (1699) depicts a study of the anatomy of an ape, one that "enables us to investigate the qualities attributed to the ape—qualities which brought it, despite empiricism's best efforts, dangerously close to the human."[25] According to Haraway, "Monkeys and apes…occupy the border zones between [nature and culture,] those potent mythic poles…. [and] have been subjected to sustained, culturally specific interrogations of what it means to be 'almost human.'"[26] The threat of the collapse between species, Fudge notes, is instigated by the similarities between these species.[27]

Although the monkey offers perhaps the most nurturing and sympathetic gestures that Gulliver experiences in Brobdignag, the nature of this sympathy promotes humiliation and dis-ease, not comfort.[28] Brown describes how such an encounter destabilizes human identity and thus poses a particularly vexing problem for the diminutive Gulliver: "'Monkies, Lap Dogs, and Parrots' are the collective protagonist of a cultural fable that explores the nature of being in relation to humanity. This exploration entails a sustained intimacy with alterity, an intimacy that provides a counterpoint to the repudiation of difference that we observed in the representation."[29] For the empowered Gulliver, the cows and sheep from Blefuscu have the potential to represent the exotic and the profitable; for the dependent Gulliver of Book 2, the monkey represents Gulliver's otherness and his lack of agency. Both the monkey and Gulliver also signify economic excess, as they are favorite exotic playthings in the queen's lavish court. In this way, Gulliver comes to symbolize the distinctively feminine frivolity that Swift maligns throughout his writings: Gulliver here is an economized body because he is a rarity, a toy, and a symbol of wealth and leisure for the queen. Underlying this excess, however, is violence. Gulliver embraces the destruction of this being that seems so like him; it is an ominous portent of events to come that he relishes the monkey's execution.

Gulliver becomes another type of commodity in his interactions with women in Brobdignag, as he is denied both human and sexual volition in the court of the maids of honor. Treating him like "a creature of no consequence" (132), the young women in his presence change their clothing, urinate, and defecate. Worst of all, he tells us, one particular girl would use him, against his will, as a human sex toy: she would "set me astride upon one of her nipples, with many other tricks, wherein the reader will excuse me for not being over particular" (132). In all of these examples, Gulliver's narration loses independent agency, a narrative characterization that anticipates the so-called "It-Narrators" found in mid-century sentimental works: in both cases, the narrators are very small and lack volition; they "circulate through society, binding together narratives of otherwise disparate individuals and [are] subject to the mechanisms of exchange."[30]

More colonized than colonizer, Gulliver repeatedly experiences dehumanizing and objectifying situations in Book 2. Upon being discovered by his first Brobdignagian master at the beginning of the book, Gulliver likens himself to an animal. Swift writes, "He considered me a while with the caution of one who endeavours to lay hold on a small dangerous animal in such a manner that it shall not be able either to scratch or to bite him, as I my self have sometimes done with a weasel in England" (107). He continues, "I apprehended every moment that he would dash me against the ground, as we usually do any little hateful animal which we have a mind to destroy" (107). Gulliver soon suspects that his pleading and polite gestures of humility convince the Brobdignagian master of his rationality; to his master, these seemingly polite gestures signify not humanity and rationality, but rather an imitation of humanity and human reason. An advertisement announcing his display as a sideshow describes him as a "strange creature … not so big as a splacknuck (an animal in that country very finely shaped, about six foot long), and in every part of the body *resembling* a human creature, could speak several words, and perform an hundred diverting tricks" (115, emphasis added). Like the monkey who can bow to an audience and drink from a goblet, or the parrot who can mimic human language, Gulliver is a commodified body, signaling the wealth of others and the subordination of a "native" figure that signifies economic and colonial conquest.

If Gulliver's body recalls colonialism and consumerism within the Queen's chambers and the side shows of Brobdignag, then in the royal court of the king, he becomes an equally objectified body through more standard scientific methods of inquiry. Initially, because of his education in philosophy and mathematics, the king believes that Gulliver is "a piece of clock-work contrived by some ingenious artist" (120). Once he realizes that Gulliver exhibits countless examples of human behavior, the king sends for "three great scholars" (120)—presumably natural philosophers—who contemplate the nature of his being:

> They all agreed that I could not be produced according to the regular laws of nature, because I was not framed with a capacity of preserving my life, either by swiftness, or climbing trees, or digging holes in the earth. They observed my teeth, which they viewed with great exactness, that I was a carnivorous animal; yet most quadrupeds being an overmatch for me, and field mice, with some others, too nimble, they could not imagine how I should be able to support myself, unless I fed upon snails or other insects. … After much debate, they concluded unanimously that I was only *relplum scalath*, which is interpreted literally, *lusus naturae*[.] (120–121)

Through this extensive recounting of scientific inquiry and scholarly debate, Gulliver's narration reveals that the Brobdignagian scientists can view him only in non-categorical terms: he is neither a human or an animal, but rather a "lusus naturae," or "freak of nature." In so doing, Swift's rhetoric demonstrates how easily such inquiry destabilizes any sort of classifiable identity. This tenuous categorization as a kind of spectacular monster therefore aligns Gulliver's body with other beings that troubled the human/animal divide, such as Mary Toft, the Englishwoman who "gave birth" to over a dozen rabbits and thus signified a seemingly monstrous case of human and animal bodies colliding.[31]

Gulliver's categorization as an uncategorizable monster gives license to the king to control him sexually through breeding.[32] Gulliver notes that the king "was strongly bent to get me a woman of my own size, by whom I might propagate the breed: but I think I should rather have died than undergone the disgrace of leaving a posterity to be kept in cages … and perhaps in time sold about the kingdom to persons of quality for curiosities" (150). The king's breeding plan, while an outlandish (and ultimately failed) project in itself, alludes to both Gulliver's lack of agency and his lack of place within in the Brobdignagian world that considers him a "freak of nature," rather than a normative part of it. The breeding scheme would also use scientific methods of agriculture and husbandry not to improve society but to create spectacle and further material evidence of the luxury of the court.

Gulliver's use of the term "breeding" to describe the king's plan here recalls Petty's work on developing specific populations in *A Treatise of Ireland* (1687). For example, Petty outlines the importance of breeding the masses for the benefit of England. He writes,

> Of 600 People, the Sixth Part (vizt 100) are teeming Women, which (if they were all marry'd) might bear 40 Children per Ann. (vizt) 20 more than do dye out of 600, at the rate of one out of 30; and consequently in 16 Years the Increase will be 320, making the whole 920. And by the same Reason, in the next 9 Years, the said 920 will be 280 more, in all 1200, vizt double of the Original Number of 600. Upon these Principles, if there be about 19000 Births per Ann. at London, the Number of the marry'd teeming Women must be above 38000; and of the whole Stock of the teeming Women must be above 114000, and of the whole People Six times as many vizt 684000; which agrees well enough with 696000, which they have been elsewhere computed to be.[33]

Petty concludes that since Great Britain and Ireland can produce enough food for twenty million people, the best way to handle the development of the population would be for all "teeming women [to] be marry'd, since there are in Effect 560 Males to 325 Females."[34] Writing of this passage, Mary Poovey notes that this "theory-dependent, theory producing" fact suggests "Petty's foundational theoretical proposition: that the 'value' of human beings should be figured in monetary, not religious or ethical, terms."[35] With this logical chain of suggestions, Petty treats child-bearing women much the way he treats livestock development in other political treatises; this manner of economic thought promotes the "idea that biological reproduction could be aligned with national productivity."[36] Breeding also had a specific institutional precedent at least as far back as Cromwell's reign. In March 1656, Cromwell ordered that 2,000 young English women ship to Barbados to help populate the colony; reportedly, 400 were recruited and shipped to Barbados within a few days.[37]

Gulliver reacts to the breeding scheme by articulating two methods of economic theory and colonial practice: first, he anatomizes England and its inhabitants in the style of Petty, dividing it into the islands of Great Britain and Ireland, followed by the three kingdoms of Ireland, England, and Scotland, along with the "plantations in America" (139). Then, when the king is unimpressed by England's government and its people, he turns to a description of militaristic and colonial power. When the Brobdignagian king interviews Gulliver about the operations of state and society in England, Gulliver shocks him with his use of economic theory and his detached representation of wars of expansion and colonialism. Gulliver narrates, "He laughed at my odd kind of arithmetic (as he was pleased to call it) in reckoning the numbers of our people by a computation drawn from the several sects among us in religion and politics. He said, he knew of no reason, why those who entertain opinions prejudicial to the public should be obliged to change, or should not be obliged to conceal them" (143). Also outraged by Gulliver's description of the English government, the king exclaims, "I cannot but conclude the bulk of your natives to be the most pernicious race of little odious vermin that nature ever suffered to crawl upon the surface of the earth" (144).

In an attempt to defend England and to assert both its and his own considerable powers, Gulliver describes how England uses gunpowder to subdue and overtake other nations. He tells the king, "We often put this powder into large hollow balls of iron, and discharged them by an engine into some city we were besieging, which would rip up the pavement, tear the houses to pieces, burst and throw splinters on every side, dashing out the brains of all who came near" (145). Rather than reaffirming him as an empowered, rational human, the story has the opposite effect. The king is so horrified, Gulliver tells us, that he cannot believe "so impotent and groveling an insect as I could entertain such inhuman ideas" (146). The words "impotent" and "inhuman" here are crucial in the king's estimation of Gulliver. Gulliver's impotent size relates to all levels of his bodily economization: as an object of fascination that represents wealth and luxury; as a sexual object; and as a commodity to be bred and propagated. These varying levels of impotence relate to his equally impotent, inhuman ideas of using gunpowder to conquer nations and whole groups of people. Gulliver sees these scientific improvements as a last-ditch effort to assert his humanity through his narrative of England's militaristic authority, without considering the populations that this power would destroy. Conversely, the king can only envision the human consequences of such power: injury, death, and destruction.[38] Through his use of these loaded terms, Swift thus suggests that population science itself is bereft of all value; it is intellectually, practically, and morally impotent.

In Book 2, intersecting discourses of colonialism, science, and economics thus impact Gulliver's body and his own use of economic and colonial theory. In Book 4, the practice of such theories upon the inhabitants of Houyhnhnmland, including Gulliver himself, leads him on a trajectory of physical and mental degradation. Through his experiences as a victim of economic and colonial logic, Gulliver implements further inhumane colonialist practices. As mentioned above, in one of the many infamous examples from the last book, Gulliver uses the skins of baby yahoos in order to create sails that will help him leave the island.[39] These affronts to Gulliver's humanity result in his invocation of the economic theories of breeding and transportation, and they finalize his status as an economized body that has no location within society.

Gulliver begins to dissociate from humanity soon after his introduction to the yahoos, a "deformed" species that he has found to be entirely abhorrent to him. Despite the overt similarities between the yahoos' bodies and his own, Gulliver does not immediately recognize that the yahoos are humans. Only when one of the Houyhnhnms compares Gulliver to a yahoo side-by-side does he realize that "in this abominable animal, [was] a perfect human figure" (226). Swift's language here is telling, as he equates the "perfect human figure" with an "abominable animal": in this statement alone, Gulliver begins to lose his ability to keep the categories of human/animal fixed. Cristina Malcomson observes that in passages like this, Swift exposes the "compulsive effort to control experience, establish personal importance, and assert the superiority of the English mind."[40] Gulliver can recognize some physical differences—"the face of it flat and broad, the nose depressed, the lips large, and the mouth wide" (226)—yet fundamentally, he realizes that only his clothes and shoes distinguish him physically from the yahoos. Size prevents Gulliver from being a human in Brobdignag, and clothes are the only element that helps distinguish him from the inhuman yahoos. From this point on, Gulliver begins to detest both himself and humanity, turning his hatred inward. He narrates, "When I happened to behold the reflection of my own form in a lake or fountain, I turned away my face in horror and detestation of myself, and could better endure the sight of a common yahoo, than of my own person" (264). After viewing his reflection and confirming this resemblance for himself, Gulliver begins conceptually to fragment his identity; at times he identifies physically and mentally with the yahoos, while at other times, he identifies with the Houyhnhnms, even to the extent that he begins to mimic their gait and their *whinnying speech*. As in Book 2, Gulliver becomes a kind of *lusus naturae*, a being that cannot be firmly categorized as either human or animal.

Also recalling events in in Book 2, a sexual encounter in Houyhnhnmland further dehumanizes and disempowers Gulliver. In this infamous incident, the encounter is not with a giant, oversexed princess but rather with a prepubescent female yahoo. As Gulliver bathes "stark naked" in a river, a "young female yahoo … inflamed by desire … came running with all speed, and leaped into the water within five yards of the place where I bathed. … She embraced me in a most fulsome manner" (254). This moment of sexual threat is crucial in sparking Gulliver's use of economic theory and language to negotiate his own objectification: his encounter with this young female yahoo is the catalyst that leads to him recommending the domination and slow extermination of the yahoo race through another form of population control. When Gulliver experiences both his reflection in the river and his nakedness through the encounter with the female yahoo, he loses the ability to relate to humanity, whether that includes his family and fellow Englishmen or the yahoos. Put simply, "The gaze of the animal offers to [his] sight the abyssal limit of the human."[41] Gulliver's encounter with the naked female yahoo presents him with the limits of the categories of rational man and irrational beast.

Without these conceptual categories of identification, Gulliver remains an unquestioning bystander when his Houyhnhnm master attempts to solve the question of how to exterminate the yahoos.[42] His master has, in fact, appropriated and modified Gulliver's suggested technique of using castration to tame "European Houyhnhnms." His master explains, "this invention might be practiced upon the younger yahoos here, which, besides rendering them tractable and fitter for use, would in an age put an end to the whole species without destroying life" (260). Significantly, Gulliver sees this use of animal husbandry as a perfectly rational plan. Gulliver's perspective, which sees neither English humans nor yahoos as "rational" or Houyhnhnm-like, enables him to embrace fully a core concept of political arithmetic: to use "practical" methods of population control in order to create a more dominant nation, often at the expense of individuals or groups within that nation. Like the language of breeding, the language of population control through forms of mass extermination is explicit in much of Petty's writing. For instance, in *Political Arithmetick* (1690), Petty leads up to his own plans for improving Ireland by saying, "Some furious Spirits have wished, that the Irish would rebel again, that they might be put to the Sword"; later, he writes, "I have heard Wise Men … wish, that *Island* were sunk under water."[43] Fascinatingly, in the sixth *Drapier's Letter* (the only letter he officially signed with his own initials), Swift directly echoes this language: "there is a Vein of Industry and Parsimony, that runs through the whole people of *England*; …As to *Ireland*, they know little more than they do of *Mexico*; further than that it is a Country subject to the King of *England*, full of Boggs, inhabited by wild *Irish Papists*; … And their general Opinion is, that it were better for *England* if this whole Island were sunk into the Sea."[44] Although Petty never specifically advocates for such a barbaric strategy, his economic treatises are occasionally punctuated by discourses of how the obliteration of the Irish people and culture would facilitate the economic growth of England.

While the use of animal husbandry to decimate the yahoos is one key component of the plan to solve the yahoo problem, the corollary to the solution—breeding a race of docile mules to act as servants—further complicates the colonialist use of economic theory within the last book. During the late seventeenth and early eighteenth centuries, the expansion of colonial practices to the Americas and other parts of the world meant that governments needed to devise new ways of creating sustainable labor for these colonies. The question, as David W. Galenson puts it, was "how to people a new world?", and the answer, in part, was to set up a system of indentured servitude specific to the colonies.[45] Unlike the European system of indentured servitude, in which the servant was treated as an apprentice, indentured servants in the colonies had longer indentures and were used specifically for agriculture. This new type of indenture system "resulted from the efforts of early British colonizers of America to transplant the English system of service in husbandry to the New World."[46] What is perhaps most damning about their use of reason in this context is that the Houyhnhnms seek to create a species of servant asses, a species that would presumably be very close to their own.

The creation of indentured servants and their subsequent transportation to the colonies posed an economic concern for many commentators on the Irish situation in the 1720s. During the time that Swift was composing the *Travels*, there was similarly anxiety that the poorer members of Irish society were emigrating, either as hired soldiers or as indentured servants: "In the eighteenth century, Irish magistrates and others often commented with alarm on the "great numbers" of people—particularly Ulster Presbyterians—leaving Ireland for America."[47] Indeed, there was such great concern about the Presbyterian emigration in 1728 that law officers of Ireland were asked, "what laws are in force for preventing the subjects of this Kingdom for transporting themselves, and carrying away their Money and Effects abroad, and to Report … what Method is to be taken upon the said Laws, or in any other legal manner to prevent the same."[48] Historian L. M. Cullen observes, "Irish out-migration of the seventeenth and eighteenth centuries represented a higher proportion of the total movement of people who crossed national boundaries within and out of Europe than did the nineteenth-century outflow."[49] Mention of the creation of a new servant class therefore had an important resonance for readers knowledgeable of the dire situation of Ireland in the 1720s, a time that was filled with famine and a multitude of economic crises.

So too, then, did the notion of transporting whole bodies of people in general have an important significance for Swift and his readers. Of course, Swift was keenly aware of the common relationship between economic need and emigration: Ferguson notes that "Swift had been concerned about the danger of depopulation as early as 1720."[50] Indeed, Gulliver travels because of his "narrow fortune" (49), and in *Directions to Servants* (1745), Swift notes that a reliable excuse for a servant's delay would be to say, "you were taking leave of an old fellow-servant, who was shipping for Barbados."[51] Theories of transport also feature heavily upon Gulliver's return to Redriff. While purportedly detesting humanity, Gulliver nevertheless creates a project for reforming the yahoos of England, one that includes the prospect of transporting the Houyhnhnms to England as a means of "civilizing Europe, by teaching us the first principles of honour, justice, truth, temperance, public spirit, fortitude, chastity, friendship, benevolence, and fidelity" (278). While this idea perhaps most obviously alludes to other plans for transporting missionaries to civilize non-Christian nations, there are several reasons that Swift might also be invoking the problematic concepts of political arithmetic and colonial theory in general. First, Gulliver's proposal occurs during a discussion of how England might perform militaristic endeavors in order to dominate the countries that Gulliver has visited, thus linking the act of transportation not with religious aims but rather with a specific colonial and economic agenda. Second, just two paragraphs later, Swift inserts an even more damning representation of the abuses of British political and colonial power, feigning praise of the nation's "caution in stocking their provinces with people of sober lives" (278–9), or transporting criminals to colonies, thereby linking the act of transporting individuals with political abuse and the depopulation of Ireland.

I suggest that the scheme of coercively transporting bodies is Swift's most subtle example of how economic theory enables colonized people to be treated as objects that can and should be moved and consumed for the purported "good" of the nation. Gulliver's plan to transport the Houyhnhnms would entail a loss of European identities that would mirror the loss of Irish identity about which Petty speculated.[52] In *The Political Anatomy of Ireland*, for example, Petty outlines his plan for transplantation as a means of complementing colonialism and further strengthening England's landholdings and monetary worth. Referring to his plan "rather as a Dream or Resvery [*sic*], than a rational Proposition," Petty argues for the mass transportation of the Irish to England: "if all the *moveables* and People of *Ireland*, and of the Highlands of *Scotland*, were transported into the rest of *Great Britain*; that then the King and his Subjects, would thereby become more *Rich* and *Strong*, both *offensively* and *defensively,* than now they are."[53] In Petty's understanding, the ultimate goal was not to benefit the people of England and Ireland but rather to benefit the economic soundness of England.

Petty further develops his transportation plan in *An Essay in Political Arithmetick concerning Ireland* (1687; pub. 1899). The inherent goal of dominating and conquering other nations and people informs this plan throughout. Petty writes, "Conquerors of ancient Times and even now in the Oriental Countreys, do execute their Conquest, by Carrying away Captives into their own Countreys, … especially, when the Conquerors have Land enough, to employ all the Hands both of their Conquering and Captive Subjects."[54] This passage overtly calls attention to the colonialist logic that underpins his entire plan of transportation. Petty primarily objects to the cost of maintaining armies in other countries; in order to avoid this cost and to increase the wealth of each nation, he uses statistics to demonstrate how all of the people involved—the native English, the transported Irish, and the two countries as a whole—will benefit. No one, he imagines, could possibly object. Here, Petty anticipates that his rational argument of mutual benefit will persuade people that his plan is in their own best interest: "Wherefore, we shall rather shew, That it will be the Profit, Pleasure, and Security of both Nations and Religions to Agree herein."[55]

Beyond the economic value, in which England will gain 100 million pounds, with 10 million being designated specifically for Ireland, this solution will eradicate the tension between the English and the Irish by erasing Irish identity. Petty assures, "The Manners, Habits, Language, and Customs of the Irish (without Prejudice to Religion) will be transmuted into English, within less than an Age, and all Old Animosities forgotten."[56]

This last detail, the erasure of a collective national identity, links both of Gulliver's politically projected plans together. Gulliver's silent endorsement of the plan to exterminate the yahoos through castration would guarantee the erasure of their presence in Houyhnhmland in one lifetime; his plan for transporting the Houyhnhnms to Europe would negate the "European yahoo" presence in England and elsewhere.

The text of the *Travels* itself, Gulliver tells us, was intended to function in a similar way. "A Letter from Capt. Gulliver to His Cousin Sympson," which first appeared in the 1735 edition of the Travels, is a document that editors usually append to the opening of the satire. Within the chronology of the satire, however, Gulliver writes this letter in response to the first published "loose and uncorrect account of my travels" from 1726 (39). The letter logically ought to appear as a kind of postscript, after the closing of the final chapter. In this letter, Gulliver laments not only the errors in the published texts ("Brobdignag" should have been "Brobdingrag," for example) but also the work's inability to reform human behavior. In the closing sentence, he writes, "I should never have attempted so absurd a *project* as that of reforming the yahoo race in this kingdom; but I have now done with all such visionary schemes forever" (42, emphasis added). Gulliver's scheme to transplant the yahoos is one founded in political arithmetic and steeped in the Royal Society's rhetoric of "improving mankind." Likewise, his choice to publish his "scientific" travelogue is grounded in his desire to use his status as a projector to benefit the people of England.

Like the projectors in the Academy of Lagado, who fail to produce anything worthwhile, Gulliver also fails in his economic, scientifically-inspired project. Swift's satire, on the other hand, portrays these failures for his own productive ends. By virtue of its generic aims, one that links the individual with society, as well as scientific practice with governmental policy, Swift's satire exposes the relationship among economic, scientific, and colonial modes of hegemony. Through his outrageous depictions of Gulliver's alternately commodified, animalized, and disenfranchised body, Swift creates a text that works to question the moral and practical implications of colonial science's problematic relationship with Irish society. Rather than using economics to promote practical, prescriptive methods to combat the economic and political problems of Ireland, Swift's Gulliver functions as a projector who represents both the problematic logic of the colonizer and the problematic effects of projection on the colonized.

NOTES

I thank Monica Najar and Linda Troost for organizing the panel "Male Bodies under Scrutiny" at the 2009 ECASECS conference, which helped me to rethink and expand the initial parameters of this paper. For their always thorough, patient, and kind feedback on both early and more final drafts of this paper, I thank my doctoral dream team: Susan Greenfield, Frank Boyle, Julie Kim, and Eve Keller. The revised version of this paper also benefitted from incisive and lightning-fast comments from John Bugg, friendly conversations with Moshe Gold and Andrew Clark about everything from Derrida to Levinas, and encouraging discussions with Maija Birenbaum, Angela Monsam, Erica DaCosta, Anne Thell, and Judy Stuchiner. Finally, I thank the ever-cheerful and ever-helpful Lisa Cody for her guidance and support during the final drafts of this work.

1. Along with the *A Proposal for the Use of Irish Manufacture*, *The Drapier's Letters*, and *A Modest Proposal*, the most well-known works in this genre, these texts include *The Swearers-Bank: or, Parliamentary Security for Establishing a new Bank in Ireland* (1720); *On English Bubbles* (1721); *The Present Miserable State of Ireland* (1727); and *A Short View of the State of Ireland* (1727). Swift consistently pronounced his interest in Ireland's economic, political, and religious situation. In addition to his "Verses on the Death of Dr. Swift," in which he writes of "The Dean by his pen did defeat / an infamous destructive cheat" (407–8), Swift's acceptance speech for being named a freeman of Dublin in 1730 immodestly bragged about his importance as an Irish patriot and economic liberator. See Oliver W. Ferguson, "Jonathan Swift, Freeman of Dublin," *Modern Language Notes* 71, no. 6 (June, 1956): 405–9.

2. On this economic discourse, see Patrick Kelly, "Swift on Money and Economics," in *The Cambridge Companion to Jonathan Swift*, ed. Christopher Fox (New York: Cambridge University Press, 2003), 128–45, esp. 134. Joseph McMinn comments on the relationship between these two themes in *The Drapier's Letters*: "What began as a minor economic and diplomatic miscalculation on the part of London was transformed by Swift's Drapier into a fundamental issue of national sovereignty" (24). See McMinn's "Swift's Life," in *The Cambridge Companion to Swift*, ed. Christopher Fox (New York: Cambridge University Press, 2003), 198–214.

3. In *Jonathan Swift and Ireland* (Chicago: University of Illinois Press, 1962), Oliver W. Ferguson notes that especially during the summer of 1725, Swift moved between composing Book 3 of *Travels* and *The Drapier's Letters*. He observes that although Wood was defeated during this time, negating the necessity for the envisioned final Letter, "it afforded Swift the opportunity to add an episode to the Third Voyage" (135).

4. Swift, "Gulliver's Travels," in *Gulliver's Travels and Other Writings*, ed. Clement Hawes (New York: Houghton Mifflin Company, 2004), 177. Hereafter cited in the text.

5. In addition to offering a seminal reading of the discourses of genocide and extermination in Book 4 of *Gulliver's Travels*, Claude Rawson has noted the link between Swift's 1726 text and *A Modest Proposal* in *God, Gulliver, and Genocide: Barbarism and the European Imagination*, 1492–1945 (New York: Oxford University Press, 2001), 282. Frank Boyle considers the logic of mass extermination in Swift's writing with a more sustained focus on Swift's concern about the moral and cultural implications of the scientific revolution functioning as the pre-eminent modern project in *Swift as Nemesis: Modernity and its Satirist* (Stanford, Stanford University Press, 2000), 142.

6. Swift, "A Modest Proposal", *Gulliver's Travels and Other Writings*, ed. Clement Hawes, 325, 326.

7. For one of the few recent studies of the relationship between economics and the *Travels*, see Gregory Lynall, "Swift's Caricatures of Newton: 'Taylor', 'Conjuror', and 'Workman at the Mint,'" *The British Journal for Eighteenth-Century Studies* 28, no. 1 (Spring 2005): 19–32. Other work includes Arthur E. Case, "Personal and Political Satire in Gulliver's Travels," in *Four Essays on "Gulliver's Travels*," (Princeton: Princeton University Press, 1945; repr. Gloucester, MA: Peter Smith, 1958), 69–96; J. M. Treadwell, "Jonathan Swift: The Satirist as Projector," *Texas Studies in Literature and Language* 17 (1975): 439–60; and Pat Rogers, "Gulliver and Engineers," *Modern Language Review* 70 (1975): 260–70.

8. The foundational studies of Swift's general economic writings are Louis Landa's "A Modest Proposal and Populousness," *Modern Philology* 40, no. 2 (Nov. 1942): 161–70 and his "Swift's Economic Views and Mercantilism," *ELH* 10, no. 4 (December 1943): 310–35. There is a long critical history of the relationship between economics and *A Modest Proposal*. Recent work includes Peter M. Briggs, "John Graunt, Sir William Petty, and Swift's Modest Proposal," *Eighteenth-Century Life* 29, no. 2 (2005): 3–24. Studies of Swift's engagement with Ireland's vexed colonial status include S. J. Connolly, "Eighteenth-Century Ireland: Colony or ancien régime?" in *The Making of Modern Irish History: Revisionism and the Revisionist Controversy*, ed. D. George Boyce and Alan O'Day (New York: Routledge, 1996),15–34; Carole Fabricant, "Speaking for the Irish Nation: The Drapier, the Bishop, and the Problems of Colonial Representation" in *Gulliver's Travels and Other Writings*, ed. Clement Hawes (New York: Houghton Mifflin Company, 2004), 465–501; Clement Hawes, "'Three Times Round the Globe: Gulliver and Colonial Discourse" in *Gulliver's Travels and Other Writings*, 438–64; and Robert Mahony, "The Irish Colonial Experience and Swift's Rhetorics of Perception in the 1720s," *Eighteenth-Century Life* 22, no. 1 (1998): 63–75.

9. J. T. Gilbert notes that Thomas Prior founded the Dublin Society for the Promotion of Agriculture, Manufactures, Arts and Sciences in 1731 (a revised model of the Dublin Philosophical Society that Petty co-founded in 1683) and concentrated the majority of his writing efforts on trade in Ireland through such works as *List of the Absentees of Ireland* (1729). (*Oxford Dictionary of National Biography*, Vol. 46: 401–2). Arthur Dobbs (1689–1765) was a colonial governor and wrote extensively on trade. His Essay on the *Trade and Improvement of Ireland* (Part 1, 1728; Part 2, 1730) aimed to address the deplorable economic conditions of Ireland by addressing the land tenure system (*Oxford Dictionary of National Biography*, Vol. 15: 130–32). Ferguson suggests that "Swift shared many of their economic theories" (477) in his "Swift's Saeva Indignatio and "A Modest Proposal," *Philological Quarterly* 38, no. 4 (October 1959): 473–79.

10. Charlotte Sussman, "The Colonial Afterlife of Political Arithmetic: Swift, Demography, and Mobile Populations," *Cultural Critique* 56 (2004): 96–126, esp. 103–08. While Sussman considers the colonial relationship between England and Ireland, her language is relevant to Swift's broader moral and epistemological concerns about economic and colonial thought.

11. Recent interest in animal studies has drawn attention to the importance of literary depictions of the "human/animal divide." Marianne DeKoven suggests that in literature, representations of animals can underscore human suffering: "A primary approach to the study of animal representation takes as its object the ways in which literary animals are used to reinforce the denigration of subjugated people or to point toward greater human equality. This approach can be motivated by a concern for human oppression or a simultaneous concern for all animal suffering and mistreatment, human and nonhuman" (363). She also carefully observes that "The term nonhuman itself is ideologically loaded: only from the point of view of the human are other animals nonhuman" (363). I use the words "dehumanized," "animalized," and "inhuman" with this concept in mind. See DeKoven's "Guest Column: Why Animals Now?" *PMLA* 124, no. 2 (March 2009): 361–69.

12. Ann Cline Kelly and Jonathan Lamb have offered two optimistic readings on animals in the *Travels*. Kelly argues that Gulliver becomes his master Houyhnhnm's pet, a sympathetic relationship that helps him find solace with his own horses upon his traumatic return to Redriff and human society. Lamb also considers the sympathetic bonds with animals forged in Book 4, but he does so by demonstrating the cumulative effects of Gulliver's otherness in Books 1–3 that help him create this sympathetic bond with animals. Lamb believes that through this sympathetic bond, Swift suggests that all definitions of humanity are contingent upon understandings of the animal. Within the context of an economic consideration of the text, however, I suggest that animals function less as ideal, sympathetic figures and more as representatives of disenfranchisement. See Kelly, "Gulliver as Pet and Pet Keeper: Talking Animals in Book 4," *ELH* 74 (2007): 323–49 and Lamb, "Gulliver and the Lives of Animals," in

Humans and Other Animals in Eighteenth-Century British Culture: Representation, Hybridity, Ethics, ed. Frank Palmeri, (Burlington, VT: Ashgate, 2006), 169–78.

13. Ingrid H. Tague, "Companions, Servants, or Slaves? Considering Animals in Eighteenth-Century Britain," *Studies in Eighteenth-Century Culture* 39 (2010): 110–30,111,112.

14. Boyle argues that Swift's "antihumanist cultural discourses" are products of what Swift sees as modernity's pet project, New Philosophy. Boyle, *Swift as Nemesis*, 81.

15. George Wittkowsky's "Swift's Modest Proposal: The Biography of an Early Georgian Pamphlet," *Journal of the History of Ideas* 4 (1943): 75–104 is still cited as the foundational article on Swift's interest in and knowledge of Petty and other proto-economic projectors.

16. On the personal relationship between Swift and Petty's children, see Briggs, "John Graunt," 9. On Swift's holdings of Petty's writing, see Briggs, 22n9, and Harold Williams's *Dean Swift's Library, with a Facsimile of the Original Sale Catalogue* (Cambridge: Cambridge University Press, 1932), catalog items 412 and 453.

17. Kelly, "Swift's Life," 129.

18. Ian Hacking, *The Emergence of Probability*, 2nd ed. (New York: Cambridge University Press, 2006), 102. The importance of Petty's economic work cannot be overstated; see also Antoin E. Murphy, *The Genesis of Macroeconomics: New Ideas from Sir William Petty to Henry Thornton* (New York: Oxford University Press, 2009), esp. 21–42, and Mary Poovey's *A History of the Modern Fact: Problems of Knowledge in the Sciences of Wealth and Society* (Chicago: University of Chicago Press, 1998), esp. 120–43.

19. William Petty, "The Political Anatomy of Ireland," vol. 1 of *The Economic Writings of Sir William Petty*, ed. Charles Henry Hull (New York: Augustus M. Kelley, 1963), 129.

20. Petty, "Political Anatomy," 129–30.

21. Briggs, "John Graunt," 17. Briggs also explains that in *A Modest Proposal*, "every time the modest proposer pauses to calculate the number, weight, or trade value of Irish babies or to speculate concerning possible marketing strategies, Swift is in fact mimicking Petty's gradual conversion of Baconian values ('Number, weight, or measure') into mercantile values" (16). I suggest that Gulliver has a similar habit when he expounds upon his economic theorems.

22. Hawes, *Gulliver's Travels and Other Writings*, 99n.

23. In "The Frailty of Human Beings in Gulliver's Travels," Paul Fussell discusses how each of the *Travels* depicts Gulliver of being in some grave physical danger; my reading expands on this observation to show the link between physical, sexual, and mental distress, and how this relates to the broader philosophical issues regarding colonialism and economics within the text. For Fussell's work, see *Readings on Gulliver's Travels*, ed. Gary Wiener (San Diego: Greenhaven Press, 2000), 91–92.

24. Laura Brown, *Fables of Modernity: Literature and Culture in the English Eighteenth Century* (Ithaca: Cornell Univeristy Press, 2003), esp. 221–66; Donna Haraway, *Primate Visions: Gender, Race, and Nature in the World of Modern Science* (New York: Routledge, 1989); and Erica Fudge, *Perceiving Animals: Humans and Beasts in Early Modern English Culture* (New York: St. Martin's Press, 2000).

25. Susan Wiseman, "Monstrous Perfectibility: Ape-Human Transformations in Hobbes, Bulwer, Tyson," in *At the Borders of the Human: Beasts, Bodies and Natural Philosophy in the Early Modern Period*, ed. Erica Fudge, Ruth Gilbert, and Susan Wiseman (New York: St. Martin's, 1999), 215–38, 215.

26. Haraway, *Primate Visions*, 1–2.

27. Fudge, *Perceiving Animals*, 30.

28. This type of sympathy stands in stark contrast to the sympathy that Cline Kelly and Lamb observe in Book 4.

29. Brown, Fables of *Modernity*, 223.

30. Liz Bellamy, "It-Narrators and Circulation: Defining a Sub-Genre," in T*he Secret Life of Things: Animals, Objects, and It-Narratives in Eighteenth-Century England*, ed. Mark Blackwell (Lewisburg: Bucknell University Press, 2007), 117–46, 121.

31. After receiving much attention from newspapers and medical authorities, the Toft case was finally determined to be a hoax. For more on the relationship between science, medicine, and monstrosity, see Dennis Todd, *Imagining Monsters* (Chicago: University of Chicago Press, 1995), esp.1–38; Lisa Forman Cody, *Birthing the Nation* (New York: Oxford University Press, 2005), esp. 123–44. Swift was well aware of the Toft incident, as depicted in a November 1726 exchange of letters exchanged between Swift and Mrs. Howard. See *The Works of Jonathan Swift*, ed. Thomas Roscoe, (London, 1843), 1: lxxii, lxxiii.

32. Jenny Davidson describes the ways in which the Houyhnhnms control their own reproduction as they attempt to do the same for the yahoos as an attempt to create a perfect caste system and a perfect society. See Davidson's *Breeding: A Partial History of the Eighteenth Century* (New York: Columbia University Press, 2009), esp. 69–82.

33. Petty, "A Treatise on Ireland," vol. 2 of *The Economic Writings of Sir William Petty*, ed. Charles Henry Hull (New York: Augustus M. Kelley, 1963), 605. *A Treatise on Ireland*, though written in 1687, was not published until 1899. This type of economic discourse, however, is found in many of Petty's other tracts, and thus the content, if not the exact example, was familiar to readers of Petty. Of course, Swift exploits this concept in *A Modest Proposal* as well.

34. Petty, "A Treatise on Ireland," 605.

35. Poovey, *A History of the Modern Fact*, 130, 131.

36. Sussman, "The Colonial Afterlife," 113.

37. Hilary Beckles, *White Servants and Black Slavery in Barbados, 1627–1715*

(Knoxville: University of Tennessee Press, 1989), 47–8. According to Beckles, local rumor had it that the women were shipped to Barbados to breed indentured servants.

38. For other readings of the relationship between Gulliver's size, impotence, and science in the *Travels*, see Marjorie Nicolson's foundational "The Microscope and the English Imagination," *Smith College Studies in Modern Languages* 16.4 (July 1935): 1–92, later republished in Nicolson's *Science and the Imagination* (Ithaca: Great Seal books, 1956), 155–234. See also Frederik N. Smith, "Science, Imagination, and Swift's Brobdignagians," *Eighteenth-Century Life* 14, no. 1 (1990 Feb.): 100–14; Douglas Lane Patey, "Swift's Satire on 'Science' and the Structure of *Gulliver's Travels*," *ELH* 58, no. 4 (Winter 1991): 809–39; Christopher Fox, "Introduction: How to Prepare a Noble Savage: The Spectacle of Human Science," in *Inventing Human Science: Eighteenth-Century Domains*, ed. Fox, Roy Porter, and Robert Wokler (Berkeley: Univeristy of California Press, 1995), 1–30; and Deborah Needleman Armintour, "The Sexual Politics of Microscopy in Brobdignag," *SEL: Studies in English Literature, 1500–1900* 47 no. 3 (Summer 2007): 619–40.

39. Sean Moore notes that the reference to cannibalism in the Irish economy related very specifically to the taxation structure; Dublin's Archbishop William King "had also been circulating unpublished manuscripts to friends for several decades, complaining that the Irish were so overtaxed that "I cannot see how any more can be got from them, except we … flay them and sell their skins" (401). This cannibal metaphor for overtaxation, which has been cited as the source of Swift's inspiration for the scene of Gulliver skinning yahoos and the *Modest Proposal*'s baby-eating scheme, was clearly being disseminated in Anglo-Irish circles in this period to describe their ethical dilemma: "the problem of how Anglo-Irishmen were passing their responsibility for funding the British empire down to the poor" (401). See Moore, "Swift and Ireland's Revenue: The Public-Finance Context of Irish Economic Pamphleteering," *Reading Swift: Papers from the Fifth Munster Symposium on Jonathan Swift* (Munich: Wilhelm Fink, 2008), 393–403.

40. Cristina Malcomson, "Gulliver's Travels and Studies of Skin Color in the Royal Society," in *Humans and Other Animals in Eighteenth-Century British Culture: Representation, Hybridity, Ethics*, ed. Frank Palmeri (Vermont: Ashgate, 2006), 45–67, 52.

41. Jacques Derrida, "The Animal that Therefore I Am (More to Follow)," trans. David Wills, *Critical Inquiry* 28 (Winter 2002): 369–418, 381.

42. Richard Nash's recent work perhaps accounts for Swift's association of the Houyhnhnms with reproductive control, particularly the ways in which horse breeding became a way to control cultural anxieties about patrilineal heritage; "Honest English Breed: The Thoroughbred as Cultural Metaphor" in *The Culture of the Horse: Status, Discipline, and Identity in the Early Modern World*, ed. Karen Raber and Treva J. Tucker (New York: Palgrave, 2005), 245–72,

43. Petty, "Political Arithmetick," vol. 1 of *The Economic Writings of Sir William Petty*, ed. Charles Henry Hull, (New York: Augustus M. Kelley, 1963), 155, 285.

44. Swift, *Drapier*, 128. Ferguson contextualizes this passage as a source for Swift's own mixed feelings (bordering on disdain) on both the broader Irish situation and on his specific fate of being appointed the Deanery in Ireland. See Ferguson, *Jonathan Swift and Ireland*, 6.

45. David W. Galenson, *White Servitude in Colonial America: An Economic Analysis* (New York: Cambridge University Press, 1981), 5.

46. Galenson, *White Servitude*, 171.

47. Kerby Miller and Líam Kennedy, "Appendix 2: Irish Migration and Demography, 1659–1831," in *Irish Immigrants in the Land of Canaan: Letters and Memoirs from Colonial and Revolutionary America, 1675–1815,* ed. Kerby A. Miller, Arnold Schrier, Bruce D. Boling, David N. Doyle (New York: Oxford University Press, 2004), 656.

48. Dickinson quoted in Sussman, "The Colonial Afterlife," 113.

49. L. M. Cullen, "The Irish Diaspora of the Seventeenth and Eighteenth Centuries," in *Europeans on the move: studies on European migration, 1500–1800*, ed. Nicholas P. Canny, (New York: Clarendon Press, 1994), 113.

50. Ferguson, *Jonathan Swift and Ireland*, 162.

51 Swift, *Directions to Servants* (1731. New York: Pantheon Books, 1964), 28.

52. Poovey's *History of the Modern Fact* has discussed how the use of political arithmetic in general, which emphasizes "the source of income, sought to transform the Irish into economic beings instead of religious, political, or even national subjects,... [encouraging] the Irish to see themselves as Petty saw them; and this perspective would enable them to realize that their true interest lay not in clinging to their Irishness but in embracing habits that would make them like the English" (Poovey 136). For obvious reasons, transporting whole groups of people would have a very practical erasure of identity. See also Sussman, "The Colonial Afterlife," 102–3.

53. Petty, "Political Anatomy of Ireland," 285

54. Petty, "An Essay Concerning Political Arithmetick concerning Ireland," vol. 2 of The Economic Writings of Sir William Petty, ed. Charles Henry Hull, (New York: Augustus M. Kelley, 1963), 562.

55. Petty, "An Essay Concerning Political Arithmetick concerning Ireland," 562.

56. Petty, "An Essay Concerning Political Arithmetick concerning Ireland," 563.

Print and Oral Culture in the Eighteenth-Century Irish Ballad

JULIE HENIGAN

Adam Fox states the obvious when he comments that the implications of literacy "vary between societies and over time" and "depend upon the particular circumstances of their dissemination and use."[1] Thus, although printed balladry in Ireland initially depended almost entirely on imports from Britain (London in particular), it increasingly displayed cultural, linguistic, and literary qualities of its own—qualities that in turn came to exercise a strong influence on printed ballads in Britain. Moreover, despite the fact that Irish printed ballads embraced a broad linguistic and artistic spectrum, there is ample evidence to indicate that the audience for these songs became increasingly heterogeneous during the course of the century, reflecting not only growing literacy but also dynamic social interaction. This interchange belies the notion that the educated classes and the peasantry inhabited two wholly discrete cultural worlds, one literate and the other oral.

Unfortunately, as Hugh Shields notes, "The ballad press of the eighteenth century, so far as we know it, gives a patchy view of song repertory, for sheets and songbooks are unevenly preserved."[2] Despite early allusions to ballads, few ballad sheets or either prose or song chapbooks (of either British or Irish provenance) survive in Ireland from before 1700—indeed, not in any numbers until the latter part of the eighteenth century. We know from several references that ballads were reasonably widespread in Ireland from at least the late seventeenth century. Limerick-based Dáibhí Ó Bruadair disparaged *sráidéigse* ("street poetry") and, in a poem from 1675 or '76, he took aim at "aos órtha an fhuairsceidill" ("the chanters of the frigid sheets").[3] In 1692, a poet—possibly Cormac Ó Luinín—addressed Sir Richard Cox (Lord Chancellor of Ireland from 1703–07) thus:

> Ná raibh tú et cailleach an hata
> Ag crois margaidh lá geimhriota,
> Is caimbeul ort go suighe do chluais,
> A' bollsaireact bailéd go chrithfhuar.[4]
>
> May you not find yourself and the hag with the hat
> At the market cross on a winter's day,
> Grimacing from ear to ear,
> Bawling ballads, and shivering with the cold.

Other indirect evidence of the early Irish ballad trade exists in the form of newspaper reports and printers' advertisements. Of the former, perhaps the most interesting is a piece in the *Dublin Gazette* of 1712/13, which mentions the Dublin printing of two murder ballads, both in the Palatine, and while refuting their validity, relates their contents. The first title is especially designed to pique prurient interest:

> A true Discovery of this Barbarous and Bloody Murder on the Body of Sarah Walker, by a Palatine innkeeper in the County of Kildare, who is suspected to make it his common way of devouring and trappaning of several men and women that pass'd that way. Together with the manner of his Salting their Bodies in Barrels, and made use of the same for eating.[5]

Meanwhile, an advertisement by a ballad-singer named John Hicks, of "Smoke-Alley" (Smock Alley) appears in the *Dublin Flying Post* of 6 July 1708, recommending "all sorts of the Newest Song Books and Ballads" to "Country Chap-Men" and others. The Reindeer at Mountrath Street is mentioned several times: in c. 1722, as the publisher for "The Weaver's Lamentation"; in the same year, for the "Printing and Selling a Seditious Ballad,"[6] in 1723, in relation to the piracy of a speech "learnedly compil'd and Publish'd 3 Months ago by the Ingenious Society of Ballad-Singers of Mountrath Street; and later still, in connection with Goldsmith's putative youthful ballad-making in the 1740s. It is thus clear that the Mountrath establishment was a site of ballad-printing for several decades,[7] and the dearth of surviving sheets probably reflects the ephemerality of such "low-grade publications" rather than a lack of trade.[8] Ballad sheets in the Gilbert Library in Dublin from the 1720s (albeit of the more upmarket variety) contribute a number of printers' names, including George Faulkner in Pembroke-Court Castle-street, Elizabeth Sadlier, on Blind-Key, S. Powell in Crane-lane, Tho. Fleming at the Salmon in High Street Dublin, and John Harding, in Molesworth Court. As Hugh Shields comments, "Evidence is available … that printers were numerous from the late seventeenth century. … [although] it is a measure of the domestic scale of the industry that the same person appears, at one time as a printer or seller, at another as a singer, of ballads."[9]

The earliest Irish-printed ballad we can date with any certainty is "Mount Taragh's Triumph, which bears a Dublin 1626 imprint. Set to the tune of "Mr. Basse, His Career" or "Hunting the Hare," it describes a "loyalty pageant" held in honor of Charles I at the Hill of Tara.[10] Like many of the ballads printed in Ireland or imported from England through at least the first quarter of the eighteenth century, it is topical and obviously aimed primarily at an educated, English-speaking audience. Many of the political ballads printed in Ireland during the same period are no less "loyal," and (when dealing with matters Jacobite) frankly anti-Catholic. Typical is "Labour Lost: Or, A New Ballad upon the Abdication of three Blunderbs A——n, and Scurvy R——r; together with their Wives, who are gone to the Bath, to Improve their tails, as their Husbands are gone London, to Improve their Understandings":

> God prosper long our Noble QUEEN,
> Our Lives and Safeties all;
> A damn'd Rebellion once there did
>   In IRELAND befall.
> To Vex the QUEEN, and Check the State,
> The Whigs have found a way,
> The Child may rue that is unborn,
> Their having so much sway.[11]

By contrast, the London-printed "Blackbird, or the Flower of England flown" (c. 1718), which is still current in Irish oral tradition, presents a perspective that is at once thoroughly Jacobite—and Irish—in tone. The song employs the blackbird as a figure for James III (the Old Pretender) and is composed in an elegant, Latinate style employing internal rhymes similar to those typical of later "hedge schoolmaster" songs:[12]

Upon a fair morning for soft recreation,
I heard a fair lady making her moan,
With sighing and sobbing and sad lamentation
Saying, my Black Bird most royal is flown;
My thoughts they deceive me,
Reflections do grieve me,
And I am over-burthened with sad misery,
Yet if death it should blind me,
As true love inclines me,
My Black Bird I'll seek out wherever he be.[13]

During the 1720s, there was a flurry of topical balladry in Dublin associated both with Jonathan Swift and his various causes, as well as with other polemicists, satirists, and political commentators. There is some dispute over the attribution of a number of ballads to Swift, but items like "Ireland's Warning … an Excellent New Song, upon Wood's Base Half-pence" and "An Excellent New Song Upon His Grace Our good Lord Archbishop of Dublin" (both attacking Wood's unregulated coinage) are commonly accepted as his own productions. More dubious is the "Song Upon the Late Grand-Jury"—which, if it is by Swift, is an example of his writing "two degrees above Grub Street":

There's Donevan, Hart, and Archer and Blood,
And Gibson and Gerard all true Men and good,
All Lovers of Ireland and Haters of Wood.
Which no body can deny.[14]

Irish-language poets, too, dabbled in this kind of balladry, including Peadar Ó Doirnín, whose "The Independent Man" also seems to have had a very specific genesis. Kieran Clendinning suggests that Ó Doirnín composed this ballad "as an advice" to his patron, William Brownlow of Lurgan, who stood in a particularly ugly county bye-election in 1753 for a seat in the Dublin Parliament.[15] The ballad urges the wisdom of remaining aloof from party politics and factions of all kinds:

In Heaven's great name, how can they blame
The poor man, or shame him, in the long run?
Ambition's their game, what else do they mean,
But purchase high fame, great power and fun?
They may swear a big oath that never they'll loath
The poor dupe that votes for them, 'tis their plan;
But I'll keep my own vote, I'll give it to none,
Then what need I care for a Parliament man?[16]

As Shields observes, "This 'municipal' tradition was anything but polite; it took invective and vituperation in its stride."[17] Not surprisingly, the idiom could also run towards indelicacy. One highly entertaining satirical ballad on Hugh Boulter, the then newly minted Archbishop of Armagh, printed in 1725–26 and set to the tune of "The Bishop of Canterbury," includes such verses as:

> One Day Importun'd by his L---day and -----r,
> To see Tinny Park and the great fall of Water.
> He begg'd their excuse but to please 'em he made,
> By the help of their W---r a Noble Cascade.[18]

Sub-genres of this tradition include both "good-nights" like the "Last Speech Confession and Dying Word of Francis McCade, William Cunneen and Edward Fox who are to be hung ... 14th ... May 1726, near St. Stephen's Green" and elegies on such figures as "The famous userer J——S——will who died raving mad" and "Madame Bently who Broak her neck Rideing towards Doney-Brook." This last contains a passage commenting wryly not only on the commonness of elegies but also on their sometimes cynically premature nature:

> Since it's grown a fashion so common
> That not a Whore, or Huckster Woman
> Or Bawd, or Butcher of the Town,
> Nor Thief, nor Rascal of Renown;
> But sometimes living, sometimes dead,
> Their Elegies are sung or said:
> And Ballad-makers for small fees,
> Do sing their Funeral Obleques.[19]

Many of the elegies I have examined from this period are—like the political ballads—more clearly poetic than balladic, obviously intended to be read rather than sung. A case in point is the 1720 elegy for James Cotter (also commemorated in multiple literary Gaelic laments) which appeared on a Cork-printed ballad-sheet, probably to be circulated at his execution. Its author seems to have been trying (vainly) to sound more like Shakespeare than Pope, but it served its purpose as topical commentary:

> And must he silent Dye, and Pitiless fall,
> No muse to Sum up now his Virtues all,
> He who the Poor's Chiefest support was,
> Supply'd their Wants, and Maintained their cause,

Lo! tho' ingratitude's the basest Crime,
That infects the most, in our Modern Times;
His Manhood, I hope, no Man will deny,
Nor dispute his Heroick Magnanimity?[20]

Other middle- to high-brow genres that appear in relatively cheap print in the early part of the century include the far more singable hunting and drinking songs, such as "The Drinking Match, A New Ballad in Imitation of Chevy Chace," written by "a Person of Quality." The long version of Ned Ward's "The Tipling Philosophers" was printed in Dublin in 1710, and the one-page setting of the original, short version in 1720. This version, "set by Mr. Leveridge and Sung at the Theatre in Dublin," apparently gave rise in 1721 to "The Ancient Philosophers Vindicated against Tipling, Written by a Young Lady," a riposte with all the charms of a temperance tract:

Now Tippling so common is grown, and Drunkenness is no
  more a Vice,
And Men must their Senses disown, if they would be thought
  to be wise,
A Drunkard is then a Divine, Religion in Liquor consists,
And Mankind may come in good Time, to be on the Leval with
  Beasts.[21]

The "Kilruddery Hunt" (1744) first turns up on the flyleaf of a copy of Allan Ramsay's *Tea-Table Miscellany* (with words by Dublin actor Thomas Mozeen and the air of "Síle Ó Ghadhra"). Commemorating a real hunt, the song later appeared in a 1762 Dublin ballad opera called *Midas*,[22] and was printed in at least one nineteenth-century chapbook.[23]

Hark, hark, jolly sportsmen, a while to my tale,
To claim your attention I'm sure it can't fail;
It's of lads and of horses and hounds that ne'er tire
O'er stone walls or hedges, through dales, bogs or briar;
A pack of such hounds or a set of such men--
It's a shrew chance if ever you meet such again;
Had Nimrod the mightiest of hunters been there,
'Fore Gad, he'd have shook like an aspin for fear.[24]

In the late 1720s we also begin to see printed evidence of the ballad opera craze: most of the popular English ballad operas of the day were performed and reprinted in Ireland. *The Beggar's Opera* was performed and published in Dublin in 1728, the year of its London debut. Gay's new theatrical genre was already being imitated by Dublin playwrights when, in 1729, first Chuck, or *The School-Boy's Opera*, then Charles Coffey's *The Beggar's Wedding*, were performed in Dublin at Smock-Alley.[25] Coffey incorporated not only the air of the British "Abbot of Canterbury" into his opera, but also Irish tunes like "Ellen a Roon" and "Lilliburlero." Later Irish-composed ballad operas, like the 1749 *Conspirators*, featured a song set to the tune of the popular "Rakes of Mallow" (still known in Irish tradition as a polka); while John O'Keefe's 1796 *Wicklow Mountains* used the air of "Éamonn an Cnoic" ("Ned of the Hill," a still popular eighteenth-century historical song) for one of its numbers.[26] Many of these songs, which reflect an increasing presence of Irish music and culture in printed balladry, were, one assumes, marketed initially to the middle-class ballad market.

Yet theater songs may well have also circulated orally before becoming available in chapbook form in the later part of the century. According to Sean Connolly, while the Dublin theater of the seventeenth and eighteenth centuries depended "heavily" on the upper classes, "there was also, from an early stage, a significant popular audience for its productions." In 1698, John Dunton remarked that the theater was "free to all classes and gives entertainment as well to the broom man as the genteel peer." During the same period, Thomas Arne's aria "Water Parted from the Sea" was celebrated—along with an Italian castrato closely associated with it—in a Dublin street song set to the tune of "Over the Hills and Far Away," which itself was, of course, recirculated by *The Beggar's Opera*:

> Tenducci was a Piper's son,
> And he was in love when he was young,
> And all the tunes that he could play
> Was "Water parted from the *Say*."[27]

Not surprisingly, many British theater and pleasure-gardens songs found their way into the Irish-printed miscellanies that began to appear in mid- to late-century, such as *The Merry Companion* (Dublin, 1752), which included "Songs sung by Mr. Beard at Ranalagh-Gardens" and *The Chearful Companion* (Cork, 1770 and 1772), which advertised itself as a collection of "the most Favourite Songs and Airs Lately sung at the Theatres and Gardens." Collections from the last years of the century contained songs of a more popular stamp than those of the earlier anthologies, reflecting broader, less purely patrician tastes. These included *The Billington: or, Vocal Enchantress; and Town and Country Songster* (Dublin, 1787/90) and *The Irish Nosegay: Or, Songster's Companion. Being a Select Collection of the Newest and Best Songs of Every Species, and Adapted to Persons of Every Kind and Taste* (Dublin, 1789). The United Irishman anthology *Paddy's Resource* (printed in several editions in both Ireland and the United States, from 1795) is—in its political focus—somewhat anomalous amongst these songsters, but it is clear that it aimed at roughly the same class: its melodies are drawn primarily from the Vauxhall repertoire and Ramsay's *Tea-Table Miscellany* (perhaps via Johnson's *Scots Musical Museum*), while its lyrics reflect influences from Burns, topical balladry, theater songs, and neoclassical poetry.

By the later part of the century, we also find an increasing number of less expensive eight-page songsters. Although they may have existed in Ireland since the early 1700s,[28] a mere three survive from the 1750s, and only thirty-five more from the 1760s. There are a few extant songbooks from the '70s, although far more from the '80s and '90s, followed by a notable increase in production until slip ballads gradually displaced them from about 1825.[29] In appearance, these little books are comparable to those produced in Britain, often featuring songs as "new," with woodcuts on their title pages, sometimes an indication of the melody to which the song is to be sung, and more rarely an author's or performer's name. Remarks John Moulden, from "the generally poor paper, the poor quality of the impressions, the type faces and decorations, the misprints, misspellings and omissions[,] it is obvious that, in the main, the section of the printing trade which generated them was at its cheap and limitedly skilled extreme."[30]

Because of their cheapness, it is easy to assume that these small songbooks were marketed solely to the less affluent. While this is probably true to a large degree, it is also possible that the widest possible public was intended. For example, some songbooks featured only pastorals and sentimental songs, or—as in the case of one songbook printed in 1784 (probably in Dublin)—mainly theater songs, including Hook's "To the Greenwood," "The Western Dame," "Jockey and Moggy," "Vauxhall Watch," and "Willy's Rare," and sporting a classical-theatrical woodcut somewhat more refined than the cruder variety usually associated with eight-page songbooks of the era. In other words, printers may have been identifying "niche" markets—in this case, a specifically middle-class one. On the other hand, members of the less prosperous classes—perhaps those who frequented the upper galleries in Dublin—may also have enjoyed such fare and thus have constituted potential buyers. By issuing such songs in both chapbook and the more expensive miscellany form, printers could embrace the broadest possible market. Some of the earlier topical single-sheet ballads of the period also reflect varying degrees of poetic and linguistic sophistication, leading me to believe that even in the early part of the century a range of registers rather than a dichotomy of elite and popular characterized the ballad trade.

Although fewer than two hundred Irish-printed eight-page songbooks survive from the period and generalizations are therefore provisional, there is clearly a preponderance of British material in many of the surviving late eighteenth-century chapbooks.[31] Toward the end of the century, however, we begin to see more Irish-composed narrative ballads both in imitation of British ballads and in new Anglo-Irish hybrid styles. A good example of the first category is a garland entitled *The Dublin Tragedy, or the Unfortunate Merchant's Daughter*, which tells "of a rich Merchant's Daughter in the town of Belfast, who was deluded by an Ensign in the army, and for love of him, dressed herself in man's apparel, and sailed with him to England." In style it could easily be taken for an early to mid-century British ballad, except for the slight awkwardness and artificiality of the diction:

> Ye lovers far and near, unto me lend an ear,
> Whilst I relate a doleful tragedy.
> 'Twill make your hearts to bleed
> It's known full well to be no falsity.[32]

More sure-handed are songs like the good-night ballad "The Dublin Baker" (also known as "The Wild and Wicked Youth" or "The Irish Robber's Adventure"):

> In Dublin sity I was bred and born,
> In Stephen's Green I died in scorn;
> I served my time to the baking trade
> And was always counted a roving blade.[33]

A ballad of comparable quality is "Sewball" (better known as "Skewball"), which describes a horse race that took place in the Curragh in 1752:[34]

> Come gentlemen sportsmen, I pray listen all,
> And I'll sing you a song in praise of Sewball,
> And how he came over you shall understand,
> It was by Lord Melvin the peer of the land.[35]

In fact, by the second half of the century, the narrative broadside ballad or "come-all-ye" form, with its long lines and typical aabb rhymes, had become so naturalized in Ireland that its adoption there amounted to "something like a takeover."[36] Some ballads of Irish composition (especially of the returned sailor type) are almost indistinguishable from their British counterparts—and in some cases represent mere localizations. The sharing of ballad airs can make provenance even more difficult to determine. As John Moulden puts it, "There is a case, in the evidence of influence from Britain upon the English language song culture of Ireland, and in evidence of the reverse process, for considering the English language song culture of Ireland and Britain as that of a unified area."[37] To this area may be added the United States: A solitary verse of the song "Rose Connelly," long thought to be an American ballad, appears in the Bunting/Lynch manuscripts.[38] Dating from the late eighteenth or early nineteenth century, it contains a warning verse typical of the murder ballad genre:

> All you young men and maidens I pray you take warning by me
> and never court your true love down under a Hogier [ozier] Tree.
> The devil & his temptations it was that came over me
> And I murdered my Rosey Conolly all under a Hogier Tree.[39]

In the last two decades of the century, however, a number of extant chapbooks, particularly from Limerick and Monaghan, include increasing amounts of Irish-composed material that reflect the influence of Irish language, poetry, and culture. Ornate hedge schoolmaster songs (see note 12), like "Castlehyde" and "The North Country Beauty," are plentiful. "The North Country Beauty" begins with what amounts to a set piece for such songs, including a standard apostrophe to the muses:

> You inspired Muses of sense and knowledge
> To me your mighty aid impart,
> To praise a Maiden who has inslaved me,
> And stole away my tender heart;
> Her majestic carriage is so enticing,
> Surpasses Hellen that Grecian queen,
> Or the bright Awrelia in all her splendor,
> Could never equal this comely Dame.[40]

A few songs of the hedge schoolmaster type contain a line or two of Gaelic, spelled phonetically according to an orthography based on English—a practice reflecting the emphasis on literacy in that language. One such is "Pearlha Nhe Kilthee Bawne" ("The Pearl of the Yellow Tresses," Monaghan, 1788):[41]

> One morning as I roved down by a shady grove,
> Where birds did sing harmonious,

Within their downy throats they warbled pretty notes,
In concert they sang melodious;
Encompassed by a shade I saw a comely maid,
Whose charms did soon trepan me,
In cruel Cupid's chain, all for that blooming dame,
Called Pearlha nhe kilthec bawne.[42]

The composer of "Terry O'Brien's Adventure," a genuine macaronic song (that is, containing a significant amount of both Gaelic and English lyrics), had an earthier approach to romance:

It was in Ennis Clare on an Easter Sunday morning,
There I drank full plenty with Molly my darling
Of punch and liquor of the best till we both grew hearty,
Then to bed we did repair, I cared not for her party,
But sported till break of day
Law an Ennish caur er mhading donough causka
Diolas f an ma youghante molly creenaf partee
Da lin morshin er licbo veen, keanh clooher faustah,
Eg ery dooh er mhadin da leg she gaureal
Agus dolemur flauna no gea.[43]

Shields, in evaluating these sometimes indecipherable macaronic texts, speculates that "Prestige value must have dominated these Irish sheets … Perhaps the macaronic sheets, with alternating lines or verses in the respective languages, represent a compromise between intelligibility and cultural prestige."[44] One song completely in Irish phonetics ("Eibhlín a Rún" or "Ducatu no vanutu") appears in the 1776 edition of *The Charms of Melody*, probably because of the popularity of the air after its inclusion in Coffey's *Beggar's Wedding* in 1729. "Ileen Oge" or "Savourneen Deelish," which appeared in a 1791 opera by George Colman and was later reprinted in both English and Irish slip ballads and chapbook collections, contains a one-line refrain in phonetic Irish. David Cooper notes that there was a "craze for Irish folk music" in Britain during the 1780s, which may account for the greater number of Irish and pseudo-Irish songs that appear in British-printed eight-page songbooks of this period.[45] The "craze" itself may have been at least partly due to the popularity of Irish ballad operas, many of which, as we have already seen, drew upon exotic "native" melodies.

Remarkably, a few singable translations of a number of Irish-Gaelic songs also appear in several surviving chapbooks, including "Byncheen Louahrea" ("An Binsín Luachra," or "The Little Bunch of Rushes"),[46] "The Mayo Maid Deceived" ("Idir Caiseal agus Durlas"—"Between

Cashel and Thurles"),[47] and a particularly elegant English version of "Tá Daoine a' Rádh" ("The People Are Saying") by one "Mr. Doyle," which was printed in Monaghan in 1789. The only known Irish version of this song was collected and published by Enrí Ó Muirgheasa in 1934. It begins:

> Tá daoine a' *rádh* go bhfuil *grádh* ag mo *mhui*rnín orm *fhéin*,
> Go deimhin má *tá* chan *grádh* gan *cu*mann dó *é*;
> Ar neamh-chead mo *cháir*de agus a *lán* de mo *mhuin*ntir-se *fhéin*
> Mur mairidh mé *ráithe* go *sás*óchaidh mé m'*in*tinn bheag *fhéin.*[48]

Doyle's translation runs:

> This country de*clare* sin*cere* that my sweet heart loves me,
> I'm very well *pleas'd* I *swear,* the truth it may be;
> In spight of re*la*tions that *tease* us to never prove kind,
> If I live but one *quar*ter my *dar*ling will *plea*sure my mind.[49]

I have italicized assonantal rhymes in both the original and the translation. Note that while Mr. Doyle retained much of the internal rhyming of the original, he adopted the aabb perfect end-rhyme more typical of the English broadside ballad.

Other signs of native linguistic influence in Irish printed ballads, both narrative and lyric, are reflected in such linguistic traits as the anachronistic English pronunciation of "ea" to rhyme with "say," the rhyming of words like "born" and "harm," or the use of Hiberno-English expressions like "a tall a tall." P. W. Joyce, in *English As We Speak It in Ireland*, points out a number of examples of Hiberno-Irish in Irish song, including the use of "be" to stand for the indicative of the verb, as in the phrase "I'll seek out my Blackbird wherever he be";[50] or the inversion of the object and the past participle, as in the line "This lovely charming maid, who has me betrayed," from "Pearlha Nhe Kilthee Bawne." John Moulden notes the presence of Ulster dialect in the orthography of a number of northern ballads he has examined, such as the spelling of "they" as "the."[51] Dialect was, of course, also employed by the "weaver poets" of northeast Ulster for whom, however, it was often a matter of choice; like Burns, James Orr could also compose highly fluent neoclassical verse.[52] The use of characteristically Irish assonantal rhyme instead of perfect rhyme is also common, especially in the schoolmaster songs. Obviously these traits reflect not only Irish cultural influence but Irish oral influence, in that they are features of colloquial speech.

Another uniquely Irish contribution to printed balladry is the Dublin slang or dialect song, like "Larry's Ghost" and "De Night before Larry was stretch'd," which first appear in late-century eight-page songbooks. While Andrew Carpenter regards these as genuine lowlife street ballads, "collected" and printed by parties unknown,[53] Hugh Shields classifies them as middle-class compositions, to be found not only in chapbooks but also in the manuscript of a contemporary Gaelic scribe who noted that they were "quite the Ton with the elegant Inhabitants of Dublin in the year One Thousand Seven Hundred and Eighty Eight."[54] I tend to agree with Shields that such language is too contrived for these songs to represent vernacular tradition—although this does not mean they did not have broad appeal.[55] A verse from "Larry's Ghost" runs:

> May de Devil take Judges and all,
> And sweep all de Jury away,
> Dat left here poor Molly to bawl,
> And buried poor Larry in clay.
> Bekaise why he hadn't de chink.[56]

A few Irish-composed patriotic songs and even whole eight-page songbooks survive from late eighteenth century and very early nineteenth century. These include "Granua's Advice to her Children," "The Rights of Man," "The Establishment of Irish Freedom," "The Vine-Cover'd Hills," "The Irish Lamentation at Achrun," and an undated Dublin eight-page songbook called *The True Born Irishman, Containing an Excellent Collection of Patriotic Songs*. Overall, however, the proportion of such songs is slight in comparison with other genres; and occasional items like the pro-Georgian "Hibernia's Resolution" and "Hibernia's Glory," warning against a French invasion, run counter to them politically. Intriguing but exceptional are songs like "A Friendly Caution" and "The Peep-of Day Boys," both concerned with regional rather than national politics. My own examination of songs printed during this period leads me to concur with John Moulden, Hugh Shields, Georges-Denis Zimmermann, and others that patriotic songs "make up a fairly small proportion of the chapbook texts of the early nineteenth century." By contrast, as William Allingham was later to note, "Nearly one-half of the whole number [of available ballads] owe their inspiration to Cupid."[57]

Many Irish ballads reflect both British influence and native linguistic, metric, or thematic influence, constituting hybrid forms, in which British broadside ballad conventions coexist with varying degrees of Irish influence. For example, "Mc. Clure's Rambles," printed in Down around

1807, like Doyle's "The People Are Saying" (see above) combines a five-stress *amhrán* meter with aabb broadside rhyme:

> Of late a strong notion of rambling entangled my mind,
> To seek out dame fortune my strong resolution inclin'd,
> I set to the road like a rover with staff in my hand,
> And I never delay'd till I came to the town of Strabane.[58]

Such heterogeneous influence is also evident in the combination of song genres. For instance, hedge schoolmaster songs, native song genres like the *aisling* and the place-praise song, and naturalized continental song-forms like the *pastourelle* and the *reverdie* sometimes combined with the neoclassical pastoral to create new, uniquely Irish forms.[59] A number of these conventions also appear in narrative ballads: A 1789 version of a well-known heiress abduction ballad called "Willy Reilly and his Cooleen Bawn," while in most respects following both metric and narrative conventions of the British broadside form, begins with a classic *reverdie* opening:

> 'Twas on a pleasant morning all in the blooming spring
> When as the chearful songsters in consert did sing,
> The primrose and daisy bespangled every lawn,
> In [an] arbour I espied my sweet Cooleen Bawn.[60]

Some ballad-singers—and perhaps chapmen—composed their own ballads, as, apparently, did several printers.[61] Many ballads were reprinted from memory, dictation, or from stock purchased or inherited by the printer.[62] Other ballads were commissioned or sold to printers by local poets, as appears to have been the case with the songwriters J. R. R. Adams dubbed the Laggan "poet-laureates." Adams's study of several song-poets of the Laggan area in eastern Donegal during the first decade of the nineteenth century emphasizes the ease with which such poetasters could get their poems published, using printers like John and Robert Buchanan of Londonderry, who sold garlands "primarily to the chapmen," supplying them "on the lowest terms." While, as Adams comments, "Most of the garlands consisted of standard fare, pirated from many sources … a proportion were severely local, plainly intended for circulation in the Laggan."[63] Several of these indicate authorship, and some of the songs, if not actually written by hedge schoolmasters or poor scholars, certainly reflect "hedge school education in all its glory."[64]

At least one notable Irish-language poet (also a schoolmaster) contributed to the more popular end of eighteenth-century narrative balladry: Eoghan Rua Ó Súilleabháin composed "Rodney's Glory" to celebrate ("with more panegyric than narration") an English naval victory in 1782, which vice-admiral Rodney himself thought "the severest ever fought at sea, and the most glorious for England," and in which Ó Súilleabháin had participated as "an ordinary seaman." His motivation for writing the ballad seems to have been unrelated to his usual poetic business, as he hoped thereby to secure his discharge from the British navy.[65] Although he employs an unusual hornpipe meter and matching rhyme scheme for his ballad, Ó Súilleabháin's style reflects sufficient acquaintance with contemporary street ballads in general, and sea battle ballads in particular, to imitate them not only in subject and style but also in diction and scansion.[66] The earliest surviving printed text appears in a Limerick-printed eight-page songbook from 1782:

> Give ear you British hearts of gold,
> That do disdain to be controuled,
> Good news to you I will unfold,
> 'Tis of brave Rodney's glory;
> Who always bore a noble heart,
> And from his colours never would start,
> Against any foes that dare oppose,
> Or blast the bloom of the English rose,
> But now observe my story.[67]

Alas, despite Rodney's warm reception of his crewman's tribute, Ó Súilleabháin's request was denied.

In attempting to determine the impact of the printed ballad on the popular oral repertoire, some scholars have pointed to the increasing availability of inexpensive texts toward the end of the eighteenth century. As John Moulden notes, the change from ballad sheet to chapbook form "meant more songs could be sold more cheaply and it may indicate that the printers believed that the potential existed for an extension of the market."[68] This presumes not only greater literacy but also sufficient income to afford such books. According to Moulden, in the early part of the eighteeth century, the price of eight-page songbooks "seems generally to have been ½d."[69] By the early nineteenth century, many chapbooks were still sold for as little as threepence each, a figure which has led Niall Ó Ciosáin—after weighing both the average wages and expenditures of unskilled laborers at the time against the price of chapbooks—conclude that such a book, "while perhaps a luxury, was not an impossible one."[70] Chapbook culture may have at once reflected and sped the increase of literacy among the general populace. Reports of ballads or other ephemera being pasted on walls for public reading are few but telling, as in the 1736 comment of a Dublin printer who explained the poor quality of a religious leaflet which was merely designed "for pasting up in the several apartments in houses, being worthy of the perusal of old and young, who have a desire to live and die well." As early as 1716, a Dublin bishop requested that one of his tracts be reprinted as a broadside and sold for 1d, since "such papers as are designed for every body's reading ought as near as may be to be accommodated to every body's purse as well as capacity."[71]

Reading aloud was of course practiced in Ireland as well as in Britain—although obviously sung performance would have spread song far more efficiently and required even fewer copies of the text. In districts where songbooks contained unfamiliar material, children who were taught English in the schools—or the schoolmasters themselves—could have acted as mediators for illiterate and/or Irish-speaking adults. While we have no specific reports of chapmen or hawkers singing songs from the books they sold, they too might have disseminated songs and their melodies. Ultimately, however, even if a songbook failed to indicate its songs' melodies, as one twentieth-century farmer is supposed to have commented after purchasing a ballad, "I've got the words now. I can go to the mountains for the air."[72]

Unfortunately, we have little to go on when it comes to knowing precisely which printed ballads actually entered the oral song tradition during the eighteenth and early nineteenth centuries. However, some of the earlier song transcriptions in the Bunting Collection afford us some glimpses into what was popular at the beginning of the nineteenth century. This collection includes either melodies or texts collected from singers for a wide variety of songs associated with previously or currently printed ballads, including "Shule Aroon" (a descendant of a seventeenth-century British ballad called "The North-countrey Maids resolution & love to her Sweetheart," which after coming to Ireland obtained an Irish refrain),[73] "Molly Bawn," Gay's "'Twas When the Seas Were Roaring," the Scottish Jacobite ballad "My Laddie Can Fight, and My Laddie Can Sing," and such "raking" songs as "Staca an Mhargaidh" and "Whist the Cat from under the Table."[74]

Patrick Kennedy's memoirs, *The Banks of the Boro* and *Evenings in the Duffrey*, recalling events from the author's youth in County Wexford around 1819–21,[75] also gives us some insight into the repertoire of the period, since many of the songs Kennedy mentions could be found in print in England or Ireland twenty years or more before this time. Among those Kennedy quotes are variants of an unexpectedly high number of Child ballads, including "Lord Bateman," "Sir Hugh," and "Young Hunting";

versions of later British broadside ballads like "Pretty Polly Oliver," "The Faithless Sea Captain," and "The Golden Glove"; hedge schoolmaster songs, like "Castlehyde," "The Colleen Rue," "The Cottage Maid," and "Sheela na Guira,"; as well as other Irish-composed ballads like "The Bantry Girls' Lament for Johnny," "The Royal Blackbird," and "The Banks of Clody." In addition there are texts that belong to two subgenres already attested in print by at least the 1820s: comic songs, such as "The Connaught Man at the Review," "The Widow's Pig," "Billy O'Rourke" (apparently of proto-music hall or song and supper club origin); as well as songs of sensibility with an Irish patina, like "Gra Gal Machree" and "Bouchal na Gruaga dhowna," in the sentimental tradition of late eighteenth-century Vauxhall song. Kennedy also includes songs by local song-poets, like the schoolmasterly "Banks of the Urrin" by John Rogers and a verse by the more plebeian Mickey Connors.[76]

While not all of these songs were necessarily learned from print (in fact Kennedy sometimes informs the reader that they were learned from servants or were, in fact, "never seen in print"), all either had a life in printed form or were influenced by eighteenth-century genres that did.[77] Kennedy also makes it clear that both manuscript and print were sometimes employed in the composition and dissemination of ballads. *In Evenings in the Duffrey*, he describes how Mickey Connors, having been entertained by

> a poor honest goose-plucker … at Molly Finn's *public* … composed an ode in his honour on the spot; and so pleased was the poor, simple, vain creature, that he took the manuscript to Wexford town, got some quires printed, and employed himself singing it at fair and market till he became a thorough tinker.[78]

Wexford may not have been typical of Ireland generally, since it was more heavily Anglicized than many areas—and it is clear that some of the singers are modestly middle-class—but it supplies at least a partial portrait of the song tradition during the period. It is also interesting to see the overlap in repertoire in Kennedy's memoirs and Gerald Griffin's 1827 *Suil Dhuv, the Coiner*, which mentions "The Red-Haired Man's Wife," "The Colleen Rue," and "Sheela na Guira."[79] Since Griffin is primarily associated with Limerick and Cork, we can infer that at least two of the hedge schoolmaster songs popular in Wexford had currency elsewhere in the southern counties of Ireland during the beginning of the nineteenth century.

Despite the small number of these sources, they cite such a large proportion of songs found in cheap songbooks of the late eighteenth-century that—in combination with the other evidence we have seen—they confirm the impression that the printed ballad had made an appreciable impact on Irish culture in general and the song repertoire in particular in at least the more Anglicized parts of the country by the turn of the century. That these songs appeared in the context of an extensive oral tradition that absorbed and interacted with songs in print, is hardly surprising. As in Britain,

> The contents of [cheap print] did not destroy circulation by word of mouth. Sometimes it enshrined material from the oral realm; certainly it fed back into it. The written word helped instruct people in what to sing, what to retell, and how to express themselves in ways which greatly enhanced and enriched their cultural world.[80]

Examples of the interaction between vernacular and elite culture during this period in relation to ballads are relatively few and indirect: besides the presumed marketing of "low-brow" songs to the middle classes and "high-brow" ones to the commonalty, we possess only scattered accounts of the widespread popularity of theater songs, stories of Oliver Goldsmith's catholic taste in song, the participation of Irish-language poets like Ó Súilleabháin and Ó Doirnín in ballad composition, descriptions of the apparently ubiquitous ballad trade, the currency of hedge schoolmaster songs, the increasing but still patchy literacy of the country as a whole, and Patrick Kennedy's invaluable depiction of a singing community at the turn of the eighteenth century. Yet taken together they are highly suggestive of a less stratified, more "democratic" song culture than most associate with folk tradition, similar to that which Thomas Crawford has ascribed to Scotland: a tradition in which, at least in certain areas, like Kennedy's part of Wexford, "practically everybody took part," and in which literary and elite influences intermingled with more popular ones to produce a unique repertoire in the context—in some cases, at least—of a more or less heterogeneous social and cultural milieu.[81] Social historian Sean Connolly has distinguished between "an élite culture defined by transmission through the printed word, its access to the worlds of law and high politics, and its observance of a particular code of politeness and behaviour" and a "culture of the common people: not necessarily illiterate, but primarily dependent on the spoken word, governed by custom and ritual, localistic, community-minded, and conservative."[82] Yet he has also pointed out numerous nexes of cultural interchange in eighteenth-century Ireland, ranging from festivals and sporting events, to dress, diet, and music, noting complaints about dairymaids wearing hoops and harpers performing Charles Dibdin melodies.[83] "Linked by the bridges of shared interest, patronage, and emulation of social superiors," the various strata of Irish culture have never existed wholly in isolation from each other.[84]

By the late eighteenth century, the Irish had made an indelible mark upon the printed balladry of their own country, as well as that of Britain (and, ultimately, North America), contributing much that was distinctive and singular to the genre and adding richness and complexity to the singing traditions of the entire English-speaking world. This contribution was reflected linguistically and generically in the many new song-forms that emerged not only from the integration of English and Irish influences in both narrative and lyric ballads but also in the emergence of genres like the Irish macaronic song, translations from the Gaelic, Dublin slang songs, and the many sub-types of the ever-popular hedge schoolmaster song that flourished in both print and oral tradition. Throughout the eighteenth century, cultural and social interaction also led to the widespread ownership of a number of cultural forms, including the printed ballad. While this was true to a great extent of England, as well, the phenomenon was much more pronounced in the Irish and Scottish traditions, where general respect for knowledge and education of a sort that embraces both oral and written forms helped to ensure the continuing vitality of the verbal arts, read, spoken, or sung. It is no coincidence that both Scotland and Ireland retained a thriving and rich oral tradition (along with their written ones) long after that of England had become moribund.

NOTES

1. Adam Fox, *Oral and Literate Culture in England 1500–1700* (Oxford and New York, 2000), 11.

2. Hugh Shields, "Ballads, Ballad Singing and Ballad Selling," in *Popular Music in Eighteenth-Century Dublin* (Dublin: Folk Music Society of Ireland and Na Píobairí Uilleann, 1985), 26.

3. Hugh Shields, *Narrative Singing in Ireland: Lays, Ballads, Come-All-Yes and Other Songs* (Blackrock: Irish Academic Press, 1993), 43. This is Shields's translation, although *fuar* could also mean without value, profit, or interest.

4. Donal O'Sullivan, "A Courtly Poem for Sir Richard Cox," *Éigse* 4 (1943–44): 284–7. My translation.

5. Quoted in Shields, *Narrative Singing*, 97.

6. Shields, *Narrative Singing*, 99.

7. We have records of printers (primarily the Goulding family) operating at premises from 1724 to at least 1764. See John Moulden "The Printed Ballad in Ireland: A Guide to the Popular Printing of Songs in Ireland, 1760–1920" (PhD diss., National University of Ireland, Galway, 2006), 969.

8. Shields, *Narrative Singing*, 28.

9. Shields, *Narrative Singing*, 44–5.

10. Moulden, "The Printed Ballad," 176.

11. British Library (hereafter BL), shelfmark: 1890.e.5. (120), Dublin, c. 1713.

12. "Hedge schoolmaster songs" are those songs either composed by or in the style of the Irish schoolmaster poets of the eighteenth and nineteenth centuries. "Hedge schoolmasters" were illegal instructors of community-supported Catholic or non-Conformist schools. Their verse is typified by Latinate word forms, classical allusions, and flowery, sometimes grandiloquent, language.

13. BL 1876.f.1.(86), London, 1718. See also Andrew Carpenter, ed. *Verse in English from Eighteenth-Century Ireland* (Cork: Cork University Press, 1998), 126.

14. BL C.121.g.9.(188), Dublin (J. Harding), 1723.

15. Kieran Clendinning, "The Armagh Bye-Election of 1753," *Review: Journal of the Craigavon Historical Society* 2.1, <http://www.craigavonhistoricalsociety.org.uk/rev/clendinningarmaghelection.html>.

16. Seán de Rís, *Peadar Ó Doirnín: a Bheatha agus a Shaothar* (Baile Átha Cliath: Oifig an tSoláthair, 1969), 47.

17. Shields, "Ballads," 26.

18. "An Excellent New Ballad," BL 1890.e.5.(32), Dublin, 1725–26.

19. Quoted in Moulden, "The Printed Ballad," 179.

20. "On the Unfortunate, tho' much Lamented Death of James Cotter Esq., who was Executed at Cork on the 7th of May 1720 for Ravishing Elizabeth Squib a Quaker," quoted in Breandán Ó Buachalla, "The Making of a Cork Jacobite," *Cork History and Society*, ed. P. O'Flanagan and C. G. Buttimer (Cork, 1993), 490.

21. "The Ancient Philosophers Vindicated against Tipling, Written by a Young Lady," (Dublin, 1721), ECCO, Gale Group, <http://galenet.galegroup.com>.

22. Shields, *Narrative Singing*, 99.

23. Moulden, "The Printed Ballad," 593.

24. Hugh Shields, *Old Dublin Songs*, ed. High Shields (Dublin: Folk Music Society of Ireland, 1988), 12–14 and 68.

25. Although others have attributed the opera to Colley Cibber, Gagey believes *Chuck* to be of Irish origin. Edmond M. Gagey, *Ballad Opera* (NewYork and London: Benjamin Blom, 1937), 105 and 90.

26. Shields, "Ballads," 29.

27. T. J. Walsh, *Opera in Dublin 1705–1797: The Social Scene* (Dublin: Allen Figgis, 1973), quoted in Shields, "Ballads." 29.

28. That is, at least, the probable date of the song; as John Moulden points out, "the song-book could have been printed at any time after that" (Moulden, "The Printed Ballad," 182, n. 27).

29. Moulden, "The Printed Ballad," 182–3 and 294. There is general agreement that these songbooks disappeared around 1840.

30. Moulden, "The Printed Ballad," 108.

31. Of the Ulster-printed songbooks or garlands during this period, J. R. R. Adams comments, "the prevailing atmosphere is English, with a scattering of Scottish and Irish songs." See J. R. R. Adams, *The Printed Word and the Common Man: Popular Culture in Ulster 1700–1900* (Belfast: The Institute of Irish Studies: The Queen's University of Belfast, 1987), 76.

32. Quoted in Hugh Shields, *Old Dublin Songs,* 26–30.

33. Quoted in Hugh Shields, *Old Dublin Songs*, 24–5.

34. Shields, *Narrative Singing*, 97. Shields tells us that this song is "precisely datable," but doesn't provide his source for this information.

35. BL 11606.aa.24, Glasgow, 1801. For a different text see Shields, *Narrative Singing*, 97.

36. Shields, *Narrative Singing*, 86.

37. Moulden, "The Printed Ballad," 358. The same is also true of dance tunes throughout the eighteenth century, with much exchange between Ireland, Scotland, and England in evidence.

38. Edward Bunting (1773–1843), who transcribed the music performed at the 1792 Belfast Harp Festival, was the first Irish collector known to acquire melodies (and later, with the help of assistants Patrick Lynch and James Cody, song-texts) "in the field." His three published volumes of airs (and in one case newly-composed English lyrics), which appeared in 1796, 1809, and 1840, featured arrangements for pianoforte and were aimed at a middle and upper class audience. For a brief assessment of Bunting's work, see *The Companion to Irish Traditional Music*, ed. Fintan Valleley (Cork: Cork University Press, 1999), 46–8.

39. Bunting Collection 33.5 (28), Queen's University, Special Collections Belfast. Although he was not aware of this verse, D. K. Wilgus wrote an extremely informative article on the song. See his "Rose Connoley": An Irish Ballad," *Journal of American Folklore* 92, no. 2 (1979): 172–95.

40. BL 11622df,(2), Monaghan, 1788.

41. Niall Ó Ciosáin quotes the editor of a 1736 edition of *Gallagher's Sermons* as regretting the lack of Irish types, adding, however, "that scarce one in ten is acquainted with her characters." Ó Ciosáin also quotes an 1858 editor of Tadhg Gaelach Ó Súillebháin's *Pious Miscellany* as saying that "if we did adopt the Irish, those for whom the work is intended would not be able to use it, being entirely unacquainted with that character, whereas every peasant who speaks Irish and reads English can master the work in its present form." See Niall Ó Ciosáin, *Print and Popular Culture in Ireland, 1750–1850* (Houndmills, Basingstoke, Hampshire: Macmillan; New York: St. Martin's Press, 1997), 159–60.

42. BL 11622.df34.(2), Monaghan, 1788.

43. BL 11622.df.51.(9), Limerick, 1810(?). The Irish is a translation of the English. I give the orthography as found in the chapbook.

44. Hugh Shields, "Printed Aids to Folk Singing, 1700–1900," in *The Origins of Popular Literacy in Ireland*, ed. Mary Daly and David Dickson (Dublin,1990), 147.

45. David Cooper, "Lámh Dearg: Celtic Minstrels and Orange Songsters," *Celtic Cultural Studies, An Interdisciplinary Online Journal* (1999), <http://www.celtic-cultural-studies.com/papers/01/cooper-01.html>.

46. BL 11622.df.34.(5), Limerick, late eighteenth century.

47. This song appears in a folio-sized sheet Edinburgh-printed garland (BL 13476.m.7, Edinburgh, 1775) and in a Newcastle-printed chapbook, in which it is followed by a much clumsier, almost certainly not Irish-composed ballad-style "answer" (BL 11621.c.3.(5), Newcastle, 1799 [?].

48. *Dhá Chéad de Cheoltaibh Uladh*, ed. Enrí Ó Muirgheasa (1934; Dublin: Oifig Dhíolta Foilseachán Rialtais, 1974), 83–4.

49. BL 11622.df.34.(13) Monaghan, 1789.

50. P. W. Joyce, *English As We Speak It in Ireland* (London: Longmans, Green, & Co.; Dublin: M. H. Gill & Son, 1910), 86–7.

51. Moulden, "The Printed Ballad," 85–6.

52. In fact, Carol Baraniuk claims that "in over eighty-five percent of his verses Orr shows a preference for neo-classical forms and Augustan English. See Carol Baraniuk, "James Orr: Ulster-Scot and Poet of the 1789 Rebelllon," *Scottish Studies Review* 6, no. 1 (Spring 2005): 23.

53. Carpenter, *Verse in English*, 430.

54. Quoted in Shields, "Ballads," 30.

55. Shields, Narrative Singing, 90–91.

56. From "Larry's Ghost," BL 11622.df.34.(37), W. Goggin, Limerick, 1788.

57. William Allingham "Irish Ballad Singers and Irish Street Ballads" *Ceol* 3, no. 2 (1967): 5. Georges-Denis Zimmermann has estimated that only 20–40% of printed ballads concerned politics (G. D. Zimmermann, Songs of Irish Rebellion (Dublin, 1967), 22.

58. Linen Hall Library, uncatalogued, Graham and Lennin, Downpatrick, 1807. I can imagine this being sung to the air of "Bean an Fhir Rua" ("The Red-Haired Man's Wife").

59. The *pastourelle* sometimes occurs in British ballads—more often in Scottish—but more rarely than in Irish ones.

60. BL 11622.df.34.(13) Monaghan, 1789.

61. Maura Murphy, "The Ballad Singer and the Role of the Seditious Ballad in Nineteenth-Century Ireland: Dublin Castle's View," *Ulster Folklife* 25 (1975): 96–97. See also Moulden, "The Printed Ballad," 122.

62. Moulden, "The Printed Ballad," Chapter 8, especially 103 and 197.

63. J. R. R. Adams, , "The Poets Laureate of Donegal: Rural Rhymers of the Laggan in the First Decade of the Nineteenth Century, *Ulster Folklife* 34 (1988): 69.

64. Adams, "Poets Laureate," 74.

65. Shields, *Narrative Singing*, 165.

66. The hornpipe scheme was used for "The Rakes of Mallow" and its relatives.

67. BL 11622.df.34.(4) Limerick, 1790[?].

68. Moulden, "The Printed Ballad," 185.

69. Moulden, "The Printed Ballad," 137.

70. Niall Ó Ciosáin, *Print and Popular Culture in Ireland, 1750–1850* (Houndmills, Basingstoke, Hampshire: Macmillan: New York : St. Martin's Press, 1997), 22–3. We have little even in the way of anecdotal information on sales until Gavin Duffy's comments on printers in the 1840s issuing "millions of yards annually of street ballads" and John Hand's claim that some O'Connellite ballads sold up to a million copies (see Moulden, "The Printed Ballad," 255).

71. Toby Barnard, "Learning, the Learned and Literacy in Ireland, c. 1660–1760," in A *Miracle of Learning: Studies in Manuscripts and Irish Learning*, ed.

Toby Barnard, Dáibhí Ó Cróinín, Katherine Simms (Aldershot: Ashgate, 1998), 220.

72. Seán O Boyle, *The Irish Song Tradition* (Dublin: Gilbert Dalton, 1976), 28.

73. Steve Gardham, "A Veritable Dungheap 18: "'Shule Agrah,'" *Musical Traditions* 164, <http://www.mustrad.org.uk/articles/dungheap.htm>.

74. Bunting Collection, Special Collections, Queen's University Belfast. Most of the songs I have noted were transcribed by Bunting's assistant, Patrick Lynch, from 1802–03.

75. Mary Ellen Cohane and Kenneth S. Goldstein, "Folksongs and the Ethnography of Singing in Patrick Kennedy's The Banks of the Boro," *The Journal of American Folkore* 109, no. 434 (Autumn, 1996): 425–36.

76. Kennedy, *Evenings in the Duffrey* (M'Glashan and Gill, 1869), 43.

77. For example, he cites "The Lady and the Farmer" as "one of those English ballads that he never saw in print, but that had been naturalized here a long time." See Patrick Kennedy, *The Banks of the Boro: A Chronicle of the County of Wexford* (1875; Enniscorthy: Duffrey Press, 1989), 116.

78. Kennedy, *Evenings*, 199. It is interesting to see even at this date the connection made between ballad-selling and travelers.

79. From *Suil Dhuv, the Coiner* (1827), cited in Moulden, "The Printed Ballad," 259.

80. Fox, *Oral and Literate Culture*, 9.

81. Thomas Crawford, "Lowland Song and Popular Tradition in the Eighteenth Century," in *The History of Scottish Literature*, II: 1660–1800, ed. Andrew Hook (Aberdeen: Aberdeen University Press, 1987), 123.

82. Sean Connolly, "'Ag Déanamh Commanding,' Élite Responses to Popular Culture, 1660–1850," in *Irish Popular Culture 1650–1850*, ed. James S. Donnelly, Sr. and Kerby A. Miller (Dublin: Irish Academic Press, 1998), 10.

83. Connolly, "'Ag Déanamh Commanding,'" 15.

84. Connolly, "'Ag Déanamh Commanding,'" 11.

Print, Performance, Personhood, Polly Honeycombe

DAVID A. BREWER

Print, performance, personhood, *Polly Honeycombe*. Four terms in my title; not many more pages to sketch out their interrelations. In some ways it helps that the first three are already so familiar to us (or at least we tend to think of them as familiar). Print has been more or less constantly on our scholarly radar for three or four decades; performance for at least two; depending on how we define it, personhood has been a category of interest since the dawn of anthropology, or perhaps is even coterminous with the humanities themselves. But the familiarity of these terms has rarely translated into very satisfying ways of thinking about their relations with one another. In general, we have tended to regard them as either strictly opposed to one another or else as so closely intertwined as to be, in effect, identical. So, for example, print has traditionally been set against performance as letter to its spirit, disembodiment to its corporeality, permanence to its ephemerality. Yet both terms have also been treated as the very negation of personhood, as purveyors of commodified or inauthentically "stagey" selves to be poised against that within which passeth show. More recently, of course, the converse (but structurally identical) view has often appeared: that personhood is nothing but performance, or that the subject positions hailed by various kinds of print are all that historians can ever recover. I am caricaturing, of course, but not, I think, particularly unfairly. For all the ways in which we have been taught to shun binary oppositions, our professional lives are still full of them, perhaps especially when it comes to thinking about the novel and the theater, which is what most discussions of eighteenth-century print and performance boil down to. Here, both in our scholarship and our curricula, there is a distressing (and distressingly frequent) tendency to go for all too easy, and just plain wrong, stories of supercession, in which, say, the drama is where the action is up to 1740, and then the novel just takes over and we don't have to worry about the playhouse anymore—often because, either as a corollary or an explanation, *people* were supposedly externally oriented and "theatrical" up to 1740, and then they turned inward, and the modern subject was born. Again, I caricature, but I have read enough manuscripts and looked at enough syllabi to feel sadly confident that while I am painting with a broad brush, the likeness is more than recognizable.[1]

Enter *Polly Honeycombe. A Dramatick Novel of One Act.* This text, an afterpiece by George Colman the Elder, was one of the most successful farces of the entire century. In its first three seasons, it received sixty-three performances in London, and appeared in three London editions. In the same period, it ran through at least four other editions—and, I strongly suspect, performances linked to those editions—in Cork, Dublin, and Edinburgh. And thereafter, it settled into a career as a repertory staple which lasted well into the nineteenth century.[2] Now farces are not where we generally go for shrewd theoretical insight. Rather, their appeal typically lies in their slapstick and broad humor, their stock situations and flat characters. But Colman is nothing if not clever, and so I would like to propose that there is a kind of vernacular theory to be drawn from *Polly Honeycombe*, if we can only open our eyes and prick up our ears long enough to attend to how it unfolds in the time and space of Drury Lane.

Farces are, of course, fundamentally plot-driven, and so we should probably begin by just sketching out what happens in *Polly Honeycombe*. Our heroine is a pert young woman who lives with her parents in the City (i.e., the commercial center of London), and delights in the romance and intrigue offered up by the circulating library. Indeed, she triumphantly proclaims that "A Novel is the only thing to teach a girl life, and the way of the world, and elegant fancies, and love to the end of the chapter."[3] Alas, her parents—a retired merchant and his cordial-swilling wife, who are continually kissing and fondling one another despite "their hard hands" and his "old gouty legs"—have a less romantic future in mind: they have contracted a marriage for her with "young Mr. Ledger, Mr. Simeon the Rich Jew's wife's nephew" (7, 5). Polly, undeterred by these plans, thrills at the prospect of running away: after all, "every girl elopes, when her parents are obstinate and ill natur'd about marrying her. It was just so with Betsy Thompson, and Sally Wilkins, and Clarinda, and Leonora in the history of Dick Careless, and Julia in the Adventures of Tom Ramble, and fifty others—Did not they all elope?

and so will I too. I have as much right to elope, as they had, for I have as much love and as much spirit as the best of them" (6). Soon enough these competing schemes collide, with the result that Polly rejects the financially-minded Ledger as "uglier than a figure of eight, and more tiresome than the multiplication-table" and so, as punishment, gets locked into her room by her father, where—Clarissa-like—she has cleverly hidden some writing materials, although she thinks hers display "a little more ingenuity" than those of Miss Harlowe (18, 23). Here her true love, Mr. Scribble, is waiting for her, disguised as a footman, and having been snuck in by the Nurse. After a near discovery by Mr. Honeycombe, the two lovers escape in a sedan chair, only to be chased down and brought back by Ledger and the servants. When confronted, Polly is utterly unrepentant, even after it is revealed that Ledger is but an attorney's clerk and her Nurse's nephew: "Lord, Papa, what signifies whose nephew he is? He may be ne'er the worse for that.—Who knows but he may be a Foundling, and a gentleman's son, as well as Tom Jones?" (40). The play closes with Polly once again rejecting Ledger (he is "as deceitful as Blifil, as rude as the Harlowes, and as ugly as Doctor Slop"), Mrs. Honeycombe getting ever more drunkenly confused (by this point, it is early afternoon, and so she has had her "Stomachick Draught" on top of her brandy-spiked tea), Ledger renouncing all claim to Polly (he would not "underwrite her for ninety *per cent*"), and Scribble and the Nurse sneaking off, leaving Mr. Honeycombe to rave: "Instead of happiness and jollity,—My friends and family about me,—A wedding and a dance,—And every thing as it should be,—Here am I, left by myself,—Deserted by my intended son-in-law—Bully'd by an attorney's clerk—My Daughter mad—My Wife in the Vapours—And all's in confusion.——This comes of Cordials and Novels.——Zouns, your Stomachicks are the Devil—And a man might as well turn his Daughter loose in Covent-garden, as trust the cultivation of her mind to A CIRCULATING LIBRARY" (41, 33, 43, 44).

I rehearse the plot at such length in order to drive home just how utterly drenched in convention, and yet completely unorthodox this all is: a combination which, I propose, is the source of its theoretical savvy for our purposes. Not only does Polly hit all her generic marks as an aspiring novelistic heroine, but so too do her parents, her suitors, even her nurse. They all work, as characters in farce need to work, as almost instantaneously recognizable types: the quixotic young woman, whose expectations of courtship are derived from the world of romance; the young man who gains a supposedly unwarranted access to her heart because of his ability to play to those expectations; the paternal blocking figure intent on a strictly prudential match. We have seen them all before, and so had the audiences of the early 1760s.[4] The difference between these characters as they're typically staged and what we get in *Polly Honeycombe*, though (what I termed the farce's "complete unorthodoxy") comes not from any great characterological innovations, but simply from the fact that the entire dramatis personae are all explicitly presented as engaged in imitation: there is not a supposed embodiment of "nature" among them. That is, all of the characters, not just Polly, are quixotic in the sense that they are embracing the roles they desire, rather than the roles which are properly "theirs" by virtue of their rank, age, gender, or anything else. However, some of them (like Polly, Scribble, perhaps the Nurse) *know* that they are doing so, while others—Mr. and Mrs. Honeycombe, Ledger—seem wholly unaware of the scripts they are following, and in that division lies the key to both their fates and our allegiances.

Take our heroine, for example: unlike most of the other novel-reading girls gone wild of the period, Polly never comes off as deluded. She never mistakes novelistic conventions for the actual way of the world, perhaps in part because she does not confine herself to novels: when told by the Nurse that she had "better read [her] prayer-book," she replies "Why so I do; but I'm reading this now" (5). Nor does her quixotism seem a rational, pragmatic response to the social constraints under which she is operating, as Arabella's behavior in *The Female Quixote* has often been explained. Rather, Polly's conduct comes off as high-spirited play, an acting out of novelistic form *as if* it could adequately capture her situation, knowing all the while that it cannot (but wouldn't it be pretty to think so?). Similarly, Scribble is not, at least primarily, the fortune-hunting cad that such cynically-attuned-to-novelistic-convention suitors are generally presented as being. Rather, he too seems to self-consciously enjoy the sheer theatricality of it all, the ways in which the whole affair "is like making love in a pantomime" or "a little amour" at the masquerade (26, 27). Far from being dismayed by the revelation of his true identity, he delights in Polly's vow to have him "though we go through as many distresses as Booth and Amelia," and he thinks her final rejection of Ledger "prodigious humour!" and "high fun"—presumably because it allows their show to go on (41).

Polly's parents and Ledger, on the other hand, betray no such awareness of their own entanglement in prior generic conventions, and therein lies their folly. So, for example, both of the Honeycombes are presented to us as cits imitating the vices of their betters. Mr. Honeycombe instructs his servant to tell visitors that he is "not at home," and invites Ledger to breakfast at the fashionable hour of 11:00, while Mrs. Honeycombe is downing cordials as a genteel way of disguising her ever more out-of-control drinking: apparently "the Hysterick Water" is not "warm enough," so she needs to "speak to Mr. Julep to order … something rather more comfortable"—i.e., higher proof (12, 31–32). These are, of course, the stock affectations of any number of upwardly mobile cits in eighteenth-century comedy, just as Ledger's inability to complete a sentence without recourse to metaphors drawn from his profession is an age-old comic tic. But none of these three seem at all self-conscious about their unwitting imitation of these highly conventionalized types. After all, they do not read novels, they do not go to the theater, their only interactions with media seem to be restricted to forms as unreflexive as they are: the marriage announcements of other cits in the newspaper, the pre-printed blank forms recording the transfer of stock from one owner to another.

All this, I would like to suggest, can help explain the otherwise rather puzzling ending to the farce, and so underscore the theoretical point about print, performance, and personhood which I would like us to draw from *Polly Honeycombe*. Clearly the ending (always an important moment in plot-driven forms) was especially charged for Colman. In the Preface to the printed play, the as of then still anonymous author went out of his way to highlight how, in the supposed words of his mother (who does not seem to bear much of a resemblance to the actual Mary Colman), he had attempted to

> violate the received laws of the Drama——That the *Catastrophe* (that was really her word) is directly contrary to all known rules—That the several Characters, instead of being dismissed, one by one, should have been industriously kept together, to make a bow to the audience at the dropping of the curtain——That, not withstanding any confusion, created by the Girl's whimsical passion for Novels, in the course of the Piece, all parties should be perfectly reconciled to each other at last. Polly, having manifested her affection for him, should, to be sure, have been married to Scribble; and the Parents should have been thoroughly, though suddenly, appeased by the declared reformation of both. Ledger might, with much propriety and great probability, have been disposed of to the Nurse: and the whole Piece, instead of concluding bluntly with a sentence in Prose, should have been tagged with a Couplet or Two; and then every thing would have gone off smoothly and roundly, *á lá mode du Théatre*. (vi–vii)

Alas, as my plot summary should have suggested, nothing of the sort transpired. Rather, as a puff in *The Public Ledger* (in which I have to imagine Colman had a hand) puts it, "the conclusion, so droll and diverting" is "so different from every thing else!"[5] What explains this difference? Why not offer the standard coupling-off of the characters amidst a general reconciliation (or expulsion of the killjoys), perhaps with a sensory delight—a dance or a couplet—to punctuate the whole? Why, in other words, should Polly and Scribble get to triumphantly exit at the peak of their powers (with Polly even able to come back and speak the epilogue), while Ledger and Mrs. Honeycombe can only depart in disarray, and Mr. Honeycombe cannot even leave, but remains downstage impotently sputtering as he pleads for compassion from the audience? The answer, I think, has to lie in their respective relations to the performance of generic convention. *Everyone* here is quixotic. Those who are knowingly and self-consciously so in order to further the fun are the ones who triumph (and, I suspect, the ones we like). Those who are obliviously or even hatefully so are the ones who lose out. And ultimately, the point here for our lovers *is* having fun, pursuing what Polly terms "Adventures." Such adventures are what is "charming" or "fine," not marriage, and so it hardly matters that Scribble does not ultimately get paired off with Polly. He has furnished her with "materials for the next chapter," and that is as much as anyone can do in this world (18).

So what, ultimately, does this suggest about print, performance, and personhood? I would like to close with four quick proposals:

First, the relationship between print and performance in a world of universal quixotism, such as the one *Polly Honeycombe* is inviting us to see, is nothing if not reciprocal. Print turns into performance; performance turns into print; the cycle begins anew, each time adding new elements. Any attempt to fix these terms, much less reify them into dubious abstractions like "print culture" or "theatricality," is doomed not only to lose the forest for the trees, but probably lose the trees for the twigs as well, by ignoring how, for example, later editions of printed texts often bear "the form and pressure" of their prior performances, both on-stage and off-.

Second, in a world of universal quixotism, the most attractive and pleasurable kinds of personhood are those which knowingly embrace and play up their quixotism, especially when it comes to texts that are themselves marked by play (e.g., the literary). That is, Polly is not just a figure of fun (in the conventional sense of the phrase), she is also a figure *for* fun, and the source of most of the delight to be had in her world. Indeed, for confirmation, we need only consider the original casting: Polly was played by Jane Pope (then sixteen or eighteen) and Scribble by Thomas King (then thirty). Both were attractive; both were comparatively new to Drury Lane; both were already known for playing sprightly pert roles of the sort associated with Kitty Clive and Henry Woodward. The Honeycombes and Ledger, on the other hand, were played by actors who were far older, less charismatic, less conspicuously talented, or simply not as pretty (Elizabeth Kennedy, who played Mrs. Honeycombe, apparently had a highly visible skin condition).[6] In a form, like farce, which values the young and attractive, it is not hard to imagine where most members of the audience placed their investments: sympathetic, erotic, and otherwise.

Third, quixotic personhood is not just a characteristic of other, sillier readers or playgoers at whom one can laugh, and from whom one can readily distinguish oneself, but rather a general phenomenon of the age, to which the largely West End-based audiences of Drury Lane are as much subject as the cits on the stage. All of the action and all but one of the places even mentioned in the play are in the City—just look at all the numbered circles in (fig. 1) and compare them to the circled "A" which marks the location of the theater, and which was about as far east as many of its habitués would routinely venture.[7] And yet the final line of the play returns us to the environs of not only the theater, but also one of the chief purveyors of the novelistic in London: John Noble's circulating library at the sign of Dryden's Head in St. Martin's Court—marked by the circled "B" in (fig. 1) (Covent Garden itself is the open space midway between Noble's shop and the theater in Drury Lane). Turning one's daughter loose in Covent Garden *was*, in effect, trusting the cultivation of her mind to a circulating library, because that was where the real-life counterparts of Polly would go to get their books. That is, Covent Garden was not only the center of theatrical, courtesanal, and vegetal pleasure, but also literary pleasure to be rented by the half-bound volume, the chief customers for which were drawn from the same demographic as frequented the theater.[8]

Finally, given the ways in which print, performance, and personhood are intertwined, both in the world of the play and in the world of Covent Garden (which is to say, the world of "the Town" more generally), it seems safe to presume that no forms are exempt from quixotic use, that there is no refuge to be sought in, say, something apparently satiric like *Polly Honeycombe*. As evidence for this, I would simply offer up (fig. 2), which shows the front cover of Ohio State's copy of the first edition of the play. If you look closely, it quickly becomes apparent that this copy bears all the signs of having been the property of . . . a circulating library: its shelfmark (number "35"), its half-binding with marbled paper boards, its general state of being "much thumbed, and in a greasy condition" (viii–ix). These are the visual traces of the circulating library, which leaves us with the delightful prospect that this play which turns universal quixotism into a source of delight was, in its printed form, itself the script for further (I hope delighted) quixotic performance.

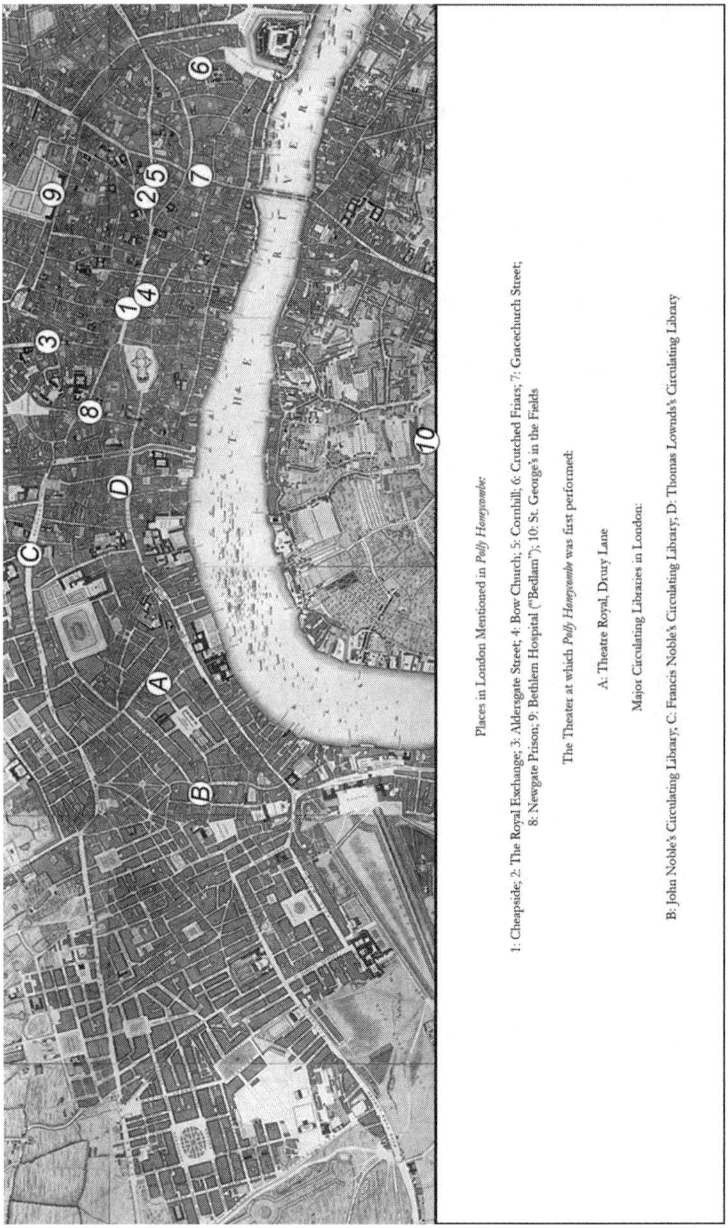

Figure 1. This map is based upon the Motco Enterprises digital version of John Rocque's *A Plan of the Cities of London* and *Westminster and the Borough of Southwark* (1747).

Figure 2. The front cover of Ohio State's copy of the first edition of *Polly Honeycombe*. Courtesy of The Ohio State University Rare Books and Manuscripts Library.

NOTES

1. For some welcome recent exceptions to this tendency, see Jane Moody, "Stolen Identities: Character, Mimicry, and the Invention of Samuel Foote," in *Theatre and Celebrity in Britain, 1660–2000*, ed. Mary Luckhurst and Jane Moody (Houndsmills, Basingstroke: Palgrave Macmillan, 2005): 65-89; Daniel O'Quinn, *Entertaining Crisis in the Atlantic Imperium, 1770–1790* (Baltimore: Johns Hopkins University Press, 2011); Stuart Sherman, "Garrick Among Media: The '*Now Performe*r' Navigates the News," *PMLA* 126.4 (2011): 966–82; and Tiffany Stern, *Documents of Performance in Early Modern England* (Cambridge: Cambridge University Press, 2009).

2. For details of the London performances, see *The London Stage, 1660–1800: A Calendar of Plays, Entertainments, and Afterpieces Together with Casts, Box-Receipts, and Contemporary Comment Compiled from the Playbills, Newspapers, and Theatrical Diaries of the Period*, Part 4: 1747–1776, ed. George Winchester Stone, Jr. (Carbondale: Southern Illinois University Press, 1962), and Part 5: 1776–1800, ed. Charles Beecher Hogan (Carbondale: Southern Illinois University Press, 1968).

3. [George Colman the Elder], *Polly Honeycombe, A Dramatick Novel of One Act, As it is now Acted at the Theatre-Royal in Drury-Lane* (London, 1760), 4. All subsequent citations will be from this edition, and will be made parenthetically.

4. For a useful survey of different kinds of mid-century comedy, see Richard Bevis, *The Laughing Tradition: Stage Comedy in Garrick's Day* (Athens: University of Georgia Press, 1980).

5. "A letter from a young Lady to her friend, on the subject of the New Farce of POLLY HONEYCOMB, performed at Drury-Lane theatre," *The Public Ledger* (8 December 1760).

6. For more on all of these performers, see their respective entries in Philip H. Highfill, Jr., Kalman A. Burnim, and Edward A. Langhans, *A Biographical Dictionary of Actors, Actresses, Musicians, Dancers, Managers, and Other Stage Personnel in London, 1660–1800* (Carbondale: Southern Illinois University Press, 1973–93).

7. For a provocative account of the geography of London pleasure-seeking, see Vic Gatrell, *City of Laughter: Sex and Satire in Eighteenth-Century London* (New York: Walker, 2006).

8. For some suggestive comments on the social composition of the theatrical and novel-reading publics, see Robert D. Hume, "The Economics of Culture in London, 1660–1740," *Huntington Library Quarterly* 69.4 (2006): 487–532.

Whose Story? The Game of Fiction in Early Eighteenth-Century French Literature

ZEINA HAKIM

Seventeenth- and eighteenth-centuries imaginary journeys, pseudo-memoirs, secret stories, and even heroic and humorous novels have in common their claim to "adhere exactly to historical truth"[1], to "have all the characteristics of a true story"[2], or to describe "the naked truth"[3]. Certain authors, dissatisfied with the general nature of the presumed veracity of their works, even go to considerable lengths to cite their historical sources[4], for instance, or refer to themselves as the editors[5], translators, or correctors of forgotten manuscripts[6]. In short, these fictional works are presented, through all sorts of devices, as authentic documents.

And yet, the hypothesis I wish to defend in the following pages is that the claim to truthfulness expressed at the end of the seventeenth and the beginning of the eighteenth centuries must be understood as a "game" and the relationship between the author and the reader considered as playful. More specifically, examined in the light of the important and pioneering work by Jan Herman and his fellow researchers[7], the claim to truthfulness is grounded on what Philippe Lejeune calls a "pact"[8] between author and reader, whose aim is not to deny the fictional character of the work but rather to emphasize it[9].

Thus understood, any member of the reading public would not be fooled by the claims to truthfulness in prefaces, the usual location where the "game" begins. On the contrary, he would recognize a rhetorical strategy at work and be conscious of the fundamentally ambivalent nature of all fictional writing[10]: the author's aim is to tell a fictional story, which the reader well knows, but he nonetheless requires that it be told "as if it were true". A great number of works of many genres used similar devices (or devices that a reader might presume are similar, but actually are not). For example, a foreword by a fictional editor was very common in the eighteenth century, as can be seen in certain philosophical works of a satirical nature—Montesquieu's *Lettres persanes* (1721)[11] is a good example—or later on, in epistolary novels whose supposed aim was "moral," such as *La Nouvelle Héloïse* (1761)[12] or *Les Liaisons dangereuses* (1782)[13].

I have, however, chosen here to focus on two works that exemplify two fictional models, which are usually contrasted. By comparing the strategies used in the prefaces to *Mémoires et aventures d'un homme de qualité qui s'est retiré du monde* (1728–1731) by Antoine François Prévost and *La Vie de Marianne* (1731–1742) by Pierre de Marivaux, I aim to distinguish certain narrative processes and rhetorical devices adopted by those writers in order to play with their readers' expectations.

Prévost and the Role Assigned to the Reader

At first glance the Abbé Prévost, as a novelist, does not seem to seek original means for "proving" the authenticity of his narratives, given the frequency with which he uses such traditional devices as the *topos* of the discovered manuscript or the preface attributed to a fictional editor. Such is, in any event, the case of the two preliminary texts that precede his *Mémoires et aventures d'un Homme de Qualité*. The first of these preliminary texts is the "Letter from the Editor" ("Lettre de l'Éditeur"), which can be found at the very beginning of volume 1, published in 1728. This text is a fictional preface, in which a character not figuring in the narrative presents the story as the true memoirs of the Marquis:

> Cet ouvrage me tomba, l'automne passé, entre les mains, dans un voyage que je fis à l'abbaye de … où l'auteur s'est retiré. La curiosité m'y avait conduit. […] Tous ceux qui ont quelque commerce avec les Pères … ne sauraient ignorer le nom de cet illustre aventurier: je serai néanmoins fidèle à la promesse que je lui ai faite, de ne le pas placer à la tête de son Histoire. Je ne l'ai

> obtenue de lui qu'à cette condition ; et l'honneur ne me permet pas d'y manquer. [...] Le style est simple et naturel, tel qu'on le doit attendre d'une personne de condition, qui s'attache plus à l'exactitude de la vérité, qu'aux ornements du langage[14].

The Man of Quality is thus designated as the "author" and the style of the memoirs is described as being "as one would expect from a person of his condition." Nowhere is it suggested that the manuscript might need some reworking in order to be publishable. The second preliminary text, also called "Letter from the Editor" ("Lettre de l'Éditeur"), which appears at the beginning of volume 5 (1730), is also a fictional preface whose aim is to legitimate the account of subsequent events in the *Mémoires*:

> La mort de M. le Marquis de ... , l'illustre sujet de ces Mémoires, me procure la liberté d'en donner la dernière partie au public. Il l'a tenue renfermée sous la clef jusqu'à la fin de sa vie, ou s'il lui a permis de voir quelquefois le jour, ce n'a été que pour quelques moments, et dans les mains de ses meilleurs amis. J'avais l'honneur d'être de ce nombre. [...] Je m'imagine donc qu'en imprimant cette suite des Mémoires, on fera un présent agréable et avantageux au public. On y trouvera plus de variété que dans les deux parties précédentes. Le style n'en est pas moins vif ni moins soutenu[15].

By making the Marquis de Renoncour die, Prévost separates the published novel from the process of its original production.

These devices—the recourse to an outside editor who publishes the memoirs of an author unknown to him, declarations by the editor concerning his promise not to reveal the author's identity, or remarks on the author's casual style—are different manifestations of the same convention: that of the discovered manuscript. One might logically expect the preface to the *Histoire du chevalier des Grieux et de Manon Lescaut* in volume 7 to adopt the same pattern and to have a fictional editor justify, here also, the circumstances under which Renoncour and his pupil learned des Grieux's story.

The approach chosen here by Prévost, however, is different. The very title of the foreword—"Notice by the Author of the *Mémoires d'un homme de qualité*" ("Avis de l'Auteur des *Mémoires d'un homme de qualité*")—reveals its ambiguity. The formulation of the title invites the reader to identify the fictional author with the real author. By choosing to have the author speak, Prévost abandons the device of the preface attributed to an editor and attributes the preface to the producer of the story who narrates the events in which he was and still is an actor. It is indeed the chevalier des Grieux who tells his own story to a silent witness who puts it into writing

> presque aussitôt après l'avoir entendue, et qu'on peut s'assurer, par conséquent, que rien n'est plus exact et plus fidèle que cette narration. Je dis fidèle jusque dans la relation des réflexions et des sentiments que le jeune aventurier exprimait de la meilleure grâce du monde. Voilà donc son récit, auquel je ne mêlerai, jusqu'à la fin, rien qui ne soit de lui[17].

It must be recognized that, by referring to the memorialist Renoncour in his preface of 1731, Prévost did not simplify his task as he had had this character die in 1730 as explained in the "Letter from the Editor" preceding volume 5. In his critical edition of the work, Jean Sgard points out that the author never felt the need to justify the publication of this posthumous narrative[18]. This can perhaps be explained by Prévost's having wanted to create the impression of an oral account: the unexpected encounter between Renoncour and des Grieux supplied the perfect excuse for des Grieux to recount his adventures.

Indeed, as soon as they recognize each other, des Grieux feels the need of explaining to his benefactor what had happened since their first encounter in Pacy:

> J'arrivais de Londres à Calais, avec le Marquis de … , mon élève. […] En marchant l'après-midi dans les rues, je crus apercevoir ce même jeune homme dont j'avais fait la rencontre à Pacy. […] Il n'attendit point que je le pressasse de me raconter l'histoire de sa vie. Monsieur, me dit-il, vous en usez si noblement avec moi, que je me reprocherais, comme une basse ingratitude, d'avoir quelque chose de réservé pour vous. Je veux vous apprendre, non seulement mes malheurs et mes peines, mais encore mes désordres et mes plus honteuses faiblesses[19].

Prévost hereby departs from the *topoi* he had adopted previously and adheres to a different tradition, that of the author-character relating his own adventures, while entrusting their transcription to a Memorialist. If, in this case however, the circumstances justify the "oral" relation of the story, the work nonetheless remains within the boundaries of a game, recognized as such by the reader.

La Vie de Marianne, or a Warning that Things are Seldom What they Seem

Let us now consider the case, parallel although different, of *La Vie de Marianne*, a novel described in its preface as a manuscript discovered by chance and edited by the prefacer who therefore is not the author. If we apply the distinction defined by Gérard Genette, we have here a typical example of a "préface dénégative," in which the prefacer declares that the text is not his doing[20] and the author refuses to give his name on the title page of the book.

The story moreover contains many reminders—indeed too many—of the supposed authenticity of the text. The editor who expresses himself in the first foreword seeks to reassure the reader:

> Comme on pourrait soupçonner cette histoire-ci d'avoir été faite exprès pour amuser le public, je crois devoir avertir que je la tiens moi-même d'un ami qui l'a réellement trouvée, comme il le dit ci-après […]. Ce qui est de vrai, c'est que si c'était une histoire simplement imaginée, il y a toute apparence qu'elle n'aurait pas la forme qu'elle a[21].

This editor refuses to be the producer of the text: at best, he admits to have played a role in the choice and organization of the material, pointing out that he only allowed himself to "correct a few words" ("quelque correction de mots")[22] and to rewrite a few passages which were "too confusing or casually formulated" ("quelques endroits trop confus et trop négligés")[23]. He claims the adventures of Marianne to be a true story because the narrator gives lessons in "morality", the work does not correspond to what readers generally enjoyed ("le goût général"), and it contains "long and frequent reflections", ("longues et […] fréquentes réflexions")[24], all of these weaknesses that a true novelist would have easily avoided. Finally, he declines responsibility for the work, stating that having the text published was his only role in its production: "je crois devoir avertir que je la tiens [cette histoire] moi-même d'un ami qui l'a réellement trouvée"[25].

After the editor excuses himself in this first foreward, the owner of the manuscript expresses himself in a second foreword and bears material witness to the authenticity of the story. He insists that it is not he but others who first discovered the manuscript and he explains the precise circumstances of its discovery:

> Il y a six mois que j'achetai une maison de campagne à quelques lieues de Rennes, qui, depuis trente ans, a passé successivement entre les mains de cinq ou six personnes. J'ai voulu faire changer quelque chose à la disposition du premier appartement, et dans une armoire pratiquée dans l'enfoncement d'un mur, on y a trouvé un manuscrit en plusieurs cahiers contenant l'histoire qu'on va lire[26.]

The owner, functioning now as the new intermediary between text, editor, and reader, took his time finding a publisher because he presumed that the "story has no interest for anyone" ("cette histoire n'intéresse personne").[27] It was only upon his friends' insistence that he finally decided to do so: "Je le lus [le manuscrit] avec deux de mes amis qui étaient chez moi, et qui depuis ce jour-là, n'ont cessé de me dire qu'il fallait le faire imprimer"[28].

If he sheds new light on the text that we are about to read—"Nous voyons par la date que nous avons trouvée à la fin du manuscrit, qu'il y a quarante ans qu'il est écrit"[29]—and if he indicates that two names have been changed,[30] he disavows responsibility for the work itself. On the contrary, he declines any connection with it: "je ne suis point auteur, et jamais on n'imprimera de moi que cette vingtaine de lignes-ci"[31]. This statement confirms to the reader that a brilliant game is being played out between the lines, which is to be understood as the opposite of what is said.

In the end, it is Marianne herself who speaks "as author" but she, like the other mediators, defers responsibility for telling her story. Her very first sentence in her first letter resembles that of the publisher and owner in the first and second forewards:

> Quand je vous ai fait le récit de quelques accidents de ma vie, je ne m'attendais pas, ma chère amie, que vous me prieriez de vous la donner tout entière et d'en faire un livre à imprimer[32].

Marianne thus insists, as do her prefacers, that the manuscript tells a true story, and she justifies having put her life into writing only through the request from a friend. In referring to "you, dear friend," she flags that the text we are about to read exists in spite of her will, because a third party has wanted it to exist.

Thus the manuscript is passed on from author to author. It is not one, nor two, but three voices which attest to the authenticity of the document[33]. Because the means of its transmission are far from simple, its style acquires the appearance of an "inspired patchwork" ("un bricolage inspiré")[34]. It is difficult to attribute the text to a sole narrator given that, in Jenny Mander's words, "la voix qui s'exprime à quelque endroit que ce soit comporte toujours la trace d'autres voix."[35] When the text finally reaches the reader, it is only after having been passed back and forth among different producers. This is what Jan Herman has referred to as a "textual shuttle" ("navette textuelle"), which results in the "progressive broadening of the senders" ("l'élargissement progressif du cercle des destinateurs") and whose effect is "a shared responsibility for authorship" ("la responsabilité auctoriale éclate et est disloquée")[36].

But what is perhaps most striking about the way in which Marivaux presents his work is that the same device he uses in the Preface and Foreword is used again in the text itself. This redundancy arouses the reader's suspicion. As Jan Herman explains, "après avoir supprimé l'idée du roman dans le péritexte, on la réintoduit dans le texte narratif, et ce reflet provoque l'indécision du lecteur quant au véritable statut du texte"[37]. Indeed, despite the numerous statements to the effect that one is about to read a true story, the reader is aware that the text itself rejects such a fiction by exhorting him not to be fooled by these conventional devices. If at first the device of the discovered manuscript gives the impression of an authentic account of events which truly happened, the redundancy and repeated interruptions within the story itself, and not only outside as its frame, become obvious indications that we are dealing with fiction.

In the roles they adopt vis-à-vis the reader, the editor and the owner of the manuscript emphasize that Marianne has not written a novel but instead the story of her life: *La Vie de Marianne* is not "simply an imagined story" ("une histoire simplement imaginée")[38], rather, "it is a woman who relates her life" ("c'est une femme qui raconte sa vie")[39]. This is why Marianne appears to have no style as the editor observes in his preface to the second part: "Son amie lui demande l'histoire de sa vie, et elle l'écrit à sa manière. Elle n'a aucune forme d'ouvrage présente à l'esprit"[40]. The editor suggests that the narrator's imperfect and unadorned style is the best proof of the story's truth insofar as it owes nothing to the rules of rhetoric and to the elegant turns of phrase that denote the work of fiction.

The editor's comments in this preface end abruptly but ironically, when he concludes that "Marianne n'a point songé à faire un roman"[41]. The editor establishes an irresolvable paradox for the reader who understands that what is most emphatically asserted is not to be trusted. The knowing reader understands that the editor relies on numerous devices proclaiming the authenticity of the text, which actually indicate that he is reading avowed fiction. The use of parody, the overuse of italics, the exaggerated insistence on the veracity of the text, and the explanation that Marianne never intended to tell her life story cannot be taken literally by the reader.

In a word, if a whole series of means are used by the author to prove the authenticity of his text, the reader can never completely believe them since, at the very same time, the author countermines his own arguments by demonstrating the intrinsic artificiality of the "realistic" novel.

In the end, the discourse in the two prefaces we have examined does not appear as a device to convince the reader of the truth of a fictional account but rather as a means to make the body of the announced works recognizable as fictional. The aim of the pre-texts is, paradoxically, to guide the reader into the fiction (thereby making him take the fiction seriously) as well as to allow him to *recognize* the text is purely fiction. In this way, the preface can be understood as a dialogue between an author and a reader: the novelist seeks to act on the reader and provoke his reaction, going as far as to suggest different ways to interpret the text for the sheer pleasure of the experience.

NOTES

I would like to warmly thank Lisa Cody for her very insightful comments and Amy Laborde for her expert help in translating this essay into English.

1. Eustache Le Noble, *L'Histoire secrète des plus fameuses conspirations* (Paris: Pierre Ribou, 1698), preface (my translation). All further translations of French texts are mine.

2. Denis Veiras, *Histoire des Sévarambes* (1677. Amsterdam: Estienne Roger, 1716), "To the Reader."

3. François Tristan l'Hermite, *Le Page disgracié* (1642), ed. Auguste Dietrich (Paris, 1889; reprint: Nendeln, Liechtenstein: Kraus Reprints, 1972), 11. For a study of the relationship between truth and fiction in the French novel of the seventeenth century, see the excellent article by Günter Berger, "Préfaces et vérité: la théorie romanesque du XVIIe siècle entre la contrainte à l'apologie et la tentation de l'histoire," *Papers on French Seventeenth-Century Literature* (*PFSCL*), Biblio 17, 18.35 (1991): 275–82.

4. For instance, César Vichard de Saint-Réal does so several times in his *Dom Carlos* (1672).

5. A good example of the use of this device can be found in the works of Courtilz de Sandras. In the *Mémoires de Gaspard Comte de Chavagnac* the editor directly speaks to the reader in the following terms: "Ayant heureusement recouvré un manuscrit des Mémoires de M. de Chavagnac, ou plutôt le seul original qu'il en a laissé, j'ai cru que je devais les donner au public après en avoir obtenu le privilège du roi," ("Having fortunately discovered a manuscript of the Mémoires de M. de Chavagnac, or rather the only original he left of his memoirs, I felt I should make them

public after having obtained the king's permission"). Courtilz de Sandras, *Mémoires de Gaspard Comte de Chavagnac, Maréchal de camp et armée du roi, général de l'artillerie: sergent de bataille de celles de sa majesté catholique, lieutenant général des troupes de l'empereur et son ambassadeur en Pologne* (Besançon: François Louis Rigoine, 1699), "To the Reader."

6. For these various devices, see Günter Berger's study, "Aspects de la théorie romanesque du XVIIe siècle français. Le problème de la vérité des préfaces," *Actes du XVIIIe Congrès international de linguistique et de philologie romane*, (Tübingen: Max Niemeyer Verlag, 1988) 4: 236–42. See also, by the same author, "Genres bâtards: roman et histoire à la fin du XVIIe siècle," *XVIIe siècle*, 215 (2002): 297–305; 302–03.

7. See, as a good example, their most recent work: Jan Herman, Mladen Kozul, and Nathalie Kremer, *Le Roman véritable: stratégies préfacielles au XVIIIe siècle*, *SVEC*, vol. 8 (Oxford, Voltaire Foundation, 2008).

8. Philippe Lejeune, *Le Pacte autobiographique* (Paris: Seuil, coll. Poétique, 1975).

9. This is what Jan Herman and his fellow researchers call "le pacte du roman véritable" ("the pact of the real novel"), in which the phrase "this is not a novel" actually means the contrary. This pact can, however, be ambiguous, as Jan Herman points out when he quotes the text preceding *Les Égarements du coeur et de l'esprit* (1736) by Crebillon: "L'unique dessein que j'aie dans celle-ci, est d'annoncer le but de ces mémoires, soit qu'on doive les regarder comme un ouvrage purement d'imagination, ou que les aventures qu'ils contiennent soient réelles." ("My only intention in all of this is to announce the aim of these memoirs, whether they should be considered as a purely fictional work or whether the adventures they contain are real.") *Les Égarements du coeur et de l'esprit,* ed. René Etiemble (Paris: Folio classique, Gallimard, 1977), 41. Jan Herman sees this example as emblematic: "Neither a contract of fiction (as Genette regarded it) nor a contract of truth, but the declared absence of a pact. It seems that every effort is made to cultivate the indecision of the reader as to the true status of the text: true or fictional?" from "Illusion et désillusion: vraisemblance et vérité dans le roman-mémoires" in *Le Mensonge romanesque. Paramètres pour l'étude du roman épistolaire en France* (Amsterdam: Rodopi, 1989), 151–73; 161.

10. From fairy tales to the novel, from autobiographies to autofictions, from pseudo-documentaries to true enthnographics, the variety of objects which can be qualified as "fictional" is vast. As a result, in spite of our familiarity with the practice of fiction, there is no consensus as to what constitutes a fictional work. Moreover, the term fiction is used in a variety of disciplines in the humanities. This practice tends not only to enrich the term significantly but also to render it more complex. In addition, the difficulties encountered also stem from the great variety of usages of the term over time and space; indeed, applied to a given genre, but also

within a given culture and at a given time, the word fiction refers to very different situations. Observation of the phenomenon over time and in non-European cultures amplifies this point. It is indispensable to recognize that our notion of "fiction" is something that emerged gradually over a long period of time and cannot be taken as an ahistorical given. On this point, see, Dorrit Cohn, *The Distinction of Fiction*; (Baltimore: Johns Hopkins University Press, 1999); Thomas Pavel, *Fictional Worlds* (Cambridge: Harvard University Press, 1986); Jean-Marie Schaeffer, *Pourquoi la fiction?* (Paris: Seuil, 1999); Michael McKeon, *Theory of the Novel: A Historical Approach* (Baltimore: Johns Hopkins University Press, 2000); Catherine Gallagher, *The Industrial Reformation of English Fiction: Social Discourse and Narrative Form, 1832–1867* (Chicago: University of Chicago Press,1985);Wayne Booth, *The Rhetoric of Fiction* (1961. Chicago: University of Chicago Press, 1983); Lubomír Dolezel, *Heterocosmica. Fiction and Possible Worlds* (Baltimore: Johns Hopkins University Press, 1997); Michael Riffaterre, *Fictional Truth* (Baltimore: Johns Hopkins University Press, 1990). Furthermore, throughout this essay, I almost always refer to the seventeenth- and eighteenth-century reader as "he" rather than "she" or "they," but I of course do not assume all readers were male. Rather, because my analysis explores the relationship between author and individual readers, a more gender-neutral plural construction alters my argument here. Because my analysis is grounded in a historical context in which authors described the generic individual as male, I follow this pattern, except when a text, such as Jean-Jacques Rousseau's *La Nouvelle Héloïse*, explicitly presented itself as speaking to both female and male readers.

11. Straight away in the introduction Montesquieu raises the question of the authenticity of his text: "Les Persans qui écrivent ici étaient logés avec moi; nous passions notre vie ensemble. Comme ils me regardaient comme un homme d'un autre monde, ils ne me cachaient rien. En effet, des gens transplantés de si loin ne pouvaient plus avoir de secrets. Ils me communiquaient la plupart de leurs lettres; je les copiai. J'en surpris même quelques-unes dont ils se seraient bien gardés de me faire confidence, tant elles étaient mortifiantes pour la vanité et la jalousie persane. Je ne fais donc que l'office du traducteur: toute ma peine a été de mettre l'ouvrage à nos mœurs. J'ai soulagé le lecteur du langage asiatique autant que je l'ai pu, et l'ai sauvé d'une infinité d'expressions sublimes, qui l'auraient envoyé jusque dans les nues. Mais ce n'est pas tout ce que j'ai fait pour lui. J'ai retranché les longs compliments, dont les Orientaux ne sont pas moins prodigues que nous; et j'ai passé un nombre infini de ces minuties qui ont tant de peine à soutenir le grand jour, et qui doivent toujours mourir entre deux amis." ("The Persians who wrote this text shared my lodgings; we lived together. Because they saw me as a man from another world, they hid nothing from me. Being transplanted from far away, they could have no secrets. They let me read most of their letters, which I copied. I even got to see a few which they would undoubtedly have wished to keep from me insofar as

they were embarrassing to Persian pride and jealousy. My role was simply that of a translator: all I had to do was to make the work correspond to our norms. I relieved the reader of Asiatic language as much as possible and spared him an infinity of sublime expressions which would have carried him to the heavens. But that is not all I did for him. I trimmed the wordy compliments which Oriental people engage in no less than we do and edited out an infinite number of details which wither in the daylight and which must always die between two true friends.") *Lettres persanes*, ed. Jacques Roger (Paris, GF Flammarion, 1964), 7–8.

12. Indeed, the epistolary novel of the eighteenth century traditionally tried to give the illusion of authenticity by claiming to be a real exchange of letters found in a drawer or discovered by a third party who decided to publish them. To reinforce the appearance of authenticity which, it must be recognized, rarely fooled the reader, most epistolary novels contained a preface in which the author claimed to be the editor or the guardian of the letters. The case of *La Nouvelle Héloïse* is especially interesting in that the responses of readers were particularly fervent, many being persuaded that Julie and Saint Preux had to be real people. Indeed, in spite of Rousseau's claim to authorship in his preface ("j'ai travaillé moi-même à ce livre, et je ne m'en cache pas"—"this book is my work and I don't seek to hide that fact") many readers chose to ignore that reality in order to identify with the characters and wrote passionate letters to Rousseau asking what had become of them. Moreover, this work is essential for the problem which interests us here, for the ambiguity of "truth" is present from the outset in the epigraph Rousseau places at the beginning of his book: "J'ai vu les mœurs de mon temps, et j'ai publié ces lettres." ("I observed the mores of my time, and I published these letters.") By claiming to condemn the fictional novel, Rousseau raises the question of the status of his work: "Is this work real or is it fictional?" (Jean-Jacques Rousseau, *Oeuvres complètes*, 2: 5). This question, reiterated in each of the two prefaces, is deliberately eluded, then left in suspense, Rousseau refusing to take a stand. If *La Nouvelle Héloïse* appears especially modern to us, this is partly because of Rousseau's refusal to define its boundaries. The discussion triggered by the epigraph is particularly revealing: "Qui peut savoir si j'ai trouvé cette épigraphe dans le manuscrit, ou si c'est moi qui l'y ai mise? Qui peut dire si je ne suis point dans le même doute où vous êtes? Si tout cet air de misère n'est peut-être pas une feinte pour vous cacher ma propre ignorance sur ce que vous voulez savoir?" ("Who can know if I found this epigraph in the manuscript or if I was the one who added it? Who can say if I share your doubts or not? If the appearance of misery is not, perhaps, a sham to hide my own ignorance concerning what you wish to know?") *La Nouvelle Héloïse*, vol. 2 in *Oeuvres complètes*, ed. Bernard Gagnebin and Marcel Raymond (Paris: Gallimard, Bibliothèque de la Pléiade, 1990), 29. The status of the text is not established but remains to be defined and redefined. For futher details on that matter, see Robert Darnton, "Readers Respond to Rousseau: The Fabrication of Romantic Sensitivity", *The Great Cat Massacre: And Other Episodes in French Cultural History* (New York: Basic Books, 1984), 215–56.

13. The author of *Les Liaisons dangereuses* does not depart from this tradition but, with unmistakable irony, exposes its artificiality by supplying two preliminary texts which contradict each other. Thus, in his first preface "A Word from the Editor" ("Avertissement de l'éditeur") on the fictional nature of the letters, Laclos writes, "[…] nous ne garantissons pas l'authenticité de ce recueil et nous avons même de fortes raisons de penser que ce n'est qu'un roman. […] Plusieurs des personnages qu'il [l'auteur] met en scène ont de si mauvaises mœurs qu'il est impossible de supposer qu'ils aient vécu dans notre siècle, dans ce siècle où […] les lumières […] ont rendu, comme chacun sait, tous les hommes si honnêtes et toutes les femmes si modestes et si réservées." ("[…] we don't guarantee the authenticity of this work and even have good reason to think that it is merely a novel. […] Several of the characters which he [the author] presents have such poor conduct that it is impossible to suppose that they lived during this century, a century in which […] enlightenment has rendered, as everyone knows, all men honest and all women modest and reserved.") Then, further on, he gives us the "Preface" written by someone who calls himself the editor-corrector of the existing letters: "Cet ouvrage, ou plutôt ce recueil […] ne contient que le plus petit nombre des lettres qui composaient la totalité de la correspondance dont il est extrait. Chargé de la mettre en ordre par les personnes à qui elle était parvenue, […] j'ai presque toujours suivi [l'ordre] des dates. […] Je dois prévenir aussi que j'ai supprimé ou changé tous les noms des personnes dont il est question dans ces lettres." ("This work, or rather this collection of letters […] contains only the smallest number of the letters which composed the totality of the correspondence of which they were a part. The people who discovered it assigned me the task of re-establishing the order of the letters. In so doing, I almost always followed [the order] of the dates […] I must also warn you that I omitted or changed all the names of the people mentioned in the letters.") Choderlos de Laclos, *Les Liaisons dangereuses,* ed. René Pomeau (Paris: GF Flammarion, 1981), 14-15. Italics are mine. It should also be noted that the very subtitle of the novel (*Lettres recueillies dans une Société, et publiées pour l'instruction de quelques autres—Letters discovered in one milieu and published for the edification of several others*) announces an ironic game, raising questions about the authenticity of the text.

14. "I came upon this work last autumn during my stay at the abbey of… to which the author had retired. I was drawn to it by my curiosity. […] No one having had dealings with the Fathers …can ignore the name of that illustrious adventurer. I will nonetheless remain faithful to the promise I made to him not to name him at the beginning of his story. He let me have the manuscript on that condition and my sense of honor does not allow me to break my word. […] The style is simple and natural, as one would expect from a person of his condition who cares more about the truth than about stylistic effects," Antoine-François Prévost d'Exiles, *Mémoires et aventures d'un homme de qualité qui s'est retiré du monde*, vol. 1 of *Oeuvres de*

Prévost, ed. Pierre Berthiaume and Jean Sgard (Grenoble: Presses Universitaires de Grenoble, 1978-1986), 9.

15. "The death of the Marquis de..., the illustrious subject of these memoirs, freed me to publish the last part of the story. He had locked it up until the end of his life or, if he brought it occasionally to light, it was only entrusted, for a fleeting moment, to his best friends. I had the honor of being included among them. [...] I can therefore imagine that by printing the last part of his Memoirs, I will be giving the public a pleasant and useful gift. There is more variety in these last pages than in the two preceding parts. The style is no less lively, the content no less solid." Prévost d'Exiles, *Mémoires*, 227.

16. "[A]lmost as soon as he heard it and one can be sure as a result that nothing is more accurate and more faithful than this narrative. I say faithful to the very relation of the thoughts and feelings that the young adventurer graciously expressed. Here is his account to which, until the end, I will add nothing that is not from him." Prévost, *Histoire du chevalier des Grieux et de Manon Lescaut*, vol. 1 in *Oeuvres de Prévost*, 1: 367. SGARD EDITION The same procedure is used in Cleveland at the beginning of Fanny's story which constitutes all of book 9: "She undertook to tell this interesting tale whose unfolding I was easily able to repeat here to the very word," Prévost, *Le Philosophe anglais ou Histoire de Monsieur Cleveland*, ed. Philip Stewart, in *Oeuvres de Prévost*, vol. 2, 380.

17. "An ambiguity will be noted concerning the nature of the author of 'the Mémoires d'un Homme de Qualité': is he really Renoncour? In fact, he died in 1730 and no justification is given for the posthumous publication of this last manuscript", as Jean Sgard notes in *Oeuvres de Prévost*, 8: 62 ("On remarquera une ambiguïté sur la nature de 'l'auteur des Mémoires d'un homme de qualité': s'agit-il vraiment de Renoncour? Il est mort en 1730 et aucune justification ne nous est donnée sur l'apparition posthume de cet ultime manuscrit").

18. "I arrived in Calais from London with the Marquis de ..., my pupil. [...] In the afternoon, while walking in the street, I thought I recognized the same young man whom I had met in Pacy. [...] He didn't need prompting to tell me his life's story. Sir, he said, you have been so kind to me that I would consider myself ungrateful if I kept anything back from you. I want you to know not only my trials and misfortunes but also my misconduct and my most shameful weaknesses," Prévost, *Histoire du chevalier des Grieux et de Manon Lescaut* in *Oeuvres de Prévost*, 1: 367.

19. Gérard Genette points out the opposition between this type of preface and "préfaces assomptives", in which an author recognizes his role by confessing to be the author of the text, *Seuils* (Paris: Seuil, 1987), 169. On this matter, see also Jan Herman, "La scénographie des préfaces," *L'Art de la préface au siècle des Lumières*, ed. Ioana Galleron (Rennes: Presses universitaires de Rennes, 2007), 29–48; 30–31.

20. "As one might suspect this story to have been deliberately invented to amuse the public, I feel the duty of explaining that it was given to me by a friend who

really found it, as he says below [… .] What is true is that if the story were a simple figment of the imagination, it is unlikely that it would have the form it has." Pierre de Marivaux, *La Vie de Marianne ou les aventures de Madame la comtesse de****, ed. Frédéric Deloffre (Paris: Garnier Frères, 1957), 5.

21. Marivaux, *La Vie*, 6.

22. Marivaux, *La Vie*, 5.

23. Marivaux, *La Vie*, 5.

24. "I feel I must inform the reader that the work I have in my possession was transmitted to me by a friend who really found it," Marivaux, *La Vie*, 5.

25. "Six months ago I bought a country house several leagues from Rennes which, within a thirty year period had been owned successively by five or six people. I wanted to have certain things changed in the way the first apartment was arranged and, in a wardrobe set into a wall, a manuscript consisting of several notebooks was discovered containing the story which is about to be read," Marivaux, *La Vie*, 5.

26. Marivaux, *La Vie*, 5.

27. "I read it [the manuscript] with two friends who were staying at my place and who, since that day, kept telling me that that it should be printed," Marivaux, *La Vie*, 5.

28. "We can see by the date figuring at the end of the manuscript that it was written forty years ago," Marivaux, *La Vie*, 5.

29. "We have changed the names of two people who are mentioned, and who are dead. What is said about them, however, has very little importance; but anyway: it is still better not to reveal their true names" Marivaux, *La Vie*, 5.

30. "I am not an author, and from me nothing will ever be printed save these twenty lines," Marivaux, *La Vie*, 5.

31. "When I related several events in my life, I didn't expect you, dear friend, to beg me to tell you everything and to make it into a book to be printed," Marivaux, *La Vie*, 7–8.

32. One might even say that there are at least three voices, since the origins of the manuscript become even more complex by the fact that the house where the discovery was made had "within thirty years been owned successively by five or six people." Marivaux, *La Vie*, 7. As a result, it becomes impossible to pinpoint the origin of the manuscript.

33. The expression is Franck Salaün's in "'Le manuscrit ne le dit pas …': déni de l'auteur et création romanesque au XVIIIe siècle," in *Le Topos du manuscrit trouvé*, ed. Jan Herman and Fernand Hallyn with Kris Peeters (Louvain: Peeters, 1999), 173–82; 178.

34. "The voice we hear on any given page always contains traces of other voices," Jenny Mander, "Moi et l'ouïe: la concurrence entre l'écrit et l'oral mise en évidence par le topos du manuscrit trouvé," in Herman et al, eds, *Le Topos du manuscrit trouvé*, 149–57; 156.

35. Herman, *Le Roman véritable*, 121.

36. "The idea that we are dealing with a novel is refuted in the preface and in the foreword but the possibility that the manuscript is indeed a novel is reintroduced in the body of the text. The result is that the reader is confused and unable to decide on the true status of the work," Herman, "Illusion et désillusion," in *Le Mensonge romanesque*,167.

37. Marivaux, *La Vie*, 5.

38. Marivaux, *La Vie*, 7–8.

39. "Her friend asks for her life's story and she writes it in her own way. She has no model of a specific genre in mind," Marivaux, *La Vie*, 55.

40. "Marianne never intended to write a novel," Marivaux, *La Vie*, 55.

Direction and Diversion: Chapter Titles in Three Mid-Century English Novels by Sarah Fielding, Henry Fielding, and Charlotte Lennox

DOROTHEE BIRKE

Most readers of eighteenth-century novels will recognize a typical feature that seems designed to delight, instruct and occasionally annoy the audience: the long chapter titles in works by authors such as Henry and Sarah Fielding and Charlotte Lennox. Famously, Henry Fielding himself provided a commentary on the phenomenon: in *Joseph Andrews*, he explains that the purpose of the "Contents prefixed to every Chapter" resembles that of "Inscriptions over the Gates of Inns … , informing the Reader what Entertainment he is to expect, which if he likes not, he may travel on to the next."[1] In *Joseph Andrews* or other novels of the period, however, these titles in fact work in a less straightforward way than this quote suggests: while some do seem calculated to convey an adequate idea of a chapter's contents, others appear as ironical, superfluous, mysterious, or self-contradictory.

While interpretations of individual novels have included references to the chapter titles, the phenomenon as a whole has not received the attention it deserves. In this article, I want to offer a comparative analysis of the chapter titles in three well-known novels from the middle of the century—Henry Fielding's *Joseph Andrews* (1742), Sarah Fielding's *The Adventures of David Simple* (1744), and Charlotte Lennox's *The Female Quixote* (1752).

In doing so, I aim to show that providing summaries is only a small part of a whole complex of functions these titles serve: put briefly, they negotiate the relations between author and reader and reflect on the functions of fictional reading at a particular (and particularly interesting) point in literary history.

The theoretical basis for such an understanding of chapter titles is provided by Gérard Genette, who introduces the concept "paratext" as an overarching category to describe a text's "accompanying productions," such as titles, illustrations, prefaces, notes, and front and back covers.[2] While these different elements have (to varying degrees) been the subject of study before, Genette's theory is the first to provide a conceptual basis and a terminology for describing the relations between the text proper and the elements he defines as paratext. Moreover, it directs attention to the key functions that paratextual elements fulfill as mediating between a text and both its imagined and real historical audiences.[3] The concept of paratext thus helps to bridge the gap between narratologically informed readings of textual features and cultural-historical approaches.

Genette's work on intertitles primarily raises questions regarding typology that are too general to be useful here. Yet, his argument that those components of the book which are outside the narrative content in fact shape readers' reception of the text provides a guide to this investigation into chapter titles' use in a specific genre at a specific historical moment. To apply Genette's ideas here, it will be helpful to consider the general distinction between descriptive and connotative functions of titles. The descriptive function of titles is to "describe the text by one of its characteristics, whether thematic (this book talks about…) or rhematic (this book is…)."[4] The connotative effects, on the other hand, "stem from the *manner* in which the thematic or rhematic title does its denotating," which may implicitly provide information about the author's stance, the stance expected of the audience, the text's genre, etc.[5] This distinction helps to highlight the ways in which chapter titles fulfill, but also exceed their functions as summaries, which is probably the most obvious example of a descriptive use. For instance, the title of chapter 1.7 from *Joseph Andrews*—"Sayings of Wise Men. A Dialogue between the Lady and her Maid, and a Panegyric or rather Satire on the Passion of Love, in the sublime Style"—descriptively furnishes information about the contents (there is indeed a dialogue between two women), while the exaggerated attention to finding the right label for the kind of writing connotatively suggests that the reader is to expect a parody instead of a serious rendering of the "sublime Style."

Genette moreover provides a provocative point of departure in his brief diachronic survey of what he calls "thematic titling" in narrative fiction: a "tradition, apparently originating in the Middle Ages … perhaps parodying serious texts by historians and by philosophers of theologians."[6] Like the example cited in the last paragraph, thematic titles use noun clauses (rather than single words or phrases) to sum up the content of a chapter, but in a comic or playful way that diverges from an earlier serious use. Genette labels this the "Cervantes model", after its influential deployment in *Don Quixote*, and regards Henry Fielding's novels as the most remarkable case of its further application.[7] Toward the beginning of the nineteenth century, he further explains, thematic titling receded—a circumstance he credits to the intertitles' problematic aspect: they may "direct a little too much attention not to the text but to the fact of the *book* as such." For an author intent on creating a seamless sense of an imaginary reality for his reader, intertitles are disruptive because "an author… may wish his reader to forget about this particular truth [that 'this' is a book], and one sign of a paratext's effectiveness is no doubt its transparency: its transitivity. The best intertitle, the best title in general, is perhaps the one that goes unnoticed."[8]

What Genette does not add is that of course in cases where a writer wants to foreground the status of the book as an artifact, the disadvantage becomes an advantage. While conspicuous thematic titles may have become superfluous and appeared as old-fashioned in the nineteenth century once the novel had become a firmly established genre, in the eighteenth century they had an important function: they contributed to the reflection of the function and purpose of an emerging form of writing.[9] In this sense, the novels by the Fieldings and Charlotte Lennox that I discuss here represent a typical preoccupation of their time. Often credited with "pav[ing] the way for modern habits of reading" in terms of production, circulation, and consumption of books,[10] the eighteenth century saw controversial debates about the purpose and effects of reading. Fictional narrative, in particular the new genre of the novel, whose establishment as leisure reading was well under way around the middle of the century, was at the center of many of these debates—regarded by some as offering a valuable opportunity for self-cultivation, by others as a pernicious danger.[11] As Martin Hall describes it, the late seventeenth to eighteenth centuries were moreover

> marked by the growing anxiety which writers and critics felt as their public became more diverse and less well defined. This anxiety was particularly strong in the case of the novel, where the lack of any established tradition of reception heightened the perception that the consensus which prevailed between writers and readers in an earlier period had broken down.[12]

Debates about the role of fictional narratives in regard to moral education and contemporaries' awareness of the reader as a consumer in a literary marketplace suggested different, sometimes clashing roles for the reader of the novel. Among other roles, he or she was cast as a customer (someone to be pleased), a pupil (someone to be instructed), or as a critic (someone to be convinced on an equal footing).

The novels under consideration in this essay, each in its specific way, negotiate these different evaluative views of the reader and reading. In this sense, they are prominent examples of the novel as criticism: instances where novels, rather than simply being the objects of critical debate, also function as vehicles for participating in it.[13] In my analyses of the chapter titles in *Joseph Andrews*, *David Simple* and *The Female Quixote*, I want to highlight the important role which apparently marginal elements play in this self-reflexive endeavor.

Joseph Andrews: A Model for Addressing the Reader?

Henry Fielding's novels are the obvious choices to begin this investigation. They have been canonized and studied as prominent examples of texts which self-consciously and explicitly deal with the form and functions of narrative fiction—the passage quoted at the beginning of this article is just one example for the detailed and sophisticated commentary on the processes of reading and writing. Genette is not the only scholar who regards the chapter titles in *Joseph Andrews* and *Tom Jones* as a pre-eminent example of thematic titling. In his study on paratexts in eighteenth-century German novels, Till Dembeck, for one, names Fielding's novels as an important model for the paratexts in the work of Christoph Martin Wieland, who also uses notably complex intertitles.[14]

In keeping with the image of chapter titles as sign posts, many of the sixty-four titles in *Joseph Andrews* serve a thematic function, giving summaries of salient plot elements and often mentioning the principal characters involved. (fig. 1) shows an overview of the titles that I would assign to this category—about half of the total number.[15] Typical examples include "1.3 Of Mr. *Abraham Adams* the Curate, Mrs. *Slipslop* the Chambermaid, and others" for the chapter introducing these characters, or "1.10 *Joseph* writes another Letter: His Transactions with Mr. *Peter Pounce*, &c. with his Departure from Lady *Booby*." I designate these titles as "straight-forward" despite the fact that their summarizing function needs to be taken with a grain of salt—in the context of the whole book, they appear as comic rather than serious. This, however, is due not primarily to the phrasing of these titles

		Joseph Andrews		David Simple		The Female Quixote	
		Individual chapters	No.	Individual chapters	No.	Individual chapters	No.
	Total no. of titles		64		38		92
1 a)	Summary function fulfilled or mostly fulfilled	1.1, 1.2, 1.3, 1.4, 1.6 1.10, 1.13, 1.16, 1.18, 2.1, 2.2, 2.3, 2.5, 2.8, 2.9, 2.11, 2.14, 2.15, 3.1, 3.2, 3.3, 3.4, 3.5, 3.6, 3.11, 4.1, 4.2, 4.3, 4.7, 4.11, 4.13, 4.15 4.16 generic: 2.4, 2.6	33 2 sum: 35	1.1, 1.4, 1.5, 1.7, 2.9, 3.3, 3.6, 4.6, 4.9 generic: 2.8, 2.10, 3.1, 3.2, 3.7, 3.8, 4.1, 4.2, 4.5, 4.7	9 10 sum: 19	1.9, 1.11, 2.3, 2.10, 2.11, 3.1, 3.2, 3.4, 3.5, 3.7, 4.2, 4.3, 4.8, 5.3, 6.6, 6.10, 7.10, 7.11, 7.12, 7.14, 8.3, 8.4, 8.5 Short/generic: 1.2 (part 2), 1.3, 1.5, 1.6, 1.12, 1.13, 2.1, 2.5, 2.9, 4.4, 4.5, 4.6, 4.7, 5.6, 6.3, 6.4, 7.2, 8.8, 9.1, 9.3, 9.4, 9.12	23 22 sum:45
1 b)	Summary function not fulfilled/strongly compromised	1.5, 1.7, 1.8, 1.9, 1.11, 1.12, 1.14, 1.15, 1.17, 2.7, 2.10, 2.12, 2.13, 2.16, 2.17, 3.7, 3.8, 3.9, 3.10, 3.12, 3.13, 4.4, 4.5, 4.6, 4.8, 4.9, 4.10, 4.12, 4.14	29	exempla: 1.2, 1.3, 1.8, 1.9, 1.10, 1.11, 2.1, 2.2, 2.3, 2.4, 2.5, 2.6, 3.4, 4.4, 4.8 others: 1.6, 2.7, 4.3	15 3 sum: 18	1.1, 1.2 (part 1), 1.4, 1.7, 1.8, 1.10, 2.2, 2.4, 2.6, 2.7, 2.8, 3.3, 3.6, 3.8, 4.1, 4.9, 5.1, 5.2, 5.4, 5.5, 6.1, 6.2, 6.5, 6.7, 6.8, 6.9, 6.11, 7.1, 7.3, 7.4, 7.5, 7.6, 7.7, 7.8, 7.9, 7.13, 8.1, 8.2, 8.6, 8.7, 9.2, 9.5, 9.6, 9.7, 9.8, 9.9, 9.10, 9.11	48
2	Reference to act of story-telling/type of writing	1.7, 1.8, 1.15, 1.18, 2.7, 2.11, 3.7, 3.8, 3.9, 3.10, 3.11, 3.12, 4.4, 4.7, 4.16	15	2.5, 4.3, 4.9	3	1.1, 1.3, 1.5, 3.3, 5.2, 6.1, 6.3, 6.5, 6.7, 6.8, 6.9, 6.11, 7.1, 7.2, 7.7, 7.9, 8.1, 8.7, 8.8, 9.5, 9.6, 9.7, 9.10, 9.11, 9.12	25
3	Reference to reception/ reader	1.9, 1.12, 2.12, 3.8, 3.10, 3.11, 3.12, 3.13, 4.5, 4.6, 4.8, 4.12	12	2.1, 2.5, 4.3	3	1.1, 1.4, 1.5, 1.6, 1.9, 1.10, 1.12, 2.6, 3.1, 3.8, 5.1, 5.4, 5.5, 6.9, 7.13, 8.6, 8.7, 9.8, 9.9	19

Figure 1. Survey of the chapter titles in *Joseph Andrews*, *David Simple*, and *The Female Quixote*.

themselves, but to their juxtaposition with other titles, in which the thematic elements are compromised or undermined. The title of the penultimate chapter already slightly departs from the principle of straightforward summary: "4.15 The Arrival of Gaffar and Gammar *Andrews*, with another Person, not much expected; and a perfect Solution of the Difficulties raised by the Pedlar." These paratextual elements involve a careful balancing of revealing and withholding of information—hinting at the novel's happy ending without revealing how exactly it is going to be brought about. They thus seem designed to circumvent a fundamental problem of thematic titling in fictional narratives (in contrast to historical chronicles): how to fulfill the orienting function of summarizing without providing so much information as to diminish the audience's interest.[16]

While some of the titles solve this problem, others self-consciously engage with it. A large number of titles are inordinately long, revealing the outcome of conflicts or containing peripheral information, such as "1.15 Shewing how Mrs. *Tow-wouse* was a little mollified; and how officious Mr. *Barnabas* and the Surgeon were to prosecute the Thief: With a Dissertation accounting for their Zeal; and that of many other Persons not mentioned in this History."[17] Others work in the opposite way: they provide markedly vague information about the contents of the chapter, such as "1.14 Being very full of Adventures, which succeeded each other at the Inn" or "1.11 Of several new Matters not expected."[18] Rather than just summing up the chapters, they play with the idea that they should perform this function. In Genette's terminology, they thus invite a rhematic as well as a thematic reading: they characterize *Joseph Andrews* as a book that manipulates the reader's expectations of being informed and entertained. The self-reflexive handling of thematic and rhematic functions becomes especially obvious in a title that fuses references to both in a chiastic gesture: "2.7 A very short Chapter, in which Parson *Adams* went a great way." Like this example, a relatively large number (fifteen, i.e. almost one-quarter of the total number) not only invite a rhematic reading as a connotative effect, by evoking and undermining expected patterns, but explicitly foreground the act of storytelling or type of writing *Joseph Andrews* purports to be.

The self-reflexive tendency of the titles, which is congruent with other elements in the novel, points towards larger questions connected with the issue of the social functions of reading and writing. James Cruise has argued that in *Joseph Andrews*, Fielding set out to pit an older social order resting on paternal authority against the pervasive influence of commercialism.[19] This commercialism, Cruise argues, is represented by many of the characters encountered by Joseph and Fanny on their journey, particularly the innkeepers; the old system of authority is mainly tied to the authorial narrator, who "supervises and directs the action of the novel by watching over it in the manner of a benevolent patriarch."[20] Cruise shows that although the narrator's comments are set up as opposing "self-interested commercialism," he involves himself in the developments he deplores when he presents himself as a writer of fiction, which is tantamount to "implicat[ing] oneself in the world or to become commercial against better judgment."[21] Writing, in this view, is intimately linked to the notion of bookselling.

I would argue that the chapter titles (which are not mentioned by Cruise, who is more interested in characterization and plot development) are another place where the pervasive character of commercialism not only becomes apparent, but is self-consciously addressed. On the one hand, some titles make fun of the notion that they should help to sell a commodity, as in the hyperbolic reference in "3.9 Containing as surprizing and bloody Adventures as can be found in this, or perhaps any other authentic History." A title that dispenses with the thematic function altogether works along similar lines: "3.8 Which some Readers will think too short, and others too long" can be read as an ironic meditation on and possibly dismissal of the need to conform to the taste of a public, as a project that is ultimately doomed. On the other hand, however, the skillful handling of expectation and suspense, as well as the only half ironic inn metaphor used for the titles, suggest that they themselves admit to being shaped by the logic of a literary marketplace. The issue of the audience's desired and actual response to the text is raised even more explicitly through the sizeable number of intertitles (twelve) envisaging the reaction of an audience. Some of these contain tongue-in-cheek references to the reader as someone who must be entertained (for instance, 3.12: "More Adventures, which we hope will as much please as surprize the Reader").

The idea of appealing to the reader's desire for sensational reading and suspense, however, is not the only one that is under scrutiny. A few of the titles also bring up what is arguably the eighteenth century's central issue with regard to reading: the problem of the moral function of fictional literature, i.e. the notion that, in the words of Samuel Johnson, these texts should serve as "lectures of conduct, and introductions into life."[22] Such a notion is reflected prominently in the title "3.11 Containing the Exhortations of Parson *Adams* to his Friend in Affliction; calculated for the Instruction and Improvement of the Reader." The stance towards literature expressed here may be seen as congruent with that in the preface of *Joseph Andrews*, where the idea of moral instruction through fiction is discussed explicitly.[23] A closer look at the title itself, and especially at the chapter it precedes, however, reveals it to be anything but a straightforward comment. Adams's lectures appear to be of no greater moral value than Joseph's natural outburst of grief at the loss of Fanny, the incident against which they are directed. The reader is thus invited to take the title as ironic (that is, Adams's sermon is not really instructive). This does not necessarily mean, however, that the chapter offers no moral commentary: the reader may feel invited to draw some kind of moral lesson from the example of Joseph and Adams's behavior, for instance, by comparing and evaluating their contrasting attitudes.

Chapter titles like this thus provide a metacommentary on the purpose and the workings of fiction: while the general idea that fiction contributes to instruction is clearly supported, the problem lies in the realization of this requirement. One issue is the problem of contrasting perspectives, hinted at in the example described above. The other question is also implicit in the title of 3.11: *how* does instruction via fictional text work? The title suggests that the promised improvement does not lie in Adams's explicit statements. This also implies that fictional texts in general should not resemble sermons, in which a lesson is laid out. The already cited title "3.8 Which some Readers will think too short, and others too long," can be reconsidered in this light. In this chapter, a priest denounces people who value riches, which turns out to be a ruse designed to get Adams to lend him some money. The title can be interpreted in the light of this specific content, as projecting two opposing attitudes towards the kind of explicit sermon provided by the priest. While one kind of reader would like to see more of this kind of writing, another one would prefer to dispense with such parts altogether, presumably in favor of more action and suspense. Both of these fictional readers are in danger of missing the point of the chapter, which hinges on the juxtaposition of a person's words and his behavior: as often in Fielding, the person advertising his morality is exposed as a hypocrite by the way he acts. The kind of improvement the novel offers to the reader is then not so much predicated on an explicit moral lesson as on the idea that he or she are trained in the detection of affectation.[24] This idea of the novel as implicitly guiding the reader has often been looked at along the lines suggested by Wolfgang Iser, who analyzes Fielding's novels in the context of his theory of the "implied reader." Iser depicts the abundance of commentaries and reader addresses as elements which mimic a dialogue, pre-structuring reading experiences and allowing the author to maneuver the audience towards moral enlightenment.[25] A central problem that remains for Iser's influential approach is the degree to which it sees the reader as subjected to authorial control: which textual features should be seen as exercising such control, and which as opening up free spaces of interpretation?[26] Rather than presuming to offer an answer to the difficult question of whether and how guidance works for actual audiences, I am interested in the finding that the chapter titles themselves negotiate issues of authorial control and impact on the reader and thus both participate in and reflect on contemporary debate.

It should not be overlooked that although Henry Fielding's chapter titles are similar to thematic titles in other works, including those by Sarah Fielding and Charlotte Lennox, they are also special cases because they are highly congruent with what may be called the text proper. The scarcity of studies focusing solely on the chapter titles in *Joseph Andrews* or *Tom Jones* may perhaps even be explained by the fact that they do not appear as separate accompanying productions with special functions, as they might in other works, because the texts as a whole constantly engage in the kind of self-reflection that is offered by the titles. Neither metanarrative commentary, nor reader address or ironic moralizing are confined to the chapter headings, which almost seamlessly merge with the discourse of the narrator—constructing an authorial persona that openly presents itself as responsible for every feature of the text as artifact.[27] The full potential of the thematic chapter title thus becomes apparent only in comparison to two works that at first sight and to some readers might seem to offer less satisfying version of what Anna Uddén has termed the Fieldingesque model.[28]

The Complex Didacticism of *David Simple*

At first sight, Sarah Fielding's *The Adventures of David Simple* seems to employ a kind of thematic titling similar to that used by her brother Henry.[29] The novel features headings summing up salient points (for instance, "1.4. The first setting out of Mr. *David Simple* on his Journey; with some very remarkable and uncommon Accidents") as well as those playing with the idea of a summary of action (for instance, "2.7 The Continuation of the History of *Cynthia*, with an Account in what manner she was suddenly transformed from a Wit into a Toad-eater, without any visible Change, in either her Person or Behaviour," which features a surplus of detail that puzzles rather than helps). There is even a purely metanarrative title that is reminiscent of Henry's inn metaphor: "4.3. Containing such a Variety, as makes it impossible to draw up a Bill of Fare; but all the Guests are heartily welcome; and I am in hopes every one will find something to please his Palate."

A closer look, however, reveals major differences. Of its total of thirty-eight chapter titles, only nine feature a straightforward summary of salient plot elements. The kind of chapter title that is maybe most distinctive for *David Simple* is almost absent from *Joseph Andrews* (except for two cases, 4.10 and arguably 2.16): a relatively large number of titles (fifteen) present summaries that do not pertain to any concrete characters or elements of the plot, but instead focus on the lesson that might be drawn from the chapter. Examples include "1.2 In which is seen the terrible Consequences that attend

Envy and Selfishness" or "4.8 Which proves the great Difference of those wrong Actions which arise from violent Passions, and those which have their Source in the Malignity of a rancorous Heart." This way of titling foregrounds the notion that the characters and scenes presented in fiction are supposed to function as *exempla* and thus prefigure the reader in the role of someone who reads (or should read) not for pleasure or interest in the particularities of the fictional world, but for self-instruction through universal truths. Such a focus seems to be in keeping with the allegorical quality of the novel's episodes, which show the main character in his search for a true and honest person. Seen in this light, the paratextual elements emphasize the didactic aspect of the stories about the different people David Simple meets, which all contain lessons about human conduct.

This description, however, is in some ways misleading. It does not yet pay tribute to the fact that more than half of the fifteen titles that apparently prescribe moral interpretations of the contents are not didactic in a straightforward sense. The title of chapter 1.10, for example, is clearly ironic: "Which teacheth Mankind a true and easy Method of serving their Friends," heads a chapter describing the strange behavior of crowds at a play. The good-natured David is puzzled by a man who professes to be the playwright's friend, but is very noisy in damning the play during the performance, and later justifies his behavior as a charitable act, designed to discourage his friend from writing further plays. Clearly, this way of treating "friends" is criticized by its juxtaposition with David's notion of friendship. The title could thus be read as a case of what James Kim has called satiric irony, which "exposes disjunctions between 'appearance' and 'reality' in order to provoke ridicule and assign moral blame."[30] As Kim sees it, in contrast to her brother, Sarah Fielding was suspicious of this kind of irony because it tends to cement rather than question complacent attitudes on the part of the audience.[31] The observation that she uses it in some of her titles may seem to contradict this view. Used in the chapter title rather than in the main text, however, the satiric irony has a more complex effect than giving the reader the comfortable feeling of being on the side of a moral majority. The irony here also becomes a self-reflexive comment: it draws attention both to the promises and to the problems of fictional teaching (what, if anything, can we learn from bad examples?) and cautions against complacent judgments on the part of both the author and the reader.

This self-reflexive function of satiric irony could not, of course, be sustained by isolated appearance in one or two titles. It works because it reoccurs in other features—in the use of what Kim calls sentimental irony in another subset of chapter titles, and in the way in which the titles relate to features from the main text, especially the representation of David's education and the narrator's commentary on the behavior David encounters. A good example can be found in chapter 1.8, which is headed: "Wherein is to be seen the Infallibility of Men's Judgments, concerning the Virtues or Vices of their own Wives." The chapter juxtaposes the story of a man who is married to a lazy and disagreeable woman, but thinks her the best wife in the world, with that of another husband, who never appreciates his wife's efforts to please him. Again, the title is clearly ironic in some way—the men are anything but infallible. However, the target of the irony is not immediately obvious—is this directed mainly against the undeserving wife who fools her husband, the husband who does not appreciate the good wife, both husbands for their lack of good judgment, or more generally the belief that people commonly exercise an objective judgment of near relations?

Perhaps readers are being prompted to consider all of the above, which makes the title a case of sentimental irony in Kim's sense, as it "highlight[s] moral complexity" and "enunciate[s] psychological principles."[32] The chapter itself also leads us through all of these motions. Interestingly, it not only questions the behavior of those two characters who behave badly—the undeserving wife and the ungrateful husband—but presents these two as involved in dysfunctional relationships. The observer David tries to explain the first case by regarding the husband as a henpecked victim of deception:

> After all the Reflections that could be made on this Subject, there could be no other Reason assign'd for this poor Man's being such a willing Slave, but her [the wife's] great Pride, and high Spirit, which imposed on him, and made him afraid to disoblige her; together with a sufficient manner of talking, which made him imagine her more capable than she really was, in all respects.[33]

This clear-cut division of blame, however, is immediately challenged by the narrator, who in contrast to David figures in the asymmetrical distribution of power between the sexes: "I think it very likely, if she had known her own Deserts, and been humble in her Behaviour, he would have paid her no other Compliment, but confessing she was in the right, in the mean Thoughts she had of herself. He then would have been Master in his own House, and made a Drudge of her."[34] A confirmation of this view then follows in the second part of the story. A stock tale of satire is thus turned into a complex case that features both sociological aspects (in particular, the relation between the sexes, which is also emphasized by the allusion to the gender binary in the title) and psychological aspects (the way in which the wife's self-esteem and behavior are shown to influence her husband's image of himself and of her). A meta-dimension is added with the notion of the fallibility of judgment, which in the title refers to the husbands, but which can also be extended to David's (and by implication, the reader's) problem in finding an adequate interpretation and evaluation for the story.

Henry Fielding, who revised his sister's text for a second edition, extended this title by adding the sentence "A Scene Taken from very low Life, in which only such Examples are to be found," which seems to suggest that the main explanation for the problem is class, and that none of this applies to the circles to which the reader probably belongs.[35] Even if this was Fielding's intention when he added this line, the fact that it clashes with the rest of the chapter with its psychological and sociological complexities may also invite an ironic reading, which in turn comports with tendencies found in some of the other titles: it would then appear to be directed against a simplistic notion of moral instruction and interpretation. If one reads the addition to the title as ironic, one can even say that in alluding to the traditional class divide between comedy and tragedy, it charges texts in the comic tradition with reproducing class stereotypes rather than moral insights.

A last example, which combines a particular thematic reference with a generalizing tendency, also reflects on the possibilities and limits of a didactic stance: "2.1 Which is writ only with a View to instruct our Readers, that Whist is a game very much in Fashion." This title not only makes fun of the superficialities of urban high society, but also playfully presents the question what kind of instruction readers can or should expect from fictional narratives.

The more playful metanarrative titles in the style of *Joseph Andrews* have a different status here than in Henry Fielding's novel in part because of their smaller number, but also because the narrative voice employed in *David Simple* differs markedly from that in Henry Fielding's novel. It seems much less playful and self-reflexive, with far fewer comments on narrative technique. Instead of blending with the text proper, those paratextual elements that *are* playful and self-reflexive thus introduce a new tone. An older brand of criticism would probably have dismissed this lack of homogeneity as showing insufficient control on the part of Sarah Fielding, charging her with an incompetent mixing of her own style with elements copied from her brother.[36] I would argue, however, that instead of attributing the changes of register to a lack of skill on the part of the novel's author, one should regard them as a way of negotiating different reader roles.

There are three roles that are especially significant in this novel: that of the reader as a receptive and naive instructee, as a distanced and sophisticated critic, and as a compassionate companion. The conflict between the first two roles is addressed in the kind of title that is discussed above. The third role, interestingly, is one that is almost absent from the chapter titles, but offered to the reader in conspicuous reader addresses in the text itself: "What this poor Creature, whose Heart was naturally tender and grateful, felt at seeing himself loaded with Benefits from a Stranger, I leave to the Imagination of every Reader, who can have any Sense of Obligations; and those that have none, I am sure must think enough of Trifles, to imagine he must be pleased, after being some time in Rags, to have whole Clothes put on."[37] David himself provides a model of compassionate reception, as he is always listening to other characters' stories, and always ready to offer the emotional response that is required, to rejoice or to cry with the protagonists. Allen Michie sees this early example of sentimental writing as inaugurating a "new philosophy of reception": "using her characters as model readers, sentimental anecdotes and vignettes are seen not just as adventures to entertain or moral lessons to instruct, but also as little gifts of pure emotion we give to one another for the sake of the joy and renewal they bring."[38]

I would argue that the marked absence of the emotional dimension of reader address in the chapter titles contributes to making the novel even more multi-faceted than Michie suggests: the emotional impact of reading is juxtaposed with the moral lessons. There is one title that focuses on David's reaction to a story: "2.9 In which Mr. *Simple* gave a fresh Proof, that he was not insensible of his Fellow-Creatures' Sufferings." This proof is not connected with a lesson, but with both an emotional reaction and an empathic act on the part of the hero. Like the passage quoted above, the title contains an implicit challenge to the reader to probe the extent and limits of his or her own sensitivity and compassion. The more playful chapter titles, in turn, demonstrate a distance from the action described in the chapters they are heading, thus introducing the possibility of a more cerebral engagement with questions of human conduct and morality. The naivety of David's character as well as the oscillations in tone, finally, pose the question of how, if at all, the two positions may be reconciled. Fiction becomes a test case for probing our stance towards our "fellow-creatures."

In sum, then, like *Joseph Andrews*, *David Simple* also offers a complex engagement with the purposes and effects of fictional reading. While the chapter titles play an important part in this reflection in both works, they have a more conspicuous function in Sarah Fielding's work, both because they appear as more clearly separated from the text proper, and because they are more diverse in style. The alternation between the predominantly playful or ironic titles and the predominantly more earnest tone of main narrative, as well as the variation of satiric and sentimental irony should not be dismissed as a lack of authorial control but taken seriously as an exploration of different stances for both author and reader. In particular, *David Simple* engages with an issue that would gain more attention as the century progressed: that of the possible impact of reading on the emotions. Not only should it be seen as an important early example of the sentimental novel, as critics like Allen Michie have argued,[39] but also as offering a commentary on the poetics and reception of the kind of writing it represents.

The Interrogation of Instruction and Authority in *The Female Quixote*

Of the three novels discussed in this article, Charlotte Lennox's is the one that is most obviously concerned with reading as a problem—after all, the misadventures of a reader are at the heart of its plot. *The Female Quixote* centers on the character of Arabella, who—as the title already suggests—has grown up on a diet of French romances and now perceives the world around her in terms of the models she knows from her books.[40] On the level of the story, Arabella's reading is the subject of several discussions between the characters, which mirror contemporary debates on the effects and purposes of fictional reading. This focus on the relation between fictional text and reader may be less obvious on the level of the novel's discourse—like in *David Simple*, the narrator holds back on self-reflexive commentary concerning the book *The Female Quixote*, and the text proper contains almost no explicit reader addresses. Again, the chapter titles play a key role in that they perform a complex reflection of the novel's own status and functioning, which is in turn closely related to the issues raised by the characters. Of a total of ninety-two intertitles in *The Female Quixote*, nineteen feature explicit references to the reader or the act of reception (for instance, "1.9 In which a Lover is severely punished for Faults the Reader never would have discovered, if he had not been told what they were") and twenty-five to the act of storytelling or type of writing (for instance, "In which one would imagine the Adventure concluded, but for a promise that something else is to come"). The percentage of titles with this kind of metanarrativity is thus even higher than in *Joseph Andrews*, where it features much more consistently in the body of the text. This makes the chapter titles in Lennox's work both a privileged and a conspicuous site for conveying rhematic information.

One fairly obvious function of the chapter titles is to emphasize the difference between the kind of writing Arabella loves and the kind of writing Lennox herself has produced in *The Female Quixote*. This juxtaposition makes use of many of the well-rehearsed oppositions prominent in the novel-romance debate, such as improbable and outlandish versus plausible plot. A chapter title that casts the contrast in terms of two different systems of values would be "1.4 A Mistake which produces no great Consequences—An extraordinary Comment upon a Behaviour natural enough—An Instance of a Lady's Compassion for her Lover, which the Reader may possibly think not very compassionate." Here, the inadequacy of Arabella's responses is demonstrated by pointing out how her idea of "compassion," which is induced by romance reading, differs from the social norm, which is staged in Lennox's novel. The contrast between the "extraordinary Comment" and the "natural Behaviour" could be interpreted in the same way (and would then refer to Arabella's view of her "Lover's" behaviour), but it could also be understood in the opposite sense, as referring to the man's, Mr Hervey's, reaction to an action by Arabella. If understood in the latter sense, the chapter title would have an ironic slant, pretending to endorse Arabella's perspective and evaluation of events.

While I regard this case as ambiguous, there are others that clearly display irony. For example, "2.10 In which our Heroine is engaged in a very perilous Adventure" reproduces Arabella's expectation (ridiculed at many points in the plot) that her life should be a series of exciting and romantic adventures. The chapter title—like many others which play with the concept of "adventure"—not only makes fun of the character's view of the world, but also has a parodic effect: *The Female Quixote* itself copies the style of Arabella's French romances. In the case of some chapters, parodic titles undoubtedly serve to emphasize *The Female Quixote*'s difference from the romance model.[41] This is especially obvious in the case of the hyperbolic titles heading those chapters in which the unsympathetic character Sir George acts as an intradiegetic narrator in the romantic style, e.g "6.2 In which Sir *George*, continuing his surprising History, relates a most stupendous Instance of a Valour only to be paralleled by that of the great *Oroondates*, *Caesario*, &c. &. &c."

In other cases, however, the juxtaposition seems to collapse. The already cited title of chapter 2.10, for example, is both an ironic reference to the romance pattern *and* an adequate description of the chapter contents: because of her romantic disposition, the protagonist really does bring herself into a dangerous situation.[42] The paratext thus at least partially invites the recipient to adopt or at least consider a romance model in his or her own reading. Such paratextual blurrings of boundaries between Arabella's romances and the kind of writing represented by *The Female Quixote* itself invite the question of how far the problem with reading is really confined to a specific type of fiction. They suggest that fundamental issues with regard to fictional writing do not disappear with a transition from romance to more realist writing.

The two most central of these issues reflected in the novel are those of moral instruction and authority. They come into view if one analyses the chapter titles' relation to the text proper. First of all, many of those titles that explicitly refer to the process of reception raise the question of authorial control: "1.6 In which the Adventure is really concluded, tho' possibly not as the Reader expected", "3.8 By which, we hope, the Reader will be differently affected" or "5.5 In which will be found one of the former Mistakes pursued, and another cleared up, to the great Satisfaction of two Persons, among whom, we expect, the Reader will make a third." These paratextual elements prepare the recipient by sketching adequate responses to the chapters' content. At the same time, however, it is striking how almost every suggestion for a response is qualified with "possibly," "perhaps," "may," "we expect," and even "in the Author's Opinion." Even if these titles make no secret of the preferred reading, the hedges draw attention to the process rather than the result of emotional or moral response. Authorial control is asserted, but at the same time characterized as an imposition on the reader, and thus partially undermined.

The problem of moral instruction, in turn, is already complicated by the way in which the main character is represented. In some respects, Arabella can actually be regarded as a model reader: she fully endorses the Johnsonian idea that the purpose of reading is to emulate a moral ideal.[43] One of the complexities of *The Female Quixote* is that to a degree, the heroine actually achieves this goal—in contrast to some of the other characters, Arabella is represented as having internalized positive values in the romance such as generosity.[44] The problem is, however, that the patterns of speech and behavior she has copied from the romances are not conformable to the expectations of the people around her. From the perspective of social convention, some of the points that are innocent within a romance context, for example Arabella's expectation of adventures, appear suspect. The heroine is thus both morally superior and dangerously flawed. As Deborah Ross puts it, "A reader seeking wisdom from *The Female Quixote* would often be unsure whether to view Arabella as a model or as a warning."[45] The chapter titles that simultaneously portray her as the heroine of the story and as the object of ridicule reflect this issue.

There are a few titles that offer an ironic commentary on moral instruction as a problem. "5.2 Which inculcates, by a very good Example, that a Person ought not to be too hasty, in deciding a Question he does not perfectly understand" presents a commonplace as if it were a weighty moral insight. In the case of "2.8 Which concludes with an excellent moral Sentence," the "sentence" also turns out to be so universal that it borders on a platitude: "So little capable are poor Mortals of knowing what is best for them!"[46] In fact, this title withholds rather than offers a moral perspective on the events described in the chapter, commenting neither on foolish behavior on the part of Arabella (she invites a stranger to her castle because she mistakenly thinks that common civility requires this) nor on this stranger's dubious designs. The lesson promised by the chapter title thus turns out to be mock instruction. What appears to be ridiculed in both cases is the notion of explicit didactic sermonizing as a valid literary strategy.

By contrast, the penultimate chapter title "9.11 Being, in the Author's Opinion, the best Chapter in this History" seems to be all in favour of explicit moralizing. It heads the chapter in which Arabella is cured of her predilection for romances by the doctor, a character modeled after Samuel Johnson, who lectures her on the immoral tendencies of these works. Many commentators find fault with the authorial endorsement and see this as the worst chapter of the book—some because they disapprove of a sermon replacing learning by experience,[47] some because they feel that it establishes a patriarchal discourse that was questioned in earlier parts of the novel.[48] By contrast, Anna Uddén has suggested that the chapter title should—like many of the others titles—be read as ironic, attributing the doctor's diatribe against Arabella's reading to a dogmatic character in the story instead of giving an authorial endorsement.[49] Uddén's perceptive analysis here offers an elegant solution to the interpreter who wants to resolve contradictions in the narrative. Yet, I think it would be rash to accuse those readers who have read the ending as a straight-forward moral lesson of misinterpretation. What is characteristic of Lennox's text is precisely that it features aspects which support either kind of reading.

This reflects unsolved general problems besetting the author of fictional texts: how to find the best way of instructing audiences that include the sophisticated, educated reader who seems to be the main addressee of Henry Fielding's work, as well as the inexperienced reader (probably young and female); and how to adequately respond to the problem that notions of virtue in society are inextricably bound up with both custom and power relations. The ironical invocations of different text types appear to be addressed at an audience of skilled readers, who recognize the different modes and enjoy the frictions that are playfully set up between them. At the same time, these elements are not so disruptive as to confuse a naive reader who wants to understand Arabella as a didactic model. The heterogeneous composition thus allows for different desired modes of address, but it also points to the fact that *The Female Quixote* does not itself purport to have a solution to the debates in which it engages.

For Gérard Genette, "[t]he effect of the paratext lies very often in the realm of influence—indeed, manipulation—experienced subconsciously. This mode of operation is doubtless in the author's interest, though not always in the reader's."[50] The chapter titles in the three novels, I have argued in this paper, not only seek to exert influence, but make it visible as a challenge and a problem: they openly probe the possibilities and limits of the effect fictional texts have on their readership. All three works engage with the notion that fiction can make an important contribution to the project of self-cultivation, be it predominantly cognitive, moral, or emotional. Each in its own way seeks to find an adequate shape for the then newly emerging genre of the novel—and use the chapter titles to provide a running commentary on this endeavor. While at first sight, there are some striking similarities between the titling employed in the three works, a second look reveals significant differences. Perhaps most importantly, the works by Sarah Fielding and Charlotte Lennox utilize the titles' liminal status to raise issues of authority and instruction, while Henry Fielding blends text and paratext into a highly self-reflexive whole. Seeing *Joseph Andrews* as a model for the other two texts thus holds the danger of obscuring significant differences between the texts, or (maybe even more perniciously) of establishing a standard of evaluation that does not do justice to each of the three distinct modes of representation.

NOTES

An earlier version of this paper was delivered at the 2010 ASECS conference in Albuquerque. I would like to thank Norbert Schuerer for putting together the panel on paratext, and Lisa Cody, Monika Fludernik, Sabine Volk-Birke, and Robyn Warhol for their criticism and advice.

1. References are to the Wesleyan edition of *The Works of Henry Fielding*, gen. ed. W. B. Coley (Middletown: Wesleyan University Press, 1967–2008), here to *The Adventures of Joseph Andrews* (1967), ed. Martin C. Battestin, 90.

2. Gérard Genette, *Paratexts: Thresholds of Interpretation*, trans. Jane E. Lewin (Cambridge: Cambridge University Press, 1997). French original *Seuils* (Paris: Editions du Seuil, 1987), 1. All references are to the English translation. The examples all fall within a subcategory of paratext, which Genette designates as "peritext," i.e. elements located in the same volume as the text. "Epitext," on the other hand, while also attributable to author or publisher, originates outside the volume: interviews, advertisements, authors' letters etc. See, Genette, *Paratexts*, 5.

3. As Richard Macksey puts it in his foreword to the English translation, he "seems to be the first to present a global view of liminal mediations and the logic of their relation to the reading public" (Macksey, "Introduction," in Genette, *Paratexts*, xi–xxiv, xx).

4. Genette, *Paratexts*, 89. To be precise, this distinction is introduced in the chapter on "Titles" rather than the one on "Intertitles," but I think it can usefully be applied to intertitles – to make this clearer, one could, in the quotation given above, substitute the word "chapter" where it now says "book."

5. Genette, *Paratexts*, 89.

6. Genette, *Paratexts*, 300.

7. Genette, *Paratexts*, 301. For a narratologically informed analysis of the paratext in *Don Quixote* (which does not, however, use the term, as it was written before Genette's study appeared), cf. James Parr, *Don Quixote: An Anatomy of Subversive Discourse* (Newark, DE: Cuesta, 1988), especially 51–54. One of Parr's main theses is that Cervantes inaugurates a self-conscious fictional tradition that subverts authority, including narrative authority, and that the complex paratexts play a key role in this endeavor.

8. Genette, *Paratexts*, 316.

9. The conspicuous use of paratextual elements is carried to an extreme in Laurence Sterne's *Tristram Shandy* (1759–67), which also marks a peak in the English novel's self-reflexive engagement with itself.

10. Karin Littau, *Theories of Reading: Books, Bodies and Bibliomania* (Cambridge: Polity, 2006), 21.

11. For examples, see the comprehensive collection of contemporary commentaries in Ioan Williams, ed., *Novel and Romance 1700–1800: A Documentary Record* (London: Routledge/Kegan Paul, 1970) and in John Tinnon Taylor, *Early Opposition to the English Novel: The Popular Reaction from 1760 to 1830* (New York: King's Crown, 1943).

12. Martin Hall, "Gender and Reading in the Late Eighteenth Century: the *Bibliothéque Universelle des Romans*," *Eighteenth-Century Fiction* 14.3 (2002): 771–89, 773.

13. For a full discussion of the "novel as criticism," see Ellen Gardiner, *Regulating Readers: Gender and Literary Criticism in the Eighteenth-Century Novel* (Newark/London: University of Delaware Press, 1999).

14. Till Dembeck, *Texte rahmen: Grenzregionen literarischer Werke im 18. Jahrhundert (Gottsched, Wieland, Moritz, Jean Paul)* (Berlin: de Gruyter, 2007), 101.

15. I have not found a good way around the problem that ultimately, the judgment whether a title represents an adequate summary of salient points in the chapter, has subjective aspects. In order to make my own point of view as transparent as possible, figure 1 provides a list of the titles as well as numbers.

16. The classical reference for an explicit contemporary comment on this problem is Lessing, who insists that a title should *not* work like a bill of fare: "Ein Titel muss kein Küchenzettel sein. Je weniger er vom Inhalt verrät, desto besser ist er." ("A title does not need to be a bill of fare. The less it reveals of the content, the better it

is." [my translation]); Gotthold Ephraim Lessing, "Hamburgische Dramaturgie," in Lessing, *Werke 1767–69*, ed. Klaus Bohnen, *Werke und Briefe*, (Frankfurt: 1985), 6: 276–698, 367. See also the discussion of this passage in Dembeck, *Texte rahmen*, 106–7 and Genette, *Paratexts*, 92.

17. I have counted thirteen titles that in this sense provide too much detail (included in fig. 1 as titles with "compromised summary function"): 1.7, 1.8, 1.9, 1.12, 1.15, 1.17, 2.10, 2.13, 2.17, 3.10, 4.8, 4.10, 4.14.

18. All in all, I would classify ten titles as "vague": 1.11, 1.14, 2.7, 2.12, 3.8, 3.9, 3.12, 3.13, 4.6, 4.12. Chapter titles I would see as in some way misleading include 1.2, 1.5 (because of its ironical mention of the widow's "affectionate and mournful behaviour"), 2.3 (which focuses on peripheral rather than main elements of the plot), 4.5 (which reads like a technical introduction into "justice business," while the chapter focuses on the outrageous story of the trial against Joseph and Fanny) and 4.9 (again irony).

19. James Cruise, "Fielding, Authority, and the New Commercialism in *Joseph Andrews*," *English Literary History* 54.2 (1987), 253–276.

20. Cruise, "Fielding, Authority, and the New Commercialism," 262.

21. Cruise, "Fielding, Authority, and the New Commercialism," 269.

22. Samuel Johnson, *The Rambler*, 31.03.1750, quotation here taken from reprint of the essay in Williams, *Novel and Romance*, 143.

23. Perhaps most famously, it is discussed in the passage in ch.3.1, which declares that the purpose of representing affectation and other vices in fictional characters is to "hold the Glass to thousands in their Closets, that they may contemplate their Deformity, and endeavour to reduce it," Fielding, *Joseph Andrews*, 189.

24. See Ronald Paulson's reading of Fielding's novels in *Don Quixote in England: The Aesthetics of Laughter* (Baltimore: Johns Hopkins University Press, 1998), 60.

25. Wolfgang Iser, "Die Leserrolle in Fieldings *Joseph Andrews* und *Tom Jones*", in Iser, ed., *Henry Fielding und der englische Roman des 18. Jahrhunderts* (Darmstadt: Wissenschaftliche Buchgesellschaft, 1972), 282–318, 306.

26. See for example Garrett Stewart's criticism of Iser's theory in *Dear Reader: The Conscripted Audience in Nineteenth-Century British Fiction* (Baltimore: Johns Hopkins UP, 1996), 10–11.

27. I am here drawing on Cheryl A. Nixon's discussion of how prefaces in eighteenth-century fiction allow a "self-definition that blurs the distinction between author and character, fact and fiction, text and pretext." Cheryl A. Nixon, "'Stop a Minute at this Preface': The Gendered Paratexts of Fielding, Barker and Haywood," *Journal of Narrative Theory* 32.2 (2002): 123–53, 123. "Authorial persona" is Nixon's shorthand term to describe this phenomenon, 131.

28. Anna Uddén, "Narratives and Counter-Narratives: Quixotic Hermeneutics in Eighteenth-Century England: Charlotte Lennox, *The Female Quixote*," *Partial Answers* 6.2 (2008): 443–57, 446.

29. References are to the edition *The Adventures of David Simple and Volume the Last*, ed. Peter Sabor (Lexington: University Press of Kentucky, 1998). In my analysis, I include only the chapter titles from the first two volumes, published as *The Adventures of David Simple* in 1744. *Volume the Last*, published in 1753, should, as Peter Sabor suggests in his introduction, better be understood as a work in its own right. See, Sabor, "Introduction," vii–xxxvii, xxxi. Even a brief comparison of the two works' chapter titles bears out the idea that they have different tendencies: for example, *Volume the Last* contains a large number of thematic titles which provide an ironic summary, including 6.5 "In which Mrs. Orgueil feels some Compassion, and Orgueil does a generous Action." This captures this work's general tendency to contrast the benevolent attitudes of David and his family with the selfish behavior of most of their acquaintances, especially the Orgueils. Further, none of the titles in *Volume the Last* provide the *exempla* that I describe as typical for the first two volumes.

30. James Kim, "Mourning, Melancholia, and Modernity: Sentimental Irony and Downward Mobility in *David Simple,*" *Eighteenth-Century Fiction* 22.3 (2010): 477–502, 486.

31. Kim, "Mourning, Melancholia, and Modernity", 486.

32. Kim, "Mourning, Melancholia, and Modernity", 486.

33. Fielding, *David Simple*, 40.

34. Fielding, *David Simple,* 51.

35. See Peter Sabor, "Introduction," *David Simple*, xxx.

36. Malcolm Kelsall's 1969 introduction to *David Simple* does not explicitly mention the paratext, but portrays Sarah Fielding as being torn between her brother's satiric style and "the irresistible pull of romance," which, as he sees it, results in breaks in the plot structure. Malcolm Kelsall, ed. and intro. to *The Adventures of David Simple* (Oxford: Oxford University Press, 1969), ix–xxiii, xiii.

37. Fielding, *David Simple*, 102.

38. Allen Michie, "Far from Simple: Sarah Fielding's *Familiar Letters* and the Limits of the Eighteenth-Century Sequel," in Debra Taylor Bourdeau and Elizabeth Kraft, eds, *On Second Thought: Updating the Eighteenth-Century Text* (Newark, DE: University of Delaware Press, 2007), 83–111, 100.

39. Michie, "Far from Simple," 85.

40. All references are to Charlotte Lennox, *The Female Quixote*, ed. Margaret Dalziel and intro. Margaret Anne Doody (Oxford: Oxford University Press, 1989).

41. Deborah Ross states more generally that "[n]ever did a novel so loudly proclaim its own realism in direct opposition to the romance, which Lennox' narrator seems unequivocally to condemn." Deborah Ross, "Mirror, Mirror: The Didactic Dilemma of *The Female Quixote,*" *Studies in English Literature, 1500–1900*, 27.3 (1987): 455–73, 456.

42. As John Richetti notes, Arabella in a sense really does turn herself into a

romance heroine; John Richetti, *The English Novel in History 1700–1780* (London: Routledge, 1999), 208. The fact that the novel uses many of the romance patterns it seems to denounce has been commented upon by a number of scholars, including Laurie Langbauer, *Women and Romance: The Consolations of Gender in the English Novel* (Ithaca: Cornell University Press, 1990), 65 and Ross, "Mirror, Mirror," 458.

43. Samuel Johnson, *The Rambler*, 31.03.1750, 143.

44. Scott Paul Gordon, "The Space of Romance in Lennox' *Female Quixote*," *SEL: Studies in English Literature, 1500–1900*, 38.3 (1998): 499–516.

45. Ross, "Mirror, Mirror," 466.

46. Lennox, *Female Quixote*, 87.

47. Duncan Isles, "Appendix: Johnson, Richardson, and *The Female Quixote,*" in Dalziel, ed. *The Female Quixote*, 419–28, 426.

48. Langbauer, *Women and Romance*, 81.

49. Uddén, "Narratives and Counter-Narratives," 453.

50. Genette, *Paratexts*, 409.

Ann Yearsley's "Clifton Hill" and its Lessons in Reading

CATHERINE KEOHANE

Hannah More's patronage of the laboring-class poet Ann Yearsley and their famous, public quarrel have become familiar to scholars of the long eighteenth century and need no detailed rehearsal here. For years often relegated to a side note in accounts of More, Yearsley has gained renewed critical attention over the last twenty years with scholars examining both her writings and her relationships with More and her later patrons.[1] Although More and Yearsley's working relationship was brief, lasting about one year, it helped shape how Yearsley was seen by both contemporaries and subsequent readers and scholars. The introductory letter More wrote for Yearsley's *Poems, on Several Occasions*, the 1785 volume whose subscription publication she organized, has played an enduring role in conceptions of her one-time protégée. While Kerri Andrews rightly advocates the need for increased attention to Yearsley's later works, the rich material of the first volume still warrants attention as well—both in its own right and in its challenges not only to More's public presentation of Yearsley but also to our own reading of her work.[2] The last and longest poem in that volume, "Clifton Hill. Written in 1785," refutes More's representation of Yearsley's literary experience and presents its own readers with lessons in how to read by depicting misreadings that illustrate the failure to sympathize.

Sparked by views in and around Yearsley's native Bristol, including the Clifton Church graveyard, St. Vincent's rocks, the Hotwells, the Avon river, and Leigh Woods, among other sites, the speaker of "Clifton Hill" surveys a range of topics.[3] Some of this prospect poem's meditations feature challenges that engage concepts of reading, broadly construed, that fall into two categories: first, challenges to middling and elite contemporaries' views of Yearsley, and, second, challenges to narrow perspectives which ignore others' wishes with potentially harmful results. On one hand, reading can be seen as representative of an individual's literacy and education, or as a marker of class, making the issue of what Yearsley actually read matter. While More's catalog and appraisal of her literary experience created a limited, even caricatured understanding of Yearsley and her work among her contemporaries and later readers, the opening depiction of winter in "Clifton Hill" provides insight into Yearsley's reading, which I address in the first two sections of this article. On the other hand, reading can be understood more broadly as an interpretive activity involving not simply texts but also people, situations, and new experiences. "Clifton Hill" suggests how difficult it is to read anything or anyone sympathetically if the reader is not receptive to, or perhaps even aware of, others' points of view, needs, and desires. The speaker's meditations on the red-breast, the graveyard lesson in mortality, and Louisa of the hay-stack, which I address in the last three sections, provide examples of misreading, intentional or not, that are grounded in resistance to other perspectives. By asking its readers to engage these multiple forms of reading, "Clifton Hill" challenges readers' preconceived assumptions about Yearsley and her works; by opening ourselves to other points of view than More's (and our own), we will not only find a different, more sophisticated Yearsley but also become more attuned to the potential interference of biases in any interpretive experience.

Yearsley's Reading

"Clifton Hill" presents a model for our rethinking of inherited ideas about the poet, ideas that were largely shaped by Hannah More's efforts to win subscribers for Yearsley's first volume prior to its publication in June 1785. As her moniker reinforces, Yearsley, "the Bristol Milkwoman Poet," was clearly identified as a member of the laboring classes, an identification that inspired limited and classist biographical perceptions while playing to the growing popularity of the so-called "uneducated" poets in the late eighteenth-century.[4] More's presentation of Yearsley in her introduction to the volume, "A Prefatory Letter to Mrs. Montagu. By a Friend," established the context for the public's understanding of Yearsley. In this text More skillfully manipulates late-eighteenth-century notions about charity, the worthy poor, and uneducated poets to craft a partially fictionalized, embellished biography, which had and continues to have the power to foster possible misreadings of Yearsley through its sensationalized account and, what I focus on here, its catalog of what the poet herself had read. Since More intended her depiction of Yearsley's experience in reading to mark her as a member of the lower classes (and thus worthy of patronage and tempered praise), she crafts a limited and conventional stereotype of an autodidact that the middling and elite orders might find appealing and unthreatening. That, however, was not Ann Yearsley's entire story, and "Clifton Hill" asks the public to read her and her work from a broader perspective.

Crucially, readers need to recognize that the "Prefatory Letter" is a marketing tool: More's goal in this document is not to provide an accurate biography of Yearsley but rather to paint a portrait that would attract subscribers. But because there is as yet no other, more accurate eighteenth-century biographical source, scholars have often mined the "Prefatory Letter" for information about Yearsley. Critics Tim Burke, Richard Greene, Susanne Kord, and Linda Zionkowski have noted the constructed nature of the "Prefatory Letter" while Yearsley's modern biographer Mary Waldron has pointed to factual discrepancies.[5] Yet for the most part, scholars lean heavily on the letter and its claims without calling much attention to any potential problems in its portrayal.[6] Though the "Prefatory Letter" raises many important issues related to eighteenth-century conceptions of charity and the poor, I am more concerned here with its influence on our perceptions of Yearsley's reading (and by extension of Yearsley herself). By highlighting the letter's design to market Yearsley as an appealing member of the "uneducated" poets, we can better understand Yearsley's "Clifton Hill" as a poetic rebuttal of the filter created by More. As I argue, questioning a seemingly small biographical detail—More's version of Yearsley's reading—raises vital questions about class bias and stereotypes while also inspiring a more general wariness about More's representation of Yearsley.

Casting her introduction as a private letter to fellow Yearsley patron and "Queen of the Bluestockings" Elizabeth Montagu, More begins the "Prefatory Letter" with an account of how she came to know of Yearsley and her poems, and offers her impressions. While carefully selected, edited, and packaged, these impressions provide some insight into contemporary conceptions of the poor and of laboring-class poets—and in the portion I focus on, of their reading. More plays to her audience's anticipated class bias when she portrays herself as surprised by Yearsley's unexpectedly good, if "common," taste:

> on a more familiar acquaintance, I have had reason to be surprised at the justness of her taste, the faculty I least expected to find in her. In truth, her remarks on the books she has read are so accurate, and so consonant to the opinions of the best critics, that, from that very circumstance, they would appear trite and common-place, in any one who had been in habits of society; for, without having ever conversed with any body above her own level, she seems to possess the general principles of sound taste and just thinking.[7]

On the most obvious level, More's reported surprise reflects contemporary stereotypes of the poor and laboring classes. Not only did More and others of her class assume that the poor behaved in recognizably unpolished ways, they also assumed that the poor typically possessed only simple and simplistic thoughts. On another level, the passage would seem to challenge these stereotypes by presenting Yearsley, the Bristol Milkwoman Poet, as not only an accomplished reader but a judicious critic. But on yet another level, More's caveat that Yearsley's "remarks … would appear trite and common-place" had she been born higher, denies that Yearsley could possibly be more intelligent or more original than the educated classes. These multiple assumptions about the poor in general, Yearsley, and the polite reader encapsulate the tensions inherent in the concept of the laboring-class poet. More attempts to negotiate these tensions as she conveys an appropriate degree of praise for Yearsley's talent by depicting it as both unexpected and unthreateningly adhering to "the general principles of sound taste and just thinking."

This curious mix of prodigiousness and limits is also highlighted in More's representation of Yearsley's unexpected facility for reading. As More relates in the "Prefatory Letter," "I was curious to know what poetry she had read."

> With the Night Thoughts, and Paradise Lost, I found her well acquainted; but she was astonished to learn that Young and Milton had written any thing else. Of Pope, she had only seen the Eloisa; and Dryden, Spenser, Thomson, and Prior, were quite unknown to her, even by name. She has read a few of Shakespeare's Plays, and speaks of a translation of the Georgics, which she has somewhere seen, with the warmest poetic rapture.[8]

This presentation of Yearsley's seemingly unlikely reading materials may contribute to enhancing the overall public interest in her, helping More create an appealing portrait: not only is Yearsley a milkwoman who writes poetry, but she also has unexpected knowledge of very particular—and safe—classic texts. Although it is difficult to assess the accuracy of this catalog, literary critic and biographer Waldron rightly speculates "it may be that Yearsley was better read than More assumed."[9] It should be remembered that this catalog is at best an account of Yearsley's reading at a particular moment in time conveyed in conversation with More, and at worst it may be More's expurgated list. While Yearsley likely had read more by this point, certainly she read more after it, even before opening her own circulating library in the early 1790s.

Yet, continuing echoes of this catalog in Yearsley scholarship have the potential to reify its apparent accuracy despite the fact that certain poems in her first volume evidence Yearsley's broader reading as does private correspondence in which More discusses plans to provide Yearsley with additional reading material.[10] While the issue of what Yearsley had read most obviously concerns reading as a marker of class, this is necessarily intertwined with reading—interpretation—of Yearsley and her work. More than seeking to add individual names or titles to her patron's catalog, my concern is with the impulse to accept and repeat this information with little recognition of its constructed nature, which, as I discuss later, "Clifton Hill" itself exposes by providing strong, if indirect, evidence of Yearsley's knowledge of James Thomson's *The Seasons*.

More's "Prefatory Letter" is presented as though it were a repurposed private letter, but in fact it was a carefully crafted and edited revision, aimed at winning subscribers without unsettling some polite readers' condescending attitudes toward members of the lower ranks. Comparing More's representation of Yearsley's reading in the "Prefatory Letter" with that in her private correspondence makes the former's strategic construction apparent. While in the "Prefatory Letter" Yearsley is depicted as the "astonished" one during their conversation about books, in a private letter More presents herself as the one amazed by Yearsley's replies to her questions. An August 27, 1784, letter to Montagu provides a differently focused account of Yearsley's reading:

> I asked who were her favorite authors? "Among the Heathens," said she, "I have met with no such Composition as in Virgil's Georgics." How I stared! besides the choice was so professional. Of English Poets her favorites are Milton and Dr Young, the latter she said has an ardour and boldness in his Imagination that was very delightful to her.[11]

Notably, this account and that in the "Prefatory Letter" include different formulations of the question to which Milton and Young will be the answer: the "what poetry had she read" of the published introduction and the "who were her favorite authors" of the private letter. The "Prefatory Letter" erases the very significant difference between Milton's and Young's works being poetry Yearsley had read and Milton and Young being her favorite poets. This editing in turn has the potential to color readers' and scholars' impressions of Yearsley, perhaps causing them to discount or overlook the literary knowledge she displays in her poems or to fail to fully consider the implications of the frame in which More presents Yearsley.

In addition, the different emphases in the two commentaries raise the issue of More's ideas about the poor. Certainly More used contemporary ideas about laboring-class poets and the poor as she strategically crafted the "Prefatory Letter" to win subscribers. Yet, it also seems likely that More herself believed in some of these ideas as her private correspondence evidences a mixture of disbelief and admiration over what appear to be contradictions between Yearsley's ideas and period stereotypes about the laboring classes' capacity for thought. In this way, More's views of Yearsley's reading may help elucidate these more general ideas about the laboring classes. In commenting on the private letter, Donna Landry notes that Yearsley's choice of the *Georgics* surprised More because it was simultaneously an appropriate and an unexpected choice: "a translation of the *Georgics* is not only a 'professional' choice in that it represents some of the labors of a country life, a milkwoman's text; it is also the choice that a professional writer of georgic or working-country verse would be expected to offer in this period."[12] More edits out this sophistication and taste in her public construction of Yearsley to fit contemporary beliefs about what members of the laboring classes should and could read.

First, keeping in mind More's extensive future endeavors in educating the lower classes, Yearsley's taste and sophistication may have conflicted with her own and others' sense of what the poor should read.[13] In this light, consider the suggestions that friend Horace Walpole offers in a November 1784 letter to More:

> Give her Dryden's Cock and Fox, the standard of good sense, poetry, nature, and ease. I would recommend others of his tales, but her imagination is already too gloomy, and should be enlivened; for which reason I do not name Mr Gray's Eton Ode and Churchyard. Prior's Solomon (for I doubt his Alma, though far superior, is too learned for her limited reading) would be very proper.[14]

As he acknowledges, Walpole's choices were guided by his ideas about Yearsley's personality and also, more importantly, her class status and her presumed intellectual capabilities. Notably, the suggested Dryden and Prior poems respectively teach the price of listening to flattery and the value of humility. Whatever her literary genius, Yearsley cannot be seen to rise in class status, and what she reads (or what she is *said* to have read) must explicitly teach her this—or, at least, it must seem to teach her to not wish to rise above her station. This is suggestive for our understanding of the implications of seeing reading as representative of education or class.[15] If the "right" reading material can keep her in her place, then very possibly the "wrong" reading material will allow her to rise; contemporary fear of the latter may in turn dictate that More present a limited version of Yearsley's reading in the "Prefatory Letter" in order to fit her into the popular laboring-class poet model.

Second, More may have edited the taste and sophistication out of Yearsley's response to meet her readers' ideas about what the laboring-class could read in terms of access to reading materials. While the polite classes might assume the lower ranks had limited access to books, evidence suggests that Yearsley had access to books through her mother's customers and, as Zionkowski has found, books by Shakespeare, Milton, and Dryden were fairly widely available throughout England of the 1770s and 1780s.[16] Because what one read was a marker of class status and how one read it was a sign of interpretive ability, More needed to present Yearsley as a stereotypical member of the so-called uneducated poets. To have done otherwise by describing more extensive literary exposure and more subtle critical abilities would have possibly diminished her marketability.

Though More presented Yearsley in a limited way to reinforce the peculiar status as semi-learned that made her curious and unthreatening, and consequently ignored or did not consider how the poet actually could obtain books, readers and scholars should not be surprised to find the poet demonstrating knowledge beyond those texts More cites, even in her earliest published works. When read against the context of the "Prefatory Letter," "Clifton Hill. Written in 1785" challenges assumptions about reading. First, it evidences Yearsley's deeper experience reading, which raises questions about More's public presentation of Yearsley. Second, in part its content explores forms of misreading and misunderstanding that are based on preconceptions rather than the sympathy produced by reading openly.

"Clifton Hill" and *The Seasons*

"Clifton Hill" poses a clear challenge to More's introductory letter.[17] That Yearsley had read at least Thomson's *Winter* from *The Seasons*, whether before or after meeting More, is evident from the beginning of the poem. Although only the first thirty-four lines of her poem treat winter, receptive readers will find many echoes of Thomson's poem. For instance, Yearsley's lines, "When hoary Winter strides the northern blast, / And FLORA's beauties at his feet are cast," recall these from Thomson's first published version of *Winter*: "For, see! where Winter comes, himself, confest, / Striding the gloomy Blast."[18] While Waldron notes additional echoes of Thomson, my goal, as noted, is not to prove Yearsley read particular authors or texts. Instead, my interests in connecting "Clifton Hill" to *Winter* are, first, to demonstrate one of the ways in which the "Prefatory Letter" misrepresents the breadth of Yearsley's reading, and, second, to acknowledge the ways in which Yearsley does not simply imitate Thomson but in fact revises him.

Because "Clifton Hill" clearly reveals Yearsley's knowledge of Thomson, it is curious that More claims otherwise in the "Prefatory Letter." As it stands, More's introduction and this poem contradict each other. It might appear that this contradiction could be easily explained by the texts' respective assigned dates: as its title prominently signals, "Clifton Hill" was "[w]ritten in 1785," and the "Prefatory Letter" is given the date of 20 October 1784. That explanation, however, requires accepting More's representation of the volume's introduction as a copy of her October 1784 letter to Montagu. In fact, she adapted, revised, and expanded that letter before the book's publication in June 1785. Alternatively, it could be that Yearsley read Thomson after her conversation with More about authors. Regardless, while it is impossible to document that More read "Clifton Hill" before finishing her revisions to the introduction, certainly she read the poem before its publication and thus had the opportunity to remove the reference to Thomson being unknown to Yearsley. Apparently, presenting Yearsley's reading as prodigious and limited was a greater priority than accuracy. Yet, in this way, the "Prefatory Letter" serves, almost certainly unintentionally, as an example of the resistant or unreceptive reading that some "Clifton Hill" meditations depict. That is, by allowing this error to stand or perhaps failing to recognize it, More behaves as an unreceptive reader, someone who sees—or who in this document wishes to present—Yearsley through the limited frame of conceptions of laboring-class poets, something which seemingly requires that she ignore the evidence in the poems themselves.

Yearsley's poetic name, Lactilla, also reinforces the limits of this context. In part a marketing strategy that Yearsley herself continued to use after her split from More, Lactilla is the public persona of the Bristol Milkwoman Poet. This poetic name reinforces Yearsley's assigned laboring-class status, indeed her job, in a way that does not have a parallel in Stella, the name she uses to refer to her patron More in her poems. Although Yearsley's own class identification is not simply or unquestionably with the laboring classes, "Clifton Hill" is one example of Yearsley adopting this role in the guise of Lactilla.[19] Yet the poem also suggests another framework of identification: while the speaker is clearly a laborer, she is distinguished from other members of the working class by her ability to offer poetic reflections on the journey she takes as part of her work as a milkwoman.[20]

This is evident in how, rather than simply imitating Thomson, Yearsley presents a perspective on winter that reflects her experience as a member of the laboring classes but also seeks to instruct her readers in empathetic responses to need. While both Thomson and Yearsley note the deadening effects of winter on human emotions and activity, they use these similar characterizations to make diverging arguments that are rooted in the different ways the polite ranks and the laboring classes experience the season. For Thomson's speaker, winter is an opportunity for strengthening himself, and he prays that the "FATHER of Light and Life!" "feed [his] Soul / With Knowledge, conscious Peace, and Virtue pure, / Sacred, substantial, never-fading Bliss!" His soul is "intense, collected, cool / Bright as the Skies, and as the Season keen."[21] Unlike Thomson's speaker, Lactilla cannot see much promise in winter. For her, it is not something to be celebrated but endured, as it numbs the emotions of the nymphs and swains she depicts:

> The Swain neglects his Nymph, yet knows not why;
> The Nymph, indifferent, mourns the freezing sky;
> Alike insensible to soft desire,
> She asks no warmth—but from the kitchen fire[.][22]

Lactilla and the emotionally desensitized nymphs and swains must focus on practical needs.

In contrast, Thomson's speaker assigns such needs to the laboring classes and domesticated animals, advising, "Now, Shepherds, to your helpless Charge be kind, / Baffle the raging Year, and fill their Pens, / With Food at Will...." This contrast is reinforced by the two speakers' attitudes toward being outside in winter. When Thomson's speaker communes with nature early in the poem, he is part of a select group who can choose to be outside, who can use the cold conditions as an escape: "Then is the Time," he observes in the 1726 version, "For those, whom Wisdom, and whom Nature charm, / To steal themselves from the degenerate Croud, / And soar above this little Scene of Things." Despite his initial intent to wander, the speaker later retreats to his house and more specifically to his study, taking refuge with friends and books. Lactilla, however, does not have the luxury of such a choice. Rather, "half sunk in snow, / LACTILLA, shivering, tends her fav'rite cow."[23] By underlining both the unpleasant cold and a bond with the animals she tends, this description serves to emphasize her lack of choice; Lactilla must be outside in the cold to do her work even if she would prefer to be inside and warm, perhaps with her books.[24]

While both poets acknowledge domesticated animals' dependence on humans to feed them, Lactilla more closely aligns herself with the animals, not only by having a "fav'rite cow" but also by positioning herself as "sharing" their troubles. Consider her later address to the "nibbling flocks" on "VINCENT's rugged height" who "of scanty herbage gaine / A meal penurious from the barren plain": "Ye bleating innocents! dispel your fears, / My woe-struck soul in all your troubles shares."[25] By claiming common concerns, Lactilla demonstrates the sympathy or empathy "Clifton Hill" seeks to teach its readers. Rather than seeing divisions between humans and animals or between polite ranks and laboring classes, readers are to recognize and value shared experience or mutual dependence, a theme which lies behind some of the poem's other meditations as well, including the story of the red-breast.

The Red-Breast

In her most striking revision of Thomson, Yearsley transforms the story of the red-breast robin from a demonstration of people's bounty into an illustration of their cruelty. While the example further reveals Yearsley's literary experience, it more importantly serves as an additional lesson in reading through the use of a negative example.

In the 1746 version of *Winter*, Thomson's robin joins the human retreat from the winter storm, "pay[ing] to trusted Man / His annual Visit."

> Half-afraid, he first
> Against the Window beats; then, brisk, alights
> On the warm Hearth; then, hopping o'er the Floor,
> Eyes all the smiling Family askance,
> And pecks, and starts, and wonders where he is:
> Till more familiar grown, the Table-Crumbs
> Attract his slender Feet.[26]

Initially wary but compelled by the cycle of nature, Thomson's red-breast depends on "trusted Man" for sustenance, shelter, and survival during the winter, and clearly the "smiling Family" is receptive to his needs.

Quite the opposite awaits Yearsley's birds in their reluctant retreat from the storm: "The feather'd warblers quit the leafless shade; / Quit those dear scenes where life and love began, / And, cheerless, seek the savage haunt of man." Given the fate of the robin, this cheerlessness is justified:

> The beauteous red-breast, tender in her frame,
> Whose murder marks the fool with treble shame,
> Near the low cottage door, in pensive mood,
> Complains, and mourns her brothers of the wood.
> Her song oft wak'd the soul to gentle joys,
> All but his ruthless soul whose gun destroys.

Not fed and sheltered by "trusted Man" like Thomson's, Yearsley's robin is "murder[ed]," "destroy[ed]" by a "rough clown."[27] Unlike those whose souls are moved by the bird's song or who recognize their shared need for warmth and shelter during the winter, the rough clown is someone who feels improperly or perhaps not at all. There is a misreading on his part, a failure to recognize how winter has made the bird dependent on humans. In contrast to Lactilla who has empathy for the sheep, he does not even have sympathy for the bird; yet, more than simply ignoring the bird's plight, this individual actively harms the creature. As "Clifton Hill" continues, Yearsley reinforces how the failure to share someone else's perspective is a prominent cause of such misreadings. This is evident in those meditations that more obviously involve competing desires or ideas: Lactilla's recollection of her mother's graveyard lesson and her later critique of the assistance More provided to Louisa, the Lady of the Hay-Stack.

Heeding Churchyard Lessons

"Clifton Hill" includes a medley of poetic ruminations that are partially rooted in autobiographical fact. Just as the "Prefatory Letter" tempts readers and scholars eager to glean biographical information, so too does "Clifton Hill" tantalize with hints about Yearsley's life. Yet, while it may offer some information about Yearsley, it does so in the service of its poetic meditations, meditations whose effect may depend on Yearsley's own careful emphasis, embellishment, or exclusion of details. That is, while some of her meditations may be inspired by her history, readers of course should not assume that all the seemingly autobiographical details are true.[28] Indeed, focusing on gleaning facts misses Yearsley's design to use pieces from her life to teach her readers how to look beyond their preconceptions. About a quarter of the way into the poem, the speaker pauses to view Clifton Church and its graveyard, a place where the poet's mother was buried and where Lactilla's own resistance to reading lessons is recalled. Although not an instance of unreceptive reading of someone else's need, this example nevertheless illustrates the difficulty of reading sympathetically when doing so involves dismissing those ideas that are crucial to maintaining a personally palatable meaning.

Seeing the graveyard exposes Lactilla's incomplete acceptance of her mother's death: "Dead! Can it be?" As she remembers visiting the site with her mother, this meditation illustrates a fundamental difference between mother and daughter, one depicted as a difference in reading: "'twas here we frequent stray'd, / And these sad records mournfully survey'd. / I mark'd the verse, the skulls her eye invite...."[29] At first, this split in the two women's attention between image and verse might suggest that her mother cannot read. In fact, as Landry's research on this point suggests, Yearsley's mother, Ann Cromartie (or Cromarty), had access to books. Waldron even argues that Ann Cromartie taught her daughter to read.[30] But more than considering this passage as revealing whether Yearsley's mother was literate or not, I view the split in attention as revealing Yearsley's sense that they had two different perspectives when looking at the same gravestone.

It is not surprising that Lactilla the poet should be more caught by the verses, of course. More than that, however, the difference in perspective was determined not by profession or interests but by their ages and awareness of their mortality, evidencing how individual bias inflects the ability to acknowledge and accept other points of view. That the mother's attention is more drawn by the skulls conveys her focus on the inevitability of death, which the younger Lactilla cannot or does not want to accept, either in the past or in the present. Consider the line in the context of its complete sentence: "I mark'd the verse, the skulls her eye invite, / Whilst my young bosom shudder'd with affright! / My heart recoil'd, and shun'd the loathsome view." Lactilla here is a reader whose younger self was unreceptive to her mother's perspective because she is distressed by the thought of death. Yet while she can shift her focus from the images, her mother's words provide the reading lesson: "'Start not, my child, each human thought subdue,' / She calmly said; 'this fate shall once be thine, / My woes pronounce that it shall first be mine'."[31] According to her mother, who shows herself willing and able to consider another's opinion, Lactilla is intentionally misreading the situation because she is too influenced by those "human thoughts" that wish to deny death. She is unwilling to accept another person's perspective because it is painful to think of her mother's or her own mortality. Recalling these words serves to confirm the mother's lesson; she did die first, and hence Lactilla herself must eventually die. Yet, as Lactilla acknowledges, subduing these "human thoughts" is difficult:

> Abash'd, I caught the awful truths she sung,
> And on her firm resolves one moment hung;
> Vain boast—my bulwark tumbles to the deep,
> Amaz'd—alone I climb the craggy steep;
> My shrieking soul deserted, sullen views
> The depths below, and Hope's fond strains refuse;
> I listen'd not—She louder struck the lyre,
> And love divine, and moral truths conspire.[32]

Although initially resistant, by the end of this passage Lactilla appears resigned to her mother's lesson, perhaps finding some comfort in recalling her mother's words.

Yet, this resignation is tempered as this passage opens itself to several readings. First, as Landry argues, this meditation is in part "a text of reparation through memory: Yearsley's mother is restored to her as a figure of wisdom and power crucial to her own development as a poet—and more surprisingly—crucial to her sanity."[33] Second, the aside and the shifting between past and present in this passage suggest a continued resistance to the mother's message. Beginning in the present moment of the speaker's journey, the meditation understandably shifts to the past tense as the speaker reflects on her visits to the churchyard with her mother and on her mother's words. But in the lines beginning with the aside at line 87, the present tense returns and possibly the present moment with it: "—my bulwark tumbles to the deep / Amaz'd—alone I climb the craggy steep. . . ." These lines provide a comment on the mother's lesson, a despairing—present tense—comment, which is only partially recuperated by the concluding lines of this meditation: "She louder struck the lyre, / And love divine, and moral truths conspire."[34] In the present, the speaker is alone and, given the evidence of the grave, forced to accept the truth of her mother's words while still wishing her own views were correct.

Yearsley follows this meditation with brief remarks on the "proud Croesean crew," or the rich, those she assumes would not see her mother's death as a fit subject for poetry. Highlighting the broad understanding of reading invoked throughout the poem, Lactilla removes the rich's claim to poetry and, more importantly, aligns this "impious race" with the murderer of the red-breast in that their "bosoms others sorrows ne'er assail, / Who hear, unheeding, Misery's bitter tale."[35] Not only are they unfit subjects for poetry, unfit to be read about, they are also poor readers of situations and of people. Like the rough clown, they fail to understand because they ignore misery. Yet although the rough clown's action and the Croesean crew's inaction clearly demonstrate faulty readings of situations, the speaker's churchyard lesson and Louisa's story, to which I now turn, demonstrate that appropriate readings and responses are not always easy or clear because of the ways in which individual bias can cloud interpretation.

Louisa's Confinements

While the majority of meditations in "Clifton Hill" are short, reflecting the pace of the speaker's journey across the landscape, the final third of the poem presents an extended meditation on Louisa, a mysterious historical figure some believed was the illegitimate daughter of the German Emperor Francis I.[36] A version of her story is given in brief in a footnote in Yearsley's volume, perhaps written by More in her editorial capacity, which emphasizes the sentimental elements of the story: "The beautiful unfortunate LOUISA, fugitive Foreigner, lived three years in a state of distraction under [a] hay-stack, without going into a house. She once confessed, in a lucid interval, that she had escaped from a Convent, in which she had been confined by her father, on refusing a marriage of his proposing, her affections being engaged to another man."[37] My interest in Louisa's case lies in the argument Yearsley makes with respect to how a seemingly sympathetic response can do harm because it arises from the benefactor's perspective, not that of the charitable object. The schism results from the failure to respect the other person's wishes or, perhaps more accurately, a failure to conceive of the other as even having wishes worth considering. This argument rests in key differences between the depiction of Louisa in "Clifton Hill" and the story of Louisa, the Lady of the Hay-Stack, making certain details left out of both footnote and poem worth attention.

A few years before the 1785 date given "Clifton Hill," this same Louisa was the focus of a subscription, led by More, that was designed to support her admission to a lunatic asylum—or what society would have considered an appropriate response to a mentally ill object. Prior to More's intervention, a group of neighborhood ladies had engaged in a similar project, banding together to place Louisa in a Bristol hospital. Rejecting this assistance, Louisa had left the hospital to return to her haystack. One of More's mid-twentieth-century biographers highlights the neighborhood women's open-mindedness as she recounts this case: learning that Louisa "had been so wretched" in the hospital, "they allowed her to return to her free haystack home. Trouble and misery dwelt in houses, [Louisa] declared, and there was no happiness but in liberty and fresh air. The kind ladies, though they themselves preferred a roof, even if it did cover trouble and misery, gave in to her and clubbed together to buy the haystack."[38] While this account is certainly sentimentalized and condescending in its contrast between the civilized preference of the "ladies" and that of Louisa, who found houses miserable, it nonetheless conveys the neighborhood women's receptiveness to Louisa's feelings even if they themselves did not share them. In buying the haystack for her, they demonstrated an attempt to understand Louisa's wishes that would seem to be missing from the subscription More led on Louisa's behalf a few years later.

Yearsley's telling of Louisa's story raises questions about benefactors' responses to need that neglect their recipients' desires. Notably, Yearsley fails to mention the more receptive compassion shown by the first group of Louisa's neighbors, choosing instead to portray More as her only rescuer: "O, thou kind friend! whom here I dare not name...."[39] Yearsley has seemed willing to name More, albeit as "Stella," throughout *Poems, on Several Occasions*, so this reluctance to name her is dissonant. It in part suggests Yearsley's complicated perspective on Louisa's case given their shared position as objects of More's assistance. Other scholars have in fact argued that Louisa serves here as a warning for Yearsley—in Madeleine Kahn's words, for example, the poem presents "a powerful admonitory portrait of the mad and destitute Louisa, another protégé of More's and the figure Yearsley could so easily have become had she not written this book of poems."[40] Yet, Louisa's import for Yearsley is not just as a personal worst-case scenario but as an example of the dangers faced by the recipient whose benefactor fails to see any conflict between the subject's desires and polite society's conceptions of appropriate actions. While Yearsley was not threatened by the literal confinement of institutionalization as was Louisa, she was confronted with another form of confinement through More's public presentation of her as a laboring-class poet and charitable object, exemplified by, but not exclusive to, the "Prefatory Letter." In addition to presenting limited ideas about Yearsley with respect to her reading, the "Prefatory Letter" set limits on the poet's success—she was not to rise in her status or to become a full-time poet. Rather, as the "Prefatory Letter" assures its readers, she was to be confined to her station, although made more comfortable within it.[41] In short, both Louisa and Yearsley were subject to labeling and preconceptions, which limited understandings of them and influenced how others responded to them.

Perhaps because her apparent mental illness may have required people to make choices for the historical Louisa, Yearsley's Lactilla is not upset by the impulse to protect her but rather by how that impulse is demonstrated. Her criticism is obliquely presented in a passage that initially appears to praise More for helping Louisa but quickly turns into a challenge:

> O, thou kind friend! whom here I dare not name,
> Who to LOUISA's shed of misery came,
> Lur'd by the tale, sigh'd o'er her beauteous form,
> And gently drew her from the beating storm,
> Stand forth—defend, for well thou canst, the cause
> Of Heaven, and justify its rigid laws;
> Yet own that human laws are harshly given,
> When they extend beyond the will of Heaven.[42]

Tellingly, the seemingly positive portrait of the "kind friend" that opens this passage is syntactically subordinate. The main force of the poetic sentence is not praise but a challenge: "O, thou kind friend!... / Stand forth—defend ...." The challenge itself is oblique because it first appears to flatter More by suggesting she can defend "the cause / Of Heaven"—"for well [she] canst." But the second part of the challenge undercuts any praise, quickly replacing an apparently praised More who could defend heaven's laws with a challenged More who might not "own that human laws are harshly given"—that is, a More unwilling or unable to realize the harm of human laws, which appear here in the form of conventional attitudes about proper approaches to charitable objects.

As it continues, this meditation makes this clear by raising the question of how Louisa has been treated:

> Say, can thy pen for that hard duty plead,
> By which the meek and helpless maid's decreed
> To dire seclusion? Snatch'd from guiltless joys,
> To where corroding grief the frame destroys;
> Monastic glooms, which active virtue cramp,
> Where horrid silence chills the vital lamp... [43]

The date given Yearsley's poem is significant: since by 1785 the historical Louisa had been confined to the second asylum for two or three years, she is no longer living in her haystack. Accordingly, Lactilla knows the answer to her question: while ostensibly compassionate, More's actions have "ple[]d" for another "hard duty" for Louisa, another form of confinement most likely no less odious to her than the convent or the first hospital. The unrecorded answer, then, is that Louisa's institutionalization poses no contradiction to More, suggesting that More has misread or not been receptive to Louisa's desires. While again complicated by the likelihood that the historical Louisa may not have been capable of judging for herself (as indeed Yearsley presents her), Louisa's example nevertheless evidences how conventional responses to those in need may fail to acknowledge their desire to make their own choices.

While "Clifton Hill" ends without offering any explicit solution to the problems identified in Louisa's case, its accumulation of meditations that concern instances of misreading effectively sketches the range of such problems. While responses like that of the rough clown are obviously misdirected, Lactilla's resistance to her mother's perspective and More's apparent failure to consider the wishes of another suggest that less obvious examples can be problematic as well. In these selected examples, Yearsley challenges her readers to question how they read not only texts but also situations and individuals. Moreover, by demonstrating her literary knowledge, Yearsley offers a further, if likely unintentional, challenge to More's public presentation of her, "Clifton Hill" serving as one example of how the poems in Yearsley's first volume disprove assertions More makes in the "Prefatory Letter." The entangled forms of reading implicated in "Clifton Hill" forward a greater appreciation of how Yearsley's poems need to be read both with and against the context created by More's introduction. Moreover, in what she herself leaves out of "Clifton Hill" with respect to Louisa's situation, Yearsley creates a context for our reading, our interpretation, which requires that we read carefully, openly, and empathetically. That is, "Clifton Hill" presents corrective lessons in reading both Yearsley and situations, as it challenges us to be aware of the context of reading in its various forms.

NOTES

I thank the organizers of the 2009 EC/ASECS meeting for devoting a panel to "Eighteenth-Century Poetry," where I presented an earlier version of this paper. I am grateful to David Macey, Lisa Cody, and the anonymous reviewers for their insightful comments on various aspects of this paper, and to Michael McKeon and Carol Barash for their comments about earlier versions of this argument.

1. Scholars instrumental in bringing renewed attention to Yearsley include Moira Ferguson, Donna Landry, and Mary Waldron. Kerri Andrews, Frank Felsenstein, and William Christmas among others have contributed more recent offerings to the field.

2. Kerri Andrews, "Ann Yearsley: A Literary Career Reconsidered," *Literature Compass* 5 no.1 (2008): 90–105, 103.

3. On Yearsley's use of the genre of the prospect poem, see Donna Landry, *The Muses of Resistance: Laboring-Class Women's Poetry in Britain, 1739–1796* (New York: Cambridge University Press, 1990), 130–31; and Mary Waldron, *Lactilla, Milkwoman of Clifton: The Life and Writings of Ann Yearsley, 1753–1806* (Athens: University of Georgia Press, 1996), 108.

4. On the bias inherent in terms like *uneducated poet*, see Richard Greene, *Mary Leapor: A Study in Eighteenth-Century Women's Poetry* (Oxford: Clarendon Press, 1993), chapter 3, esp. 98–100. While Yearsley would likely reject this label and that of laboring-class poet, they are useful reminders of how she was seen by others.

5. On More's packaging of Yearsley, see: Tim Burke, "Ann Yearsley and the Distribution of Genius in Early Romantic Culture," in *Early Romantics: Perspectives in British Poetry from Pope to Wordsworth*, ed. Thomas Woodman (New York: St. Martin's Press, 1998), 215–30, 227; Greene, *Mary Leapor*, 151–2; Susanne Kord, *Women Peasant Poets in Eighteenth-Century England, Scotland, and Germany: Milkmaids on Parnassus* (Rochester, NY: Camden House - Boydell & Brewer, 2003), 106; and Linda Zionkowski, "Strategies of Containment: Stephen Duck, Ann Yearsley, and the Problem of Polite Culture," *Eighteenth-Century Life* 13 (1989): 91–108, 100. For a discussion of some errors, see Waldron, *Lactilla*, 58–59.

6. For examples of direct and filtered references, see: Moira Ferguson, *Eighteenth-Century Women Poets: Nation, Class, and Gender* (Albany: State University of New York Press, 1995), 47; A. D. Harvey, "Working-Class Poets and Self-Education," *Contemporary Review* 274 no.1600 (1999): 252–63, 254–55; Claire Knowles, "Ann Yearsley, Biography, and the 'Pow'rs of Sensibility Untaught!'" *Women's Writing* 17 no. 1 (2010): 166–84, 169; and even Zionkowski, who otherwise recognizes aspects of the construction, in "Strategies of Containment" (107 n. 17).

7. Hannah More, "A Prefatory Letter to Mrs. Montagu. By a Friend." in *Poems, on Several Occasions*, by Ann Yearsley, 2nd ed. (London: T. Cadell, 1785), vi.

8. More, "A Prefatory Letter," vi.

9. Waldron, *Lactilla*, 29.

10. For one example of More's ideas about what books to give Yearsley, see her letter to Montagu reproduced in Mary R. Mahl and Helene Koon, eds., *The Female Spectator: English Women Writers Before 1800* (Bloomington: Indiana University Press, 1977), 279.

11. More, quoted in Mahl and Koon, eds., *The Female Spectator*, 278.

12. Landry, *Muses of Resistance*, 129; see also Andrews, "Ann Yearsley," 94.

13. Consider, for example, the *Cheap Repository Tracts*, which More began publishing in 1795, that in part sought to teach the poor to remain content with their lot as well as the value of hard work. As critics acknowledge, the *Cheap Repository Tracts*, like some of More's other works written for the poor, had multiple audiences: the poor and the polite ranks. More deftly instructs both sets of readers in her texts,

as she tries to, in Robert Hole's phrase, "reconcile the poor to their poverty" while also instructing the polite classes in their responsibility to the poor (Robert Hole, "Hannah More on Literature and Propaganda, 1788–799," *History* 85 [2000]: 613–33, 615.) For additional scholarship on these works, see Mona Scheuermann, "Hannah More and the English Poor," *Eighteenth-Century Life* 25 (2001): 237–51; and Jane Nardin, "Avoiding the Perils of the Muse: Hannah More, Didactic Literature, and Eighteenth-Century Criticism," *Papers on Language and Literature* 36 (2000): 377–91.

14. Walpole to Hannah More, 13 November 1784, in *The Yale Edition of Horace Walpole's Correspondence*, ed. W. S. Lewis, vol. 31 (New Haven: Yale University Press, 1961), 221.

15. While Landry proposes a useful distinction between literary class and social class, the polite classes see instead a conflation (*Muses of Resistance*, 125).

16. "Character of Mrs. Yearsley, a Milk-maid on Clifton Hill," *Gentleman's Magazine* 54 (1784): 897; Zionkowski, "Strategies of Containment," 92 (see also 98–99). For further speculation on how the "uneducated" poets acquired their literary knowledge, see Carolyn Steedman, "Poetical Maids and Cooks Who Wrote," *Eighteenth-Century Studies* 39 (2005): 1–27.

17. It seems likely that Yearsley did not read the "Prefatory Letter" until its publication, making this challenge unintentional.

18. Ann Yearsley, "Clifton Hill. Written in 1785," *Poems, on Several Occasions*, 2nd ed. (London: T. Cadell, 1785), 107–26, 107 [lines 5–6]; James Thomson, *The Seasons*, *Eighteenth-Century English Literature*, ed. Geoffrey Tillotson, Paul Fussell, Jr., and Marshall Waingrow (New York: Harcourt, Brace and World, 1969), 706–25, 708 [lines 112–13]. For further comparison of Thomson and Yearsley, see Waldron, *Lactilla*, 109 11.

19. Yearsley's class status has been the subject of critical debate. While critics like Landry have identified Yearsley as a member of the working class, Waldron has made a strong case that Yearsley considered herself part of the yeomanry. For my purposes here it is important to recognize that More's vision of Yearsley is clouded by her reliance on models of what was appropriate for laboring-class poets to be and do. For more on this issue, see: Landry, *Muses of Resistance,* 125, 303 fn 19; Waldron, *Lactilla,* 14–17, 25; Mary Waldron, "A Different Kind of Patronage: Ann Yearsley's Later Friends," *The Age of Johnson*, vol. 13, eds. Paul J. Korshin and Jack Lynch (New York: AMS Press, 2002), 283–335, 284; William J. Christmas, *The Lab'ring Muses: Work, Writing, and the Social Order in English Plebeian Poetry, 1730–1830* (Newark: University of Delaware Press, 2001), 329 n 8; Julie Cairnie, "The Ambivalence of Ann Yearsley: Laboring and Writing, Submission and Resistance," *Nineteenth-Century Contexts* 27 no. 4 (2005): 353–64, 354; and Andrews, "Ann Yearsley," 91–92.

20. In "Clifton Hill," as Landry rightly points out, Lactilla is a shifting presence (*Muses of Resistance*, 131). See also Waldron on Lactilla as a "go-between" for the polite and laboring classes (*Lactilla*, 108).

21. Thomson, *The Seasons*, 1746 version, lines 217, 220–22, 702–3.

22. Yearsley, "Clifton Hill," lines 15–18.

23. Thomson, *The Seasons*, 1746, lines 265–67; 1726, 33–36; Yearsley, "Clifton Hill," lines 19–20.

24. Seeking to place "Clifton Hill" within the tradition of sensibility and reading this passage to mean that "Lactilla labours out of love, not necessity," Knowles is too quick to discount Lactilla's discomfort ("Ann Yearsley," 171).

25. Yearsley, "Clifton Hill," lines 100, 99, 100–01, 106–07.

26. Thomson, *The Seasons*, 1746, lines 249–56.

27. Yearsley, "Clifton Hill," lines 8–10, 23–28, 29.

28. For this reason, it is important to think of the poem as presenting the ideas and experiences of Lactilla, rather than of Yearsley. While there is certainly overlapping between the two, we can still view Lactilla as a constructed version of Yearsley.

29. Yearsley, "Clifton Hill," lines 77, 77–79.

30. Landry, *Muses of Resistance*, 138; Mary Waldron, "'By no means milk and water matters': the contribution to English poetry of Ann Yearsley, milkwoman of Clifton, 1753–1806," *Studies on Voltaire and the Eighteenth Century* 304 (1992): 801–04, 802.

31. Yearsley, "Clifton Hill," lines 79–81, 82–84.

32. Yearsley, "Clifton Hill," lines 85–92.

33. Landry, *Muses of Resistance*, 137.

34. Yearsley, "Clifton Hill," lines 87–88, 91–92.

35. Yearsley, "Clifton Hill," lines 97, 93–94, 98, 95–96.

36. Despite efforts made by Hannah More among others, the identity of the woman known as "The Lady of the Hay-Stack" was never determined. Her age, an accent that appeared German, and the Holy Roman Emperor's reputation as a philanderer were cited by those who wished to link her to royalty. For further speculations about Louisa, see Henry Thompson, *The Life of Hannah More: With Notices of Her Sisters* (London: T. Cadell, 1838), 50–55; and G. H. Glasse, *Louisa: a narrative of facts supposed to throw light on the mysterious history of "The lady of the hay-stack" / translated from a French work, published in the Imperial Dominions, A.D. 1785* (New York: Ward for Fenno, 1801). Glasse, notably, gives high praise to More for her efforts on Louisa's behalf.

37. Yearsley, "Clifton Hill," 121 [note]; Louisa's story does, as Landry argues, allow Yearsley to rewrite *Eloisa to Abelard* (a text which did make More's catalog); see *Muses of Resistance*, 139.

38. Mary Alden Hopkins, *Hannah More and Her Circle* (New York: Longmans, Green and Co., 1947), 126.

39. Yearsley, "Clifton Hill," line 222.

40. Madeleine Kahn, "Hannah More and Ann Yearsley: A Collaboration Across the Class Divide," in *Studies in Eighteenth-Century Culture*, ed. Syndy M. Conger and Julie C. Hayes, vol. 25 (Baltimore: Johns Hopkins University Press, 1996), 201–23, 213; see also Landry, *Muses of Resistance*, 139–43.

41. More, "A Prefatory Letter," xi.

42. Yearsley, "Clifton Hill," lines 222–29.

43. Yearsley, "Clifton Hill," lines 230–35. For Waldron, this passage addresses More's attempts to locate Louisa's family and reflects Yearsley's concern that More would be unable to convince Louisa's father not to send her back to a convent; for Landry, the silence about Louisa's fate indicates a conflict between Yearsley's discomfort with More's actions and her desire to praise her patron (*Lactilla,* 114–15; *Muses of Resistance*, 142–43).

Contributors to Volume 41

Katrin Berndt is Assistant Professor in British and Anglophone Literatures at the University of Bremen. The author of *Female Identity in Contemporary Zimbabwean Fiction* (Bayreuth 2005), she co-edited *Words and Worlds: African Writing, Literature, and Society* (with Susan Arndt, Africa World Press 2007), and *Heroism in the Harry Potter Series* (with Lena Steveker, Ashgate 2011). At present, she is writing a monograph on friendship in the British novel of the eighteenth century.

Dorothee Birke is junior research fellow in English literature at the Freiburg Institute for Advanced Studies (FRIAS) at Freiburg University, Germany. She specializes in narratology and the history of the novel and is currently preparing a book on representations of reading in the English novel from the eighteenth to the twenty-first centuries. She is the author of *Memory's Fragile Power: Crises of Memory, Identity and Narrative in Contemporary British Novels* (Wissenschaftlicher Verlag Trier, 2008) and has edited with Michael Butter and Tilmann Köppe *Counterfactual Thinking--Counterfactual Writing* (de Gruyter, 2011). She is also working on an edited volume (with Stella Butter) entitled *Realisms in Contemporary Culture*.

David A. Brewer is Associate Professor of English at The Ohio State University and the author of *The Afterlife of Character, 1726-1825* (University of Pennsylvania Press, 2005). He is currently working on the uses to which authorial names were put in the eighteenth-century Anglophone world. His edition of *The Rivals* and *Polly Honeycombe* is forthcoming from Broadview.

Jennifer Germann is Assistant Professor of Art History at Ithaca College and her research centers on issues of gender and visual culture in early modern Europe. She has published essays on the representation of Anne of Austria, Marie Leszczinska, and Madame de Pompadour. She is currently working on a project investigating the queen's bedchamber at Versailles from a material cultural perspective.

Zeina Hakim is Assistant Professor of French at Tufts University. She works primarily on the French novel in the Enlightenment, as well as on cultural history and historiography in early modern France. She has published articles on Diderot, Rousseau, literature and aesthetics, and women's studies. Her book *Fictions déjouées. Le récit en trompe-l'œil au XVIII*[e] *siècle* is forthcoming (Droz, 2012).

Julie Henigan obtained her Ph.D. in English and Irish Studies in 2009 from the University of Notre Dame. She has published a variety of articles on British and Irish literature, as well as on traditional Irish song. Her book *Literacy and Orality in Eighteenth-Century Irish Song* is forthcoming (Pickering and Chatto, 2012).

Sandro Jung is Research Professor of Early Modern British Literature and Culture and the Director of the Centre for the Study of Text and Print Culture at Ghent University. The editor of *Eighteenth-Century Poetry* and the *Journal of the Printing Historical Society*, he is also the director of the four-year funded projects "Genettian Theories of Para- and Hypotextuality and Thomson's *The Seasons*" (2011-2014) and "The Translation, Cultural Mediation, and Reception in Britain of Rousseau's *Discours sur les Sciences et les Arts*" (2012-2015). He has published widely on eighteenth-century literature. His most recent monographs are: *David Mallet, Anglo-Scot: Poetry, Politics and Patronage in the Age of Union* (University of Delaware Press, 2008) and *The Fragmentary Poetic: Eighteenth-Century Uses of an Experimental Mode* (Lehigh University Press, 2009). His most recent book, *James Thomson's 'The Seasons', Print Culture, and Visual Interpretation, 1730-1842*, is forthcoming, and he is completing a book on the paratexts of Spenserian editions in the eighteenth century for Manchester University Press.

Catherine Keohane is Assistant Professor of English at Montclair State University, where she teaches writing and literature courses, and also serves as Assistant Director for Placement. She has published articles in *ELH*, *Studies in the Novel*, *Studies in Eighteenth-Century Culture*, and *WPA*. Her current book project examines eighteenth-century depictions of charity in didactic and imaginative literature to explore the implications of form for promoting and challenging gender and class ideology.

Marc H. Lerner is Associate Professor of History at the University of Mississippi and the author of *A Laboratory of Liberty: The Transformation of Political Culture in Republican Switzerland, 1750-1848* (Brill, 2011). He is currently working on a new project about the symbolic uses of the William Tell story during the international Age of Revolution.

Danielle Spratt is Assistant Professor of English at California State University, Northridge. Her research focuses on the ways in which eighteenth-century literature engages in debates about the rise of the new scientific movement, with a focus on issues of gender, race, the body, and social justice.

Michael Yonan is Associate Professor of Art History at the University of Missouri–Columbia. He is the author of *Empress Maria Theresa and the Politics of Habsburg Imperial Art* (Penn State, 2011) and numerous articles on art and architecture in eighteenth-century Central Europe.

ASECS Executive Board 2011–2012

For information about the
American Society for Eighteenth-Century Studies, please contact:

ASECS
P.O. Box 7867
Wake Forest University
Winston-Salem, NC 27109-7867
Telephone: (336) 727-4694
Fax: (336) 727-4697
E-mail: asecs@wfu.edu
Web Site: http://asecs.press.jhu.edu

American Society for Eighteenth-Century Studies

Patron Members 2011–2012

Hans Adler
Stephen Ahern
Stanford Anderson
Mark S. Auburn
Paula Backscheider
Joseph F. Bartolomeo
James G. Basker
Denise Baxter
Barbara Becker-Cantarino
Barbara Benedict
Oliver Berghof
Kevin Binfield
Martha F. Bowden
Theodore E.D. Braun
Fritz Breithaupt
Peter M. Briggs
Jane K. Brown
Marshall Brown
Michael Burden
Joseph A. Byrnes
Ann Campbell
Susan Carlile
Vincent Carretta
Jeng-Guo Chen
Julie Choi
Michael Conlon
Brian A. Connery
E. Heckendorn Cook
Kevin L. Cope
Brian Cowan
Margaret Mary Daley
Marlies K. Danziger
Jenny Davidson
Joan DeJean
Robert DeMaria, Jr.
Julia Douthwaite
William F. Edmiston
Roger J. Fechner
Riikka Forsstrom
Bernadette Fort
Patsy Fowler
Christopher Fox
Jennifer E. Frangos
Gorden Fulton
Robert Glen
Charles E. Gobin
Scott Gordon
Sayre Greenfield
Monika Greenleaf
Anita Guerrini
Joan R. Gunderson
Phyllis Guskin
Susan Gustafson
Basil Guy
Knud Haakonssen
Wolfgang Haase
Martha Hamilton-Phillips
Corrine Harol
Phillip Harth
Donald M. Hassler
Julie C. Hayes
Robert D. Hume
Lynn A. Hunt
Sheila M. Hwang
Catherine Ingrassia
Malcolm Jack
Margaret C. Jacob
Regina Mary Janes
Annibel Jenkins
Alessa Johns
Sandro Jung
George Justice
Sarah Kareem
Gary Kates
Michael Keevak
Shirley Strum Kenny
Thomas Keymer
Heather King
Charles A. Knight
Jocelyne Kolb
David H. Koss
Thomas W. Krise
Susan Lanser
Meredith Lee
Elizabeth Liebman
Devoney K. Looser
Aino Makikalli
Elizabeth Mansfield
Marie E. McAllister
Christie McDonald
Paula McDowell
George C. McElroy
Alan T. McKenzie
James C. McKusick
Heather McPherson
Donald C. Mell Jr.
Eun Kyung Min
Dennis Moore
Anja Mueller-Muth
Yvonne Noble
Felicity Nussbaum
Mary Ann O'Donnell
Frank Palmeri
Virginia J. Peacock
Ruth Perry
Jane Perry-Camp
Stuart Peterfreund
R.G. Peterson
George W. Poe
John Valdimir Price
Ruben D. Quintero
John Radner
Bryant T. Ragan
Tilottama Rajan
Gary A. Richardson
John Richetti
James Rosenheim
Roseann Runte
Elizabeth Samet
Carole Fungaroli Sargent

Patron Members 2011–2012 (Con't)

J.T. Scanlan
Steven D. Scherwatzky
Harold Schiffman
Volker Schroder
Norbert Schurer
Richard Sher
Mary D. Sheriff
Eleanor F. Shevlin
John C. Shields
Kazuko Shimizu
Craig A. Simmons
Robert Louis Smith
Susan Staves
Masashi Suzuki
Mika Suzuki
Ruud N.W.M. Teeuwen
Linda V. Troost
Randolph Trumbach
Bertil Van Boer
David F. Venturo
Joachim Von der Thusen
Howard D. Weinbrot
Byron R. Wells
Betty E. White
J. Edmund White
Lance Wilcox
James A. Winn
Karin E. Wolfe
Larry Wolff
Servanne Woodward
James Woolley
Karin Wurst
Myron D. Yeager
Janet E. Aikins Yount
William J. Zachs
Lisa M. Zeitz

Sponsoring Members 2011–2012

Paul Alkon
Misty G. Anderson
Eve T. Bannet
Robert Bernasconi
Thomas F. Bonnell
Leo Braudy
Jill Campbell
Michael Chappell
Brian Corman
Clarissa C. Erwin
Daniel Timothy Erwin
David Fairer
Jan Fergus
Lisa Freeman
Jenna Gibbs
David Hagan
Daniel Heartz
Deborah Kennedy
Issac Kramnick
Joan Landes
Nanette C. LeCoat
Deidre Shauna Lynch
Robert Markley
Jean I. Marsden
John A. McCarthy
R.W. McHenry
Linda E. Merians
Maureen E. Mulvihill
Melvyn New
John C. O'Neal
Douglas Lane Patey
Adam Potkay
Suzanne R. Pucci
Peter H. Reill
Larry L. Reynolds
Jacqueline Rhodes
Albert J. Rivero
Wendy W. Roworth
Treadwell Ruml II
Peter Sabor
Beverly Schneller
Barbara B. Schnorrenberg
William C. Schrader
Julia Simon
John Sitter
Henry Slosser
Jeffrey Smitten
G.A. Starr
Ann T. Straulman
Dennis Todd
Raymond D. Tumbleson
Deborah M. Valenze
Cynthia S. Wall

Institutional Members 2011-12

American Antiquarian Society
Colonial Williamsburg Foundation, *John D. Rockefeller, Jr. Library*
Folger Institute
Fordham University
Newberry Library
Ohio State University Libraries, *Thompson Library*
Omohundro Institute for Early American History, *Kellock Library*
Princeton University
Smithsonian Institute, AAPG Library
Stanford University
UCLA, *William Andrews Clark Memorial Library*
University of California, Santa Barbara
University of Kentucky, *Young Library*
University of North Carolina, *Davis Library*
University of Pennsylvania Library
University of Rochester Library
University of Victoria, *McPherson Library*
Yale University Library

Index

Every effort has been made to include references to all identifiable persons living before or during the long eighteenth century, as well as to often cited contemporary critics and commentators, and to provide a selective listing of relevant concepts and keywords. Readers may also wish to consult the endnotes of each essay for more comprehensive information.

V

W

Y

Z